GREAT VEGETARIAN DISHES

GREAT
VEGETARIAN DISHES
Over 240 recipes from around the world

Kurma dasa

THE BHAKTIVEDANTA BOOK TRUST
Los Angeles • London • Stockholm • Bombay • Sydney • Hong Kong

Recognising a responsibility to preserve the environment of the earth,
and replenish it's natural resources, the publishers have planted twice
the number of trees used in the manufacture of this book.

The Bhaktivedanta Book Trust
10 Rochester St.
Botany, NSW 2019
Australia

Publisher	Naresvara dasa
Photography	Peter Bailey
Food Styling	Maureen McKeon
Art Direction & Design	Ram Prasad dasa
Food Preparation	Kurma dasa, Maureen McKeon, Sudevi devi dasi, Krsnarupa devi dasi
Illustrations	Lucy Leviska
Colour Separations	Palace Press

First published 1990: 30,000 copies

**National Library of Australia
Cataloguing-in-Publication data:**
Kurma dasa, 1952-
    Great Vegetarian Dishes

    Includes index
    ISBN 0 9593659 1 5

    1. Vegetarian Cookery. I. Title
641.5636

Printed in Singapore

Dedication

In the Vedic literatures, cooking is listed as one of the sixty-four arts. My spiritual master, His Divine Grace A.C. Bhaktivedanta Swami Prabhupada, was an excellent cook, and when he came to the West from India he used his skills to make delicious preparations for the pleasure of the Supreme Personality of Godhead, Sri Krishna. As we read in his biography by Satsvarupa dasa Goswami:

'......... So he very deftly emptied the bag of flour, and with his fingertips, cut in the butter until the mixture had the consistency of coarse meal. Then he made a well in the centre of the flour, poured in just the right amount of water, and very deftly and expertly kneaded it into a velvety smooth, medium-soft dough. He then brought in a tray of cooked potatoes, mashed them with his fingertips, and began to sprinkle in spices. He showed me how to make and form potato *kachoris*, which are fried Indian pastries with spiced potato filling. Meanwhile, in the course of the same afternoon, Swamiji brought in fifteen other special vegetarian dishes, each one in a large enough quantity for forty persons. And he had made them singlehandedly in his small, narrow kitchen.'

These preparations were then distributed to the people who had come to associate with him. By taking this *prasadam*, sanctified food, they became further attracted to Krishna consciousness. The preparation and distribution of *prasadam* is an important part of the Krishna consciousness movement, and it is the part to which I have gravitated.

I would like to dedicate this book to His Divine Grace A.C. Bhaktivedanta Swami Prabhupada and ask him to bless this endeavour.

A.C. Bhaktivedanta Swami Prabhupada
Founder/Acharya: International Society for Krishna Consciousness

v

Foreword

Whenever someone hears about a vegetarian diet, the common question is, "But what can you eat if you don't eat meat, fish, or eggs?" How sad it is to see what advertising has done to us, particularly our young folk! They grow up with the vast majority of food commercials on TV showing them the benefits of deep-fried chicken, fast-food hamburgers, "lite" beer, and the like. Rarely is there mention of the grains, beans, vegetables, and fruits that for centuries have made up the staple diet of most people around the world. So all too often youngsters end up thinking "food" means "meat".

The slaughterhouse, factory farming, and mass merchandising are pretty much unique to this century. Refrigerators are a relatively recent invention. Many societies around the world still subsist on a very simple, basic vegetarian diet. People in the Western world seldom die of starvation, but rather the opposite—over-indulgence.

But there is infinite variety in a vegetarian diet. Let's look at the international nature of the culinary world. If you study the various ethnic foods (Italian, Indian, Thai, Chinese, Mexican, etc.), they were all vegetarian-based diets. It was only after certain individuals or societies became more affluent that they added meat. Do you really think that the original lasagna or chow mein or tortillas had any meat in them? First of all, people couldn't afford it, and secondly, it wasn't something that was attractive or economically sound.

Many people today are becoming aware of the health benefits of a vegetarian diet. The vast increase in the number of deaths from cancer, heart disease, osteoporosis, etc., have woken up a lot of people. Almost everyone in the Western world has lost a loved one to one of these diseases, which are brought on by a meat-centered diet.

But a great myth persists: that meat, fish, poultry, and eggs are necessary for a person to stay well and excel. A case in point: myself. In 1970, when I switched from a predominantly meat-based diet to a vegetarian one, virtually all my fellow athletes told me how sick I was going to get, and some even said I would die! After one year as a vegetarian, I was tested at the Percival Institute in Toronto. I had the highest fitness index of any athlete in Canada! In fact, my left hand strength had increased 38%—amazing, considering I'm right-handed and didn't lift any weights during the year. But the most significant increase was in my stamina. It had increased almost 80 per cent!

Every athlete should understand that meat, fish, poultry, and eggs contain a high percentage of concentrated, pure protein, along with high levels of cholesterol. When one eats pure protein, the body cannot use it in that form; it must break it down into amino acids, expending energy with this extra step. This drain on the body's energy takes away from an athlete's performance. Also, these foods contain a lot of toxins, which the body has to work hard to eliminate. And because the cholesterol is in the lean tissue of the animal, even if you trim the fat you will still eat excessive cholesterol. The average Westerner takes in 500–600 milligrams of cholesterol a day, while the body can eliminate only 100 milligrams a day. The result is that Westerners accumulate a lot of cholesterol in their bodies, especially in the bloodstream, where it coats the arterial walls, causing arteriosclerotic build-up. As the area through which the blood flows narrows, less oxygen goes through the bloodstream, and with less oxygen getting to the muscles, the athlete will fatigue sooner. Athletes need to keep a flexible, elastic, and clean blood system, and this is accomplished on either a lacto-vegetarian or a vegan diet.

And finally, the overall perspective important for us to understand is that eating meat is an ecological crime. The purpose of the fish is to keep the ocean clean, the purpose of the chicken and pigs is to keep the land clean, and the purpose of the cow is to give us milk. Unfortunately, today we must even be concerned with the quality of milk we purchase, as so many of our factory-farmed animals are filled with hormones. *Ghee* is preferred over butter, and butter is preferred over margarine, the latter basically being plastic fat, a product that was invented in the late 1940's as a substitute for the shortage of butter.

I consider the step to vegetarianism, and in particular, the understanding of it, the most important step in my life. It has changed my health for the better, but more importantly, it has changed how I view life. Only after changing to a vegetarian diet did I truly understand the phrase "reverence for life". When I hear people say, "But a little meat won't hurt me," that may be true, but what a selfish way of looking at things. If you asked a cow or a chicken or a fish how it felt about "that little piece"...

So wherever you are in your level of understanding about nutrition, give Kurma's recipes a try. Through his TV cooking series and video tapes, he has helped thousands of people realise the sheer versatility of vegetarian cooking.

If you sincerely make the effort to follow his instructions and recipes, you'll discover a whole new world of enjoyment. You will be amazed at how good food really can be. Happy eating.

Peter Burwash
Tennis Professional
and founder of
PETER BURWASH INTERNATIONAL.

Contents

Acknowledgements

I would like to offer my heartfelt thanks to the following persons: Naresvara dasa, the publisher, and Ram Prasad dasa, the art director, (both my dear friends) without whose collaboration and direction this book would not have become a reality; Peter Bailey for his beautiful photographs and his patience; Maureen McKeon for her assistance in so many ways, especially her foodstyling; Lucy Leviska for her excellent illustrations; Tulasi Maharani dasi for typing and re-typing the manuscripts; Nada dasi and Nagaraj dasa for editing; Krsnarupa dasi, Jeff Perry, Jenny Naismith and Yadusrestha dasa for proofreading; Mark Kennedy for patiently assisting me in the long months of recipe testing; Suchi for allowing me to use his kitchen; Sudevi Dasi, Michelle and Shaun for hands-on assistance in the studio; Ujvala dasa, Rahugana dasa, Aniruddha dasa, Chakra dasa and Vijay Gopikesha dasa for their advice and technical assistance; Mrs Nancye Walmsley, Jenny Jenkins, Cecilia Caffery, John Raffaut, Subhuji dasi, Peter Burwash, Drutakarma dasa, Advaita Acharya dasa, Trevor Absalom, Russell and Della Absalom, Shreed, and others too numerous to mention.

My special thanks to:
Casa Portuguesa Pty. Ltd., Dartington Crystal, Deruta of Italy, Brighton, Georges Australia Ltd., Ishka of Prahran, J.D. Milner and Associates, Mikasa Tableware Pty. Ltd., Villeroy and Boch Australia Pty.Ltd., and Waterford Wedgwood Australia Ltd.

Introduction

You'll notice in *Great Vegetarian Dishes'* full and inviting Directory of Recipes quite a number of tantalizing Indian recipes—*South Indian Sweet-and-Sour Tamarind Rice, Gujarati Yogurt Soup, Rajasthani Spicy Dal-Stuffed Bread, North Indian Curried Cauliflower and Potato*, and many others.

There's a good reason for that. The inspiration for this superbly conceived and lavishly illustrated international vegetarian cookbook comes from the timeless spiritual philosophy of India, especially as it is represented in the enduring books of Vedic knowledge such as the *Bhagavad-gita.*

The author of the recipes, in addition to being an expert vegetarian cook, has long practiced the *yoga* most highly recommended in the *Gita*—*bhakti-yoga*, the *yoga* of devotion.

Kurma knows well that in order to experience the optimum spiritual rewards of *yoga*—or even to stay fit and healthy—one should eat properly. And with humor, patience, and enthusiasm he has successfully communicated that essential bit of knowledge to a growing and appreciative world-wide audience.

It's a message Kurma learned from his spiritual master (and mine), His Divine Grace A.C. Bhaktivedanta Swami Prabhupada (1896-1977), who introduced *bhakti-yoga* to the world outside India, starting with his arrival in the United States in 1965.

Srila Prabhupada's lucid translations of Sanskrit and Bengali classics on *bhakti-yoga* gained him a reputation among scholars. But it was Srila Prabhupada's cooking that most endeared him to his original followers in New York City's Lower East Side. In his first storefront temple and *ashram*, Srila Prabhupada trained his disciples not only in the teachings of *Bhagavad-gita*, but in the art of India's spiritual vegetarian cooking. Needless to say, everyone thoroughly enjoyed these lessons—especially the final test of tasting.

Since those early days, the movement Srila Prabhupada founded has grown impressively to a world-wide network of hundreds of temples, farm communities, and restaurants, which together provide millions of spiritual vegetarian meals each year. The delighted beneficiaries range from patrons of the movement's fine vegetarian restaurants (the newest in Leningrad) to the poor and homeless who receive nutritious free meals from Hare Krishna Food for Life in cities around the world.

As many people are aware, a vegetarian diet is healthy. But it would be a mistake to think that the health benefits of a vegetarian diet have only been recently discovered. I don't want to downplay the many modern medical and scientific reports that show so clearly the links between meat-centered diets and such implacable killers as cancer and heart disease. It's valuable research, and well worth studying. But long, long ago, the *Bhagavad-gita* identified meat, fish, and eggs as foods harmful to bodily well-being. According to the *Gita*, such foods "cause distress, misery, and disease."

The *Gita* recommends food in the mode of goodness—vegetarian foods: "Foods dear to those in the mode of goodness increase the duration of life, purify one's existence, and give strength, health, happiness, and satisfaction."

Those are the kinds of food Kurma teaches you to prepare in this book. The *Gita* says that such foods are "wholesome and pleasing to the heart." What more could one ask?

How about a more livable planet? A vegetarian diet is good for the environment.

The *Bhagavad-gita* tells us "all living bodies subsist on food grains." Even the consumer of fast-food burgers depends on vegetables for nourishment—the vegetables have simply been processed into the flesh of cows.

But getting one's vegetables in that way is harmful for our planet. Rain forests are being destroyed to make way for beef cattle ranches in developing countries.

Amogha Dasa

A bullock team working on the Hare Krishna movement's 'New Govardhana' farming community, northern New South Wales, Australia

A meat-centered diet is also wasteful of scarce agricultural resources. These days, most meat is grain-fed, and, just to give one example, it takes 16 pounds of grain to get 1 pound of beef.

A vegetarian diet is a compassionate diet. It involves less pain to our fellow creatures. That humane message is coming to mean more and more to people who love animals. But despite the recent surge of interest in animal rights, concern for animals is not new. For thousands of years the spiritual tradition of India has consistently shown an attitude of *ahimsa,* or nonviolence toward all things living.

It's nice that so many celebrities have been putting themselves on the line—speaking (or singing) out in the many campaigns to convince people to stop wearing fur, to stop eating veal and beef, to stop buying cosmetics tested on animals, and so forth. But there is a more solid and enduring foundation for our concern for God's creatures. That is the remarkable spiritual vision outlined in the *Bhagavad-gita.* Fashions in causes may change, but genuine commitment founded on real knowledge remains unshakeable in all circumstances.

Lord Krishna says in the *Gita:* "The humble sages, by virtue of true knowledge, see with equal vision a learned and gentle brahmana, a cow, an elephant, a dog, and a dog-eater [outcaste]." This vision of equality is the key to respect for all life. Animals have souls too.

True knowledge enlightens us to the fact that violence against animals is not simply a matter of abstract ethics. According to the *Vedas,* the spiritual texts of ancient India, one who kills animals directly or indirectly (by purchasing meat, for example) will experience a definite reaction—something more than moral qualms and pangs of conscience.

The destined reaction may not come immediately, but eventually it will, in the form of disease, accident, or violence. What goes around comes around—in this case, pain and suffering. This unrelenting cycle of action and reaction is called "the wheel of *karma,*" and eating meat is definitely bad *karma.*

Now that naturally gives rise to this question—what about plants? Aren't vegetarians getting *karma* for killing them? The answer is yes.

Of course, in many cases, you don't have to kill the plant in order to take the part we use for food. For example, you can pick a tomato without killing the tomato plant. But there is still some *karma* to be had for that. How would you like some creature taking part of you for food?

And in many cases you do have to kill the plant. The question then remains—what about the *karma*?

To get free from the *karma* is possible. But you must go beyond ordinary vegetarianism to spiritual vegetarianism, and the *Bhagavad-gita* tells how to do it. The underlying principle of spiritual vegetarianism is that everything in the universe is part of the energy of God. This means that everything—including food—should be used in connection with God. This is called sacrifice.

By sacrifice I mean the attitude of doing something for the sake of someone else. For example, a mother sacrifices for her children. She does things for them, to make them happy. One kind of sacrifice is to prepare food for others. It takes time and energy to shop for ingredients, to cook, wash the pots, and so on. It's an act of love. The opposite of selfishness.

So the *Bhagavad-gita* recommends that we perform the sacrifice of cooking for God, Krishna: "The devotees of the Lord are released from all kinds of sins because they eat food which is offered first for sacrifice. Others, who prepare food for personal sense enjoyment, verily eat only sin."

In other words, if one prepares vegetarian food as a sacrifice to Krishna, one stays free from *karma*. Since God is all-powerful, He can transform the material energy of *karma* into spiritual energy.

At this point, I should say a few words about Krishna. According to the *Gita*, there is one God, who is the creator of all things, material and spiritual. That God is known by many names in different parts of the world. One God, different names. Most of these names refer to God as the creator, the most powerful being, and so forth. These names are somewhat impersonal, in the sense that titles such as "king", "president", and "commander-in-chief" are impersonal. They designate the post but don't name the specific person who holds the post.

Ultimately, however, there is a person who occupies the post of God, and He has intimate, personal names. Krishna is one of these personal names, and it means "all-attractive." Krishna is the person who is God.

According to the *Vedas*, Krishna periodically descends from the spiritual world to this material world, sometimes in His original personal form and sometimes in other personal forms, such as Buddha. The most recent *avatara*, or incarnation, of Krishna was Lord Chaitanya, who appeared in India about five centuries ago and taught love of God by His own example.

Can foods other than vegetarian be offered to Krishna? In *Bhagavad-gita* Krishna says: "If one offers Me with love and devotion a leaf, a flower, fruit, or water, I will accept it." He does not say He will accept non-vegetarian foods, such as meat, fish, and eggs. He specifies vegetarian items.

But even more important, Krishna asks for love and devotion. These are the most essential ingredients in the vegetarian offerings prepared for His pleasure.

So now that I've explained the philosophy behind preparing vegetarian food as an offering to Krsna, I'll give you specific instructions on how exactly to perform a simple offering.

Let's start with some preliminaries. It's said that cleanliness is next to godliness, so keep a clean kitchen while you're working. Also, don't taste any of your preparations until after you have offered them to Krishna.

Now for the offering itself. First, if you have some hesitation about offering your food specifically to Krishna, then simply offer it to God as you understand Him.

But if you do want to offer your food to Krishna, here is how you can go about it. Somewhere in your home or kitchen you can make a small altar. On this altar you can place three pictures—one of the spiritual master, one of Krishna, and one of Lord Chaitanya. Such pictures are also available from the publisher of this book.

The spiritual master, or guru, serves as Krishna's representative, and it is through the spiritual master that Krishna receives offerings. If you seriously take up the practice of *bhakti-yoga*, you will eventually want to connect yourself with a living spiritual master through initiation. In

Amogha Dasa

Organic vegetables harvested the natural way.

that case, you would use a picture of your personal spiritual master for offering food. But until that time one may make offerings using a picture of Srila Prabhupada along with pictures of Lord Krishna and Lord Chaitanya.

For the purposes of offering, it is best to reserve a special plate that is not used for anything else. After you have finished cooking, place a little of each preparation on the plate for offering. Soups and drinks can, of course, go in special cups and bowls reserved for making offerings.

The simplest kind of offering you can make is to place the offering before the pictures of Srila Prabhupada, Krishna, and Lord Chaitanya and simply ask them to please accept it. But the usual procedure is to say some traditional Sanskrit prayers, or *mantras*. Each of the following four *mantras* should be softly repeated three times. The English translations do not have to be spoken. I have provided them simply so you will know what the Sanskrit *mantras* mean.

1) *nama om vishnu-padaya*
  krishna-presthaya bhutale
  srimate bhaktivedanta-
  svamin iti namine

"I offer my respectful obeisances unto His Divine Grace A.C. Bhaktivedanta Swami Prabhupada, who is very dear to Lord Krishna, having taken shelter at His lotus feet."

2) *namas te sarasvate devam*
  gaura-vani-pracharine
  nirvishesha-shunyavadi-
  paschatya-desha tarine

"Our respectful obeisances unto you, O spiritual master, servant of Sarasvati Goswami. You are kindly preaching the message of Lord Chaitanya and delivering the Western countries, which are filled with impersonalism and voidism.

3) *namo maha-vadanyaya*
  krishna-prema-pradaya te
  krishnaya krishna-chaitanya-
  namne gaura-tvishe namaha

"I offer my respectful obeisances unto the Supreme Lord Sri Krishna Chaitanya, who is more magnanimous than any other

incarnation, even Krishna Himself, because He is bestowing freely what no one else has ever given—pure love of Krsna."

4) *namo-brahmanya-devaya*
  go brahmana hitaya cha
  jagad-hitaya krishnaya
  govindaya namo namaha

"I offer my respectful obeisances to the Supreme Absolute Truth, Krishna, who is the well-wisher of the cows and the *brahmanas* as well as the living entities in general. I offer my repeated obeisances to Govinda [Krishna], who is the pleasure reservoir for all the senses."

After chanting these four *mantras* three times each, you can chant the following *mantra*, called the *maha-mantra*, or great *mantra*, several times:

Hare Krishna, Hare Krishna,
  Krishna Krishna, Hare Hare
Hare Rama, Hare Rama,
  Rama Rama, Hare Hare

Amogha Dasa

Sri Sri Radha-Ballabha, the presiding Deities at the Melbourne Hare Krishna temple

When the offering is completed, you and your family or guests can enjoy your meal. Be prepared for a nourishing and satisfying taste experience.

When food is offered to Krishna, it becomes transformed. It not only becomes *karma*-free, it becomes infused with positive spiritual energy. The Sanskrit word for spiritual food offered to Krishna is *prasadam*, which means "mercy."

Prasadam is especially wonderful, because simply by eating it one can make spiritual advancement. One is freed from *karma* and experiences spiritual energy and pleasure.

As Lord Chaitanya said five centuries ago: "These ingredients, such as sugar, camphor, black pepper, cardamom, cloves, butter, spices, and licorice, are all material. Everyone has tasted these material substances before. However, in these ingredients there are extraordinary tastes and uncommon fragrances. Just taste them and see the difference in the experience. Apart from the taste, even the fragrance pleases the mind and makes one forget any other sweetness besides its own. Therefore, it is to be understood that the spiritual nectar of Krsna's lips has touched these ordinary ingredients and transferred to them all their spiritual qualities."

Drutakarma dasa
Co-author of *The Higher Taste:
A Guide to Gourmet Vegetarian Cooking
and a Karma-Free Diet.*
July 29, 1990
Pacific Beach, California

Suggestions for further reading:

For more recipes from India, try *Lord Krishna's Cuisine: The Art of Indian Vegetarian Cooking*, by Yamuna Devi. This award-winning cookbook is the ultimate encyclopaedia of India's culinary tradition. The *Chicago Tribune* called it "the Taj Mahal of cookbooks."

For a brief but comprehensive overview of the philosophy of spiritual vegetarianism, along with selected international vegetarian recipes, try *The Higher Taste: A Guide to Gourmet Vegetarian Cooking and a Karma-Free Diet.* This book is a good introduction to spiritual vegetarianism for a friend or relative.

Another excellent cookbook is *The Hare Krishna Book of Vegetarian Cooking*, by Adiraja dasa. In addition to 133 recipes, it contains suggested menus and useful explanations of spices.

For information about vegetarianism and religion, see *Food for the Spirit: Vegetarianism and the World Religions.* In this wide-ranging survey, Satyaraja dasa (Steven Rosen) examines traditions of vegetarianism in Hinduism, Christianity, Judaism, Buddhism, Islam, and other faiths.

For more insight into the life of Srila Prabhupada, you can read *Prabhupada,* the first-rate biography by Satsvarupa dasa Goswami.

For further details about the practice of *bhakti-yoga* the indispensable first book to read is *Bhagavad-gita As It Is,* by Srila Prabhupada.

All of these books are available from the publishers of this book.

Please write to:

The Bhaktivedanta Book Trust,
P.O. Box 262, Botany,
N.S.W. 2019, Australia.

The Bhaktivedanta Book Trust
3764 Watseka Ave.
Los Angeles CA 90034 U.S.A.

How to Measure and Use the Recipes

Measurement of Volume

Because there is some difference between Australian, American and British cup and spoon measurements, this book gives quantities for most ingredients in Australian cups and spoons with the metric volume equivalent (litres or parts thereof) in parentheses. This avoids the troublesome business of looking up conversion charts or using kitchen scales to weigh ingredients.

To conveniently use these recipes, you will require a set of graduated spoons (1/4 teaspoon, 1/2 teaspoon, 1 teaspoon and 1 tablespoon) and a set of graduated cups (1/4 cup, 1/3 cup, 1/2 cup and 1 cup) and perhaps a glass or plastic liquid measuring container, usually containing both cup and litre markings.

Teaspoons

The Australian, American and British teaspoons all hold approximately 5 ml. I have rounded off fractions of teaspoons to the nearest ml, thus:

1/2 teaspoon (2 ml) salt

1/4 teaspoon (1 ml) black pepper

Tablespoons

Tablespoon measurements given in this book are standard Australian tablespoons, holding 20 ml. The American standard tablespoon holds 14.2 ml and the British standard tablespoon holds 17.7 ml. Thus American readers should heap their tablespoons, and British readers should slightly heap their tablespoons.

Cups

Cup measurements given in this book are standard Australian cups, which hold 250 ml. The American and British standard cups hold 240 ml. Thus American and British readers should generously fill their standard measurement cups, or in the case of liquids, should add 2 teaspoons extra for every cup required.

Measurement of Weight

Measurement for items which cannot be conveniently measured by volume, such as un-melted butter, pastry, spaghetti, ungrated cheese, etc. have been given in grams with ounces in parentheses, thus:

60 g (2 ounces) butter

400 g (14 ounces) filo pastry

Measurement of Temperature

Accurate temperatures are indicated for baking, some deep frying and for confectionery making. In this book, measurements are given first in Celcius, then in Fahrenheit, thus: 185°C/365°F.

A cooking thermometer is a useful accessory.

Measurement of Length

Measurements are given in centimetres with inches in parentheses, thus:

1.25 cm (1/2-inch) cubes

25 cm (10 inches)

Finally

Take note of the following suggestions to get the best out of these recipes:

1. Read the entire recipe first and obtain all the ingredients before commencing to cook. Measure all the spices and ingredients beforehand and place them where they can be easily reached.

2. All measurements for the spoons and cups are level unless otherwise specified.

Pan size is specified whenever important e.g. 3-litre/quart pan.

3. "*PREPARATION TIME: 15 minutes*" does not include the time needed to gather the ingredients. Some ingredients, when indicated, are pre-cooked and the assembling and chopping of most vegetables, fruits and herbs is not included in the preparation time.

4. "*COOKING TIME: 25 minutes*" is based on the time it took me to cook the dish over a household gas stove. This should serve only as a guideline. Adjust cooking time according to the capabilities and liabilities of your heat source. For instance, keep in mind that compared to gas, electric cooking elements are slow to heat up and cool down.

5. For information about unfamilar ingredients, see Glossary.

Special Notes for American Cooks

The following list will clarify any confusion that may arise because of the different cooking terms and ingredient names used in Australia and America.

Australian	American
beetroot	beet
biscuit	cookie
bulgur wheat	cracked wheat
capsicums	peppers
caster sugar	fine granulated sugar
chickpeas	garbanzo beans
cornflour	corn starch
frying pan	skillet
icing sugar	confectioners sugar
plain flour	all purpose flour
raw sugar	turbinado sugar
semolina	farina
sultanas	golden raisins
wholemeal flour	wholewheat or graham flour

Special Ingredients

Modern fast-paced living often affords us little time to spend in the kitchen. Yet the kitchen is a very special place. George Bernard Shaw said "You are what you eat". The foods that you prepare directly influence the physical and mental behaviour of those who partake. Meals prepared begrudgingly or without care, for instance, often taste poor. Therefore the most important 'special ingredient' in cooking is your good consciousness.

Fresh produce is also of primary importance; basic ingredients that can be prepared at home taste so much better than shop-bought items that can sometimes be old or stale.

Let's start with a few recipes for freshly prepared dairy products.

Home-made Yogurt

Yogurt is an indispensable ingredient in vegetarian cuisine, being nutritious, tasty, and easily digestible.

It is a source of calcium, protein, fat, carbohydrates, phosphorus, vitamin A, the B-complex vitamins, and vitamin D. The lactic acid content of yogurt aids in the digestion of calcium. Yogurt encourages the growth of "friendly" bacteria in the intestines that help destroy harmful strains. And yogurt is quickly assimilated into the body.

Yogurt is made by adding a small amount of "starter" (which can be either previously prepared home-made yogurt or commercial plain yogurt) to warm milk. Under certain temperature conditions, and after some hours, the live bacteria in the starter will transform the milk into yogurt, which can then be refrigerated and used as needed. If you prefer a slightly thicker, firm yogurt, you can add milk powder at the beginning.

Yogurt is called for in many recipes in this book, from the traditional creamy yogurt-based drinks called *Lassi* to the cooling yogurt salad called *Raita*. Drained of its whey, yogurt is transformed into a low-calorie cream cheese featured in *Syrian Yogurt Cheese* and *Greek Yogurt Dip*. When sweetened, this yogurt cheese becomes a delicious dessert called *Shrikhand*. Yogurt can be folded into vegetable dishes, such as *South Indian Vegetable Combination*, or heated into zesty *Gujarati Yogurt Soup*. A small bowl of plain yogurt is a cooling addition to any main meal.

PREPARATION TIME: 20 minutes

SETTING TIME: 4 to 10 hours

YIELD: 4 cups (1 litre)

⅓ cup (85 ml) fresh milk (optional)

½ cup (125 ml) full-cream milk powder (optional)

4 cups (1 litre) fresh milk

3 tablespoons (60 ml) fresh plain yogurt

1. If you prefer thicker yogurt, combine the ⅓ cup (85 ml) of milk with the milk powder, whisk until smooth, and set aside.

2. Bring the milk to the boil in a heavy, 3-litre/quart saucepan, stirring constantly. Remove milk from the heat and whisk in the optional powdered-milk thickener. Transfer the milk into a sterilized container and set aside to cool.

3. When the temperature of the milk has reached 46°C/115°F, add the yogurt starter and whisk until smooth. The milk temperature should not exceed 44°C/111°F, which is the ideal culturing temperature.

4. Put the container of warm milk in a warm place for 4 to 6 hours. You can place the container inside a sealed plastic bucket of warm water or wrap it in a towel or heavy blanket. The container may also be placed in an oven with the pilot light on, in a preheated electric oven which has been turned off, or in a wide-mouthed thermos flask.

5. Check the yogurt after 5 hours. It should be thick and firm (it will become thicker after refrigeration). Refrigerate, covered, and use within 3 days. After three days, the yogurt makes an ideal curdling agent for production of *Home-made Curd Cheese (Panir)*.

Note: If your home-made yogurt does not taste as nice as expected or is something other than yogurt, consider the following points:

1. Over-boiling the milk without proper stirring can cause the milk to scorch or burn. This will give the yogurt an unpleasant taste.

2. If the milk does not sufficiently cool before you add the starter culture, it will curdle.

3. If the milk cools too much before adding the starter culture, it will remain milk.

4. If you do not ensure continuous warmth during incubation, the yogurt might fall to a less-than-desired temperature. Over warming during incubation causes spoilage.

5. Over-incubation (allowing the milk and yogurt to sit for longer than required) will produce a strong-tasting, tart yogurt.

6. Non-sterile containers may introduce foreign bacteria into your yogurt, causing bad tastes. Do not disturb the yogurt while it is culturing.

Cultured Buttermilk

Cultured buttermilk is prepared in the same manner as yogurt—by inoculating milk with a special culture and allowing it to grow under certain conditions. However, the type and the amount of culture, and the temperature conditions, differ from yogurt production. Buttermilk requires twice as much culture as yogurt; it must be incubated for up to 2 to 3 times as long and at a considerably lower temperature. For these reasons, it is best to use an electric yogurt maker or a thermos when making buttermilk. Buttermilk has a milder taste than yogurt and is lower in calories because it is produced from skim- or low-fat milk. Try *Orange Buttermilk Smoothie* or substitute home-made buttermilk in any dish requiring yogurt for milder, lower-calorie results.

PREPARATION TIME: 30 minutes

SETTING TIME: 8 to 16 hours

YIELD: a little over 4 cups (1 litre)

4 cups (1 litre) fresh skim or low-fat milk

¾ cup (185 ml) commercial cultured buttermilk

⅔ cup (165 ml) full-fat milk powder

1. Heat the milk over moderate heat in a heavy-bottomed 2-litre/quart pan, stirring constantly. Don't boil the milk; just heat it until it reaches 42°C/108°F. Remove from the heat.

2. Blend the buttermilk and milk powder in a blender or food processor until smooth.

3. Whisk the warm milk with the buttermilk and milk powder, until smooth. Immediately pour the mixture into an electric yogurt machine or wide-mouthed thermos and cover loosely. Wrap the container in a thick towel or blanket and set aside at a temperature of about 26°C/80°F for between 8 and 16 hours or until it sets. Buttermilk can be refrigerated for up to 1 week.

Note: After one week, buttermilk is ideal for curdling milk in the production of *Home-made Curd Cheese (Panir)*.

Ghee

Ghee, clarified butter, is the preferred cooking medium for many dishes. Most commonly used in traditional Indian cuisine, *ghee* is also popular in Middle Eastern cooking. Whilst olive oil, sesame oil, peanut oil, and coconut oil find their way into recipes in this book, *ghee* has many advantages.

When butter is melted and slowly heated, all the moisture is evaporated, and the milk solids are separated from the clear butterfat. This residual, golden-coloured liquid, called *ghee*, is excellent for sautéeing and frying, as it can be heated to 190°C/375°F before reaching its smoking point.

Ghee will not turn rancid and will keep for months unrefrigerated; it will keep for over 6 months in the refrigerator and for over a year when frozen. *Ghee* has a delightful, slightly nutty flavour and is preferred for all traditional fried Indian sweets and savouries. *Ghee* can be purchased at most gourmet stores, Indian and Middle Eastern grocers, and some well-stocked supermarkets. Home-made *ghee*, however, is much more economical. *Ghee* can be prepared either on the top of the stove or in the oven. If you are making a large quantity of *ghee*, it is best to use the oven method. Unsalted butter makes the best *ghee*.

The following is a chart indicating how long it takes to make a batch of *ghee* and what the approximate yield will be.

have removed all the *ghee* that you can without disturbing the solids, allow the *ghee* to cool and store in a suitable covered storage container.

4. The remaining *ghee* and solids can be mixed with the crust from the top of the *ghee* in the small bowl and used for vegetables, soups, or sandwich spread. It will keep 3 to 4 days refrigerated.

QUANTITY OF BUTTER	COOKING TIME		APPROXIMATE YIELD OF GHEE
	STOVE METHOD	OVEN METHOD	
500 g (17.5 ounces)	1 1/4 hrs	1 1/2 - 1 3/4 hrs	1 3/4 cups (435 mls)
1 kilo (2 lbs 3 ounces)	1 3/4 hrs	2 - 2 1/2 hrs	3 1/4 cups (810 mls)
1.5 kilo (3 lbs 5 ounces)	2 hrs	2 3/4 - 3 1/4 hrs	5 1/2 cups (1.4 litres)
3 kilo (6 lbs 10 ounces)	3 1/4 - 3 1/2	3 3/4 - 4 1/2 hrs	12 cups (3 litres)
5 kilo (11 lbs)	5 1/2 - 6 hrs	6 3/4 - 7 1/4 hrs	19 cups (4.75 litres)

Stove-top *Ghee*

1/2-2 kg (1-5 pounds) unsalted butter

1. Cut the butter into large chunks and melt it over moderate heat in a large heavy-based saucepan, stirring to ensure that it melts slowly and does not brown. Still stirring, bring the melted butter to a boil. When the butter becomes frothy, reduce the heat to very low. Simmer uncovered and undisturbed for the required time until the solids have settled on the bottom, a thin crust appears on the top, and the *ghee* is clear and golden.

2. Skim off the surface crust with a fine-mesh wire sieve and set it aside in a bowl.

3. Turn off the heat source and remove the *ghee* with a ladle without disturbing the solids on the bottom. Pour the *ghee* through a sieve lined with paper towels. When you

Oven-Made *Ghee*

This method for making *ghee* is suitable if you want to produce a larger quantity of *ghee*. It is practically effortless and can be conducted in basically the same way as the stove-top method, except that instead of placing the *ghee* on top of the stove, heat it for the required time in a preheated 150°C/300°F oven. Skim and store in the same way as for the stove-top method.

Home-made Curd Cheese (*Panir*)

Curd cheese, or *Panir*, is the Indian equivalent of bean curd (*tofu*). It is rich in protein and extremely versatile. It can be deep-fried and used in vegetable dishes, crumbled into salads,

made into sweets, stuffed inside breads and pastries, and creamed into dips. Curd cheese is the simplest kind of unripened cheese and is made by adding an acid or other curdling agent to hot milk. The solid milk protein coagulates to form the soft curd cheese, the liquid whey is separated, and the cheese is drained, pressed, and then used as required. Because curd cheese is not available in shops outside of India, I have included the simple recipe for making your own.

The quality and freshness of the milk will determine the quality of the curd cheese. The higher the fat-content of the milk, the richer the curd cheese. Different curdling agents will produce different types of curd. The most common curdling agents are strained, fresh lemon juice, citric acid crystals dissolved in water, sour whey from a previous batch of curd cheese, and the whey residue from hanging yogurt to make *Shrikhand*, *Greek Yogurt Dip*, or *Syrian Yogurt Cheese*. Left-over yogurt or buttermilk used as curdling agents produce good curd cheese. Here are some hints in making your curd cheese.

1. Don't allow your milk to scorch or burn, as this will spoil the taste of the curd cheese.

2. Don't unnecessarily use all the prescribed acid curdling agent unless the milk stays a whitish colour. Over-curdling tends to produce an unpleasant acidic taste.

3. If you use all the curdling agent and the milk has still not completely curdled, add a little more curdling agent until the whey becomes clear.

4. Bad flavours in the cheese indicate that the milk was not fresh or that the utensils were dirty.

5. Tough or crumbly curd results from using low-fat milk or from allowing the curd cheese to remain too long over the heat once it has separated from the whey.

Home-made Curd Cheese (Panir) is featured in many recipes in this book, such as *Bengali Royal Rice*; *Eggplant, Potato and Curd Cheese*;

MILK	STRAINED FRESH LEMON JUICE	APPROXIMATE YIELD OF CURD CHEESE
4 cups (1 litre)	6 teaspoons (30 ml)	3/4 cup (185 ml)
6 cups (1.5 litres)	2 tablespoons (40 ml)	1 1/8 cup (280 ml)
8 cups (2 litres)	3 tablespoons (60 ml)	1 1/2 cups (375 ml)
10 cups (2.5 litres)	1/3 cup (85 ml)	1 7/8 cups (475 ml)
16 cups (4 litres)	6 tablespoons (120 ml)	3 cups (750 ml)

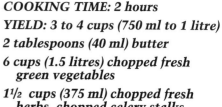

Tomato, Peas and Home-made Cheese, and *Curd Pakoras*. *Lemon Cream Cheese Fudge* (*Sandesh*) also features *panir*, smoothed into a cream-cheese consistency.

Curd cheese can also be crumbled and mixed into salads or vegetable dishes such as *Scrambled Curd* or as a substitute for ricotta cheese in *Spinach Filo Triangles*.

Here's how to prepare curd

1. Boil the milk in a heavy-based saucepan, stirring often to prevent scorching or sticking. Lower the heat and add the lemon juice or other curdling agent. (See above chart for quantities.) Stir the milk gently until it curdles; then remove the saucepan from the heat. If the liquid is not clear but is still milky, return the saucepan to the heat. If it hasn't fully cleared after another minute, add more curdling agent.

2. Place the saucepan of curds and whey aside for 10 minutes. Pour or scoop the contents of the pan into a colander lined with cheesecloth, gather the corners, and hold the bag of cheese under lukewarm water for 10 seconds. Squeeze the bag, place it back in the colander, and press it under a heavy weight for 3/4-1 1/2 hours or as desired.

3. Unwrap the curd cheese and use as required. It will last in the refrigerator for up to 4 days.

Green Vegetable Stock

Below are recipes for various vegetable broths: *Green Vegetable Stock*, *Root Vegetable Stock*, *Brown Vegetable Stock*, and *Chinese Vegetable Stock*. These recipes, however, should act only as a guide. Whenever you can, save vegetable peelings, stalks, leaves, and any water used to boil vegetables. Broths can serve as a natural flavour-enhancer for soups, rice dishes, *dals*, and stews.

COOKING TIME: 2 hours
YIELD: 3 to 4 cups (750 ml to 1 litre)
2 tablespoons (40 ml) butter
6 cups (1.5 litres) chopped fresh green vegetables
1½ cups (375 ml) chopped fresh herbs, chopped celery stalks, beans, pea pods, etc.
8 cups (2 litres) water
2 teaspoons (10 ml) salt
2 bay leaves
3 cloves
¼ teaspoon (1 ml) yellow asafoetida powder

1. Melt the butter in a heavy 6-litre/quart saucepan or stockpot and sauté the vegetables for 20 minutes over moderate heat. Turn off the heat and allow the vegetables to "sweat" with a lid on for 10 minutes.

2. Add the water and remaining ingredients and bring to a boil; then simmer for 1½ hours with a tight-fitting lid. Strain. Refrigerate the stock and use as needed.

Root Vegetable Stock

COOKING TIME: 2 hours

YIELD: about 3 cups (750 ml)

2 tablespoons (40 ml) butter

1/2 large potato, diced

1 cup (250 ml) squash
    or pumpkin, diced

2 medium celery stalks, chopped

2 carrots, diced

8 cups (2 litres) water

1 bay leaf

1/4 teaspoon (1 ml) yellow
    asafoetida powder

1/2 teaspoon (2 ml) black
    peppercorns

1 teaspoon (5 ml) minced
    fresh ginger

2 whole cloves

2 tomatoes, chopped

2 teaspoons (10 ml) salt

1. Melt the butter in a heavy 6-litre/quart saucepan or stockpot and sauté the vegetables for 20 minutes over moderate heat. Turn off the heat and allow the vegetables to "sweat" with a lid on for 10 minutes.

2. Add the water and remaining ingredients and bring to a boil; then simmer for 1 1/2 hours with a tight-fitting lid. Strain. Refrigerate the stock and use as needed.

Brown Vegetable Stock

BEAN SOAKING TIME: overnight

COOKING TIME: 2 hours

YIELD: about 2 litres/quarts

2 cups dried beans (cannelini, lima,
    borlotti, kidney), soaked in water
    overnight

3 litres/quarts water

3 tablespoons (60 ml) butter

2 celery stalks, chopped

1 cup (250 ml) squash or
    pumpkin, diced

2 small carrots, diced

2 cloves

1/2 teaspoon (2 ml) yellow
    asafoetida powder

1 teaspoon (5 ml) minced
    fresh ginger

1 bay leaf

1 tablespoon (20 ml) salt

1. Drain the beans. Boil the beans in two litres/quarts of water in a heavy saucepan. Simmer until the beans are soft (about 1 hour).

2. Melt the butter in a large saucepan over low heat. Sauté the vegetables in butter for 10 minutes. Remove the saucepan from the heat, cover it with a lid, and allow the vegetables to "sweat" for 10 min-utes. Add the remaining water and set aside. When the beans have been cooking for 1 hour, add the vegetables and water with the spices and salt to the beans and bean water and boil for another 1 hour. Strain. Refrigerate the stock and use as required.

Chinese Vegetable Stock

COOKING TIME: 1 hour

YIELD: 6 cups (1 1/2 litres)

1 1/4 cups (310 ml) mung bean shoots

1 cup (250 ml) Chinese cabbage,
    chopped

1 teaspoon (5 ml) minced
    fresh ginger

1/4 teaspoon (1 ml) yellow
    asafoetida powder

1 teaspoon (5 ml) Chinese sesame oil

10 black peppercorns

1 tablespoon (20 ml) lemon juice

1 tablespoon (20 ml) light soy sauce

1 teaspoon (5 ml) salt

Wash the bean shoots and place them in a heavy 4-litre/quart saucepan or stockpot with all the other ingredients. Bring to a boil, reduce the heat, and simmer, covered, for one hour. Strain and use as required.

From simple *Boiled Rice* to banquet-style *Royal Rice*, sautéed or fried, baked or folded with vegetables, fruits and nuts, yogurt, herbs, or spices—here the staple food for three-quarters of the world's population shows its true colours.

RICE DISHES

Pictured: Spanish Vegetable Rice

Boiled Rice

In the following recipe, the rice is half-cooked in boiling water, and lemon juice is added to keep the rice grains separate. The rice is then baked in the oven. Butter and salt can be added. Serve hot, fluffy, boiled rice with vegetable dishes, *dal*s, and soups.

PREPARATION TIME: 5 minutes
COOKING TIME: 25–30 minutes
YIELD: enough for 4 or 5 persons

1½ cups (375 ml) basmati *or other* long-grain white rice

10 cups (2.5 litres) water

1 teaspoon (5 ml) fresh lemon juice

1 teaspoon (5 ml) salt (optional)

2 tablespoons (40 ml) butter (optional)

1. Preheat the oven to 150°C/300°F. Clean, wash, and drain the rice.
2. Boil the water in a heavy 5-litre/quart saucepan and add the lemon juice and the salt. Add the rice; return the water to a boil. Boil rapidly for 10 minutes, without stirring.
3. Drain the rice in a strainer. Transfer the rice to a casserole dish. Dot with half the butter. Spread it out and cover with a tight-fitting lid. Place the rice in the preheated oven and cook at 150°C/300°F for 15-20 minutes or until the rice is dry and tender. If you are using butter, add the remaining butter, gently toss, and serve immediately.

Sautéed Rice with Poppy Seeds

Sautéeing the rice in butter, *ghee*, or oil before adding the water allows all the rice grains to remain separate.

PREPARATION TIME: 5 minutes
COOKING TIME: 25-35 minutes
YIELD: enough for 3 or 4 persons

1 cup (250 ml) basmati *or other* long-grain white rice

2 cups (500 ml) water

¾ teaspoon (3 ml) salt

1 teaspoon (5 ml) fresh lemon juice

6 teaspoons (30 ml) ghee or oil

1½ teaspoons (7 ml) poppy seeds

1. Wash, drain, and dry the rice.
2. Boil the water, salt, and lemon juice in a 2-litre/quart saucepan over moderate heat. Keep it covered to avoid evaporation.
3. Heat the *ghee* or oil over moderately low heat in a 2-litre/quart saucepan. Sauté the poppy seeds in the hot *ghee* until they become aromatic. Stir in the rice and sauté for 1 minute.

4. Add the boiling lemon juice and salt water, increase the heat to high, and allow the water to fully boil for a few seconds; then reduce the heat and allow the rice to gently simmer. Place a tight-fitting lid on the pan and cook without stirring or removing the lid for about 15-20 minutes or until the rice is tender, dry, and fluffy. Turn off the heat, allow the rice to steam another 5 minutes, and serve.

Above: Sautéed Rice with Poppy Seeds
Right: Rice with Green Peas and Almonds
(p. 13)

Thai Rice

Thai Jasmine rice is an aromatic long-grain rice from Thailand. Serve it as an accompaniment to Chinese or South East Asian savoury or vegetable dishes.

PREPARATION TIME: 5 minutes
COOKING TIME: 20-25 minutes
YIELD: enough for 3 or 4 persons

1½ cups (375 ml) Thai rice

2½ cups (625 ml) water

salt (optional)

1 tablespoon (20 ml) ghee or oil

1. Wash, drain, and dry the rice.
2. Boil the water (and optional salt) in a 2-litre/quart saucepan over moderate heat.
3. Heat the *ghee* or oil over moderately low heat in a 2-litre/quart saucepan. Sauté the rice for 1 minute.
4. Add the boiling water, raise the heat, and allow the water to boil again. Reduce the heat and allow the rice to gently simmer, covered with a tight-fitting lid. Cook the rice, without stirring, for 15 minutes. Remove the rice from the heat, leaving it covered for another 5 minutes before serving.

South Indian Yogurt Rice
(*Dahi Bhat*)

This delightful yogurt rice from South India features *urad dal*, mustard, chili, and ginger. Serve hot or cold as a refreshing accompaniment to a light lunch menu.

PREPARATION TIME: 5 minutes
COOKING TIME: 25–35 minutes
YIELD: enough for 4 or 5 persons

1½ cups (375 ml) basmati or other long-grain white rice

2¾ cups (685 ml) water

1 teaspoon (5 ml) salt

2 tablespoons (40 ml) ghee or oil

1 teaspoon (5 ml) black mustard seeds

1 teaspoon (5 ml) split urad dal

1 tablespoon (20 ml) minced fresh ginger

2 fresh green chilies, seeded and minced

1½ cups (375 ml) fresh yogurt

1. Wash, drain, and dry the rice.
2. Bring the water and salt to the boil in a covered 2-litre/quart saucepan over moderate heat.
3. Heat the *ghee* or oil over moderate heat in a 2-litre/quart saucepan. Sauté the mustard seeds in the hot *ghee* until they crackle. Add the *urad dal* and fry until golden brown. Add the minced ginger and the chilies and sauté for 1 minute. Add the rice and sauté for 1 minute.
4. Pour in the boiling salted water and increase the heat to full. When the water boils, reduce the heat, allowing the rice to gently simmer. Place a tight-fitting lid on the pan and cook without stirring for 15 minutes or until the rice is tender and dry. Remove the rice from the heat and gently fold in the yogurt with a fork. Replace the lid, allowing the rice to absorb the yogurt. Serve immediately or allow the rice to cool and serve chilled.

Yellow Rice

The delightful yellow colour in this rice dish comes from turmeric, the powdered root of the plant *Curcuma longa*. Turmeric is an essential ingredient in Indian cooking, extensively used in beans, legumes, *dals*, and various vegetable dishes. It should always be used in moderation, lending a hint of yellow and a slightly warm flavour. Excessive use of turmeric results in an unpleasant bitter taste. Turmeric is a blood purifier and is used in *Ayur Vedic* medicine as a poultice. Purchase turmeric at any well-stocked supermarket or Asian grocer. Serve *Yellow Rice* with spinach-based vegetable dishes such as *Spinach, Tomato, Eggplant, and Chickpea Stew*; or *Creamed Spinach with Curd Cheese*, along with *dal*, and a salad.

PREPARATION TIME: 5 minutes
COOKING TIME: 30-35 minutes
YIELD: enough for 3 or 4 persons

1 cup (250 ml) basmati or other long-grain white rice
2 cups (500 ml) water
3/4 teaspoon (3 ml) salt
1/2 teaspoon (2 ml) turmeric
2 tablespoons (40 ml) ghee or oil
2 tablespoons (40 ml) chopped fresh coriander leaves

1. Wash, drain, and dry the rice.
2. Boil the water, salt, and turmeric in a 2-litre/quart saucepan over moderate heat.
3. Heat the *ghee* or oil over moderate heat in a 2-litre/quart saucepan.

Sauté the rice in the hot *ghee* for 1 minute.

4. Add the boiling turmeric and salt water and increase the heat to full. When the water boils, reduce the heat to low and allow the rice to gently simmer. Place a tight-fitting lid on the pan and cook without stirring for 15-20 minutes or until the rice is tender and dry. Remove the rice from the heat, leaving the lid on for another 5 minutes to allow the grains to firm. Fluff with a fork and serve hot, garnished with fresh coriander leaves.

Rainbow Brown Rice

Compared with most white rice, brown rice is more chewy, with a delightful nutty, sweet flavour. It is also high in much-needed B-complex vitamins. It can be sautéed and cooked in the same way as white rice, the only difference being the length of time it takes to cook. Brown rice should cook for at least 45-55 minutes to become soft and flaky. Serve long-grain brown rice with a light vegetable dish accompanied by bread and salad.

PREPARATION TIME: 10 minutes
COOKING TIME: 1 hour
YIELD: enough for 6 to 8 persons

3 cups (750 ml) water
1½ teaspoons (7 ml) salt
2 bay leaves
4 tablespoons (80 ml) ghee or oil
1½ cups (375 ml) long-grain brown rice
1 teaspoon (5 ml) yellow asafoetida powder
½ teaspoon (2 ml) freshly ground black pepper
1 tablespoon (20 ml) minced fresh ginger
2 tablespoons (40 ml) each of the following: tiny cauliflower pieces, celery bits, green peas, red peppers, carrot straws, cooked corn niblets, tomato pieces, cooked chickpeas, roasted peanuts
3 tablespoons (60 ml) dry-roasted sesame seeds
3 tablespoons (60 ml) finely chopped parsley or coriander leaves
lemon or lime twists for garnish

1. Bring the water, salt, and bay leaves slowly to a boil in a heavy 2-litre/quart saucepan over moderate heat.
2. Heat half the *ghee* or oil in a 2-litre/quart saucepan over moderately-low heat. When hot, stir in the rice and sauté for about 2 minutes. Pour in the boiling salted water. Stir, raise the heat, and bring the water to a full boil. Immediately reduce the heat to low, cover with a tight-fitting lid, and gently simmer, without stirring, for 45-55 minutes or until all the water has been absorbed and the rice is tender and flaky.
3. Remove the rice from the heat, leaving the lid on for another 5 minutes to allow the rice to become firm.
4. Heat the rest of the *ghee* or oil over moderate heat in a heavy pan or wok. Sauté the asafoetida and black pepper momentarily in the hot *ghee*. Add the minced ginger and sauté for ½ minute. Stir-fry the cauliflower pieces, celery, peas, peppers, and carrot straws until tender. Add the cooked corn, tomato pieces, chickpeas, peanuts, sesame seeds, and parsley and combine well. Remove from the heat.
5. Fold together the cooked rice and vegetables and serve immediately, garnished with twists of lemon or lime.

South Indian Sweet-and-Sour Tamarind Rice

This is a well-known and favourite rice dish amongst the Iyengars of South India who are followers of the Ramanuja Sampradaya. The recipe is over 1000 years old and is traditionally called *puliogre*. The *rasam* powder called for in this recipe is home-made (see p.30); however, shop-bought *rasam* powder can be substituted for the home-made variety.

PREPARATION TIME: 15 minutes
COOKING TIME: 25-30 minutes
YIELD: enough for 4 or 5 persons

1½ cups (375 ml) **basmati or other long-grain white rice**

3 cups (750 ml) **water**

1 walnut-sized ball of **seeded tamarind pulp**

½ cup (125 ml) **hot water**

¼ teaspoon (1 ml) **cumin seeds**

¼ teaspoon (1 ml) **whole black peppercorns**

¼ teaspoon (1 ml) **fenugreek seeds**

2 tablespoons (40 ml) **raw sesame seeds**

3 tablespoons (60 ml) **dried coconut**

2 teaspoons (10 ml) **rasam powder**

1 teaspoon (5 ml) **salt**

2 tablespoons (40 ml) **brown sugar**

2 tablespoons (40 ml) **peanut oil**

2 tablespoons (40 ml) **raw peanut halves**

1 teaspoon (5 ml) **black mustard seeds**

8-10 small **curry leaves**

Right: Rainbow Brown Rice

1. Wash, drain, and dry the rice.
2. Boil the 3 cups (750 ml) of unsalted water in a heavy 3-litre/quart non-stick saucepan. Add the rice. Stir until the water returns to a boil; then reduce the heat to a simmer, put on a tight-fitting lid, and leave undisturbed for 15 or 20 minutes or until the rice is dry and tender. Remove the rice from the heat and set aside, covered.
3. Meanwhile, combine the ball of seeded tamarind pulp with the ½ cup (125 ml) of hot water, squeeze until well mixed, and leave to soak.
4. Dry-roast the cumin seeds, black peppercorns, fenugreek, and sesame seeds in a small, heavy pan over moderately low heat. Stir constantly for about 3 minutes until the sesame seeds become aromatic and the spices darken a few shades. Remove the seeds and spices from the pan, allow them to cool, and then grind them in a small coffee grinder or blender until they are powdered. Combine them with the dried coconut, mix well, and place them in a small bowl.

5. Strain the tamarind pulp through a sieve. Squeeze and scrape the underside of the sieve, collecting the juice and discarding the pulp. Combine the tamarind juice, *rasam* powder, salt, and sugar and simmer the mixture over moderate heat in a small saucepan until slightly thickened (about 3-5 minutes). Remove from the heat.
6. Pour the ground spices, seeds, and coconut mixture into the tamarind syrup and mix well.
7. Pour the peanut oil into the small pan in which you roasted the spices. Place over moderate heat. When the oil is hot, add the peanuts and stir-fry them until they are golden brown (about 2 minutes). Remove them with a slotted spoon and drain them on paper towels. Continue heating the remaining oil and add the mustard seeds and curry leaves. When the seeds crackle, pour the contents of the pan into the tamarind syrup and mix well.
8. When the rice is fully cooked, add the peanuts and spicy tamarind syrup and serve immediately.

Bengali Royal Rice (*Pushpanna*)

Pushpanna is the "queen of rice". It contains pure saffron threads and a variety of nuts, dried fruit, vegetables, and spices. It is ideal served on special festive occasions and is worth the time and effort put into gathering the ingredients.

PREPARATION TIME: 10 minutes
COOKING TIME: 40 minutes
YIELD: enough for 6 to 8 persons

1½ cups (375 ml) basmati or other long-grain white rice

½ teaspoon (2 ml) saffron threads

1 tablespoon (20 ml) hot milk

3 cups (750 ml) water

2 teaspoons (10 ml) salt

3 teaspoons (15 ml) nutmeg, freshly ground

¼ cup (60 ml) ghee

¼ cup (60 ml) cashew bits or halves

¼ cup (60 ml) raw almond slivers

3 tablespoons (60 ml) raisins

1 teaspoon (5 ml) fennel seeds

one 2.5 cm (1-inch) cinnamon stick

1 teaspoon (5 ml) cumin seeds

6 cardamom pods, bruised

6 whole cloves

1 teaspoon (5 ml) coarsely ground black pepper

½ teaspoon (2 ml) cayenne pepper

½ teaspoon (2 ml) yellow asafoetida powder

2 tablespoons (40 ml) shredded fresh coconut

¼ cup (60 ml) cooked green peas

¼ cup (60 ml) brown sugar

home-made curd cheese (panir), made from 6 cups (1.5 litres) milk cut into 0.5 cm (¼-inch) cubes and deep-fried until golden brown

1. Wash, drain, and dry the rice.
2. Soak the saffron in the milk for 5 minutes.
3. Boil the water, salt, saffron milk, and nutmeg in a 2-litre/quart saucepan over moderate heat. Keep it covered to avoid evaporation.
4. Heat half the *ghee* or oil in a 4-litre/quart saucepan over moderate heat. Add the cashews and almonds, sauté until golden brown, and then remove with a slotted spoon. Set aside. Stir-fry the raisins for a few seconds until they swell, remove them, and place them in a bowl with the cashews and almonds.
5. Add half the remaining *ghee* or oil to the pan. Sauté the rice for 2-3 minutes over moderate heat; then add the boiling water. Stir, raise the heat, and bring the water to a full boil. Immediately reduce the heat to low, cover with a tight-fitting lid, and gently simmer, without stirring, for 15-20 minutes or until all the water has been absorbed and the rice is tender and flaky.
6. Remove the rice from the heat, leaving the lid on for another 5 minutes to allow the rice to become firm.
7. Place the remaining *ghee* in a heavy pan over moderate heat. Stir-fry the fennel seeds, cinnamon stick, cumin seeds, cardamom pods, and whole cloves for 1 minute or until seeds are golden brown. Add the black pepper, cayenne pepper, asafoetida, and fresh coconut. Sauté the coconut for 1 minute; then add the peas, sugar, deep-fried *panir*, nuts, and raisins. Remove from the heat.
8. Carefully combine the cooked rice with all the other ingredients. Serve on a warmed serving dish or on individual plates .

Rice with Green Peas and Almonds

This fancy rice dish is ideal for party catering or for a special lunch or dinner.

PREPARATION TIME: 5 minutes
COOKING TIME: 30-40 minutes
YIELD: enough for 4 or 5 persons

1 cup (250 ml) basmati or other long-grain white rice

4 green cardamom pods

2 cups (500 ml) water

Left: Bengali Royal Rice, shown with Grated Cauliflower Balls in Tomato Sauce (p. 99)

¾ teaspoon (3 ml) salt

¼ teaspoon (1 ml) turmeric

3 tablespoons (60 ml) ghee or oil

one 4 cm (1½-inch) cinnamon stick

6 whole cloves

⅓ cup (85 ml) slivered or sliced raw almonds

1 cup (250 ml) fresh or frozen peas

1. Wash, drain, and dry the rice.
2. Lightly tap each cardamom pod to partially crush.
3. Bring the water, salt, and turmeric slowly to a boil in a 2-litre/quart saucepan over moderate heat.
4. Heat the *ghee* or oil in another 2-litre/quart saucepan over moderately low heat. Fry the cinnamon stick, cloves, bruised cardamom pods, and almonds in the hot *ghee* until the almonds turn pale golden brown.
5. Add the rice and sauté for about 2 minutes or until the grains turn whitish. Pour in the boiling salted turmeric water and fresh peas (defrosted frozen peas should be added after the rice has been cooking for about 10 minutes). Stir, increase the heat to high, and bring the water to a full boil. Immediately reduce the heat to low, cover with a tight-fitting lid, and gently simmer, without stirring, for 15-20 minutes or until all the water is absorbed and the rice is tender and flaky. Serve hot.

13

Savoury Cantonese Fried Rice

Use long-grain rice in this tasty fried combination with sautéed vegetables, *tofu*, and seasonings. The rice should be boiled in water, drained, and chilled overnight before frying. The *tofu* required is the firm rather than the soft or "silken" variety. It is available from any Asian grocer.

PREPARATION AND COOKING TIME: 30 minutes

YIELD: enough for 6-8 persons

4 tablespoons (80 ml) Chinese sesame oil

1 teaspoon (5 ml) minced fresh ginger

1/2 teaspoon (2 ml) yellow asafoetida powder

1 small carrot, cut julienne style

1/4 cup (60 ml) finely slivered celery

1/4 cup (60 ml) finely diced cabbage

1/4 cup (60 ml) unpeeled cucumber pieces, cut matchstick-size

2 tablespoons (40 ml) bamboo shoots, cut matchstick-size

2 tablespoons (40 ml) diced red peppers

1/4 cup (60 ml) cooked green peas

1/4 cup (60 ml) mung bean shoots

1/4 cup (60 ml) crumbled firm **tofu**

3 tablespoons (60 ml) soy sauce

2 teaspoons (10 ml) Chinese chili oil

1 teaspoon (5 ml) salt

1/4 teaspoon (1 ml) black pepper

2 cups (500 ml) long-grain rice, cooked without salt and chilled overnight

1. Heat 1 tablespoon (20 ml) of Chinese sesame oil in a wok over moderate heat. Sauté the minced ginger in the hot oil for one minute. Add the asafoetida, tossing it momentarily with the ginger. Increase the heat to full. Add the carrots, celery, and cabbage and sauté for 2 or 3 minutes. Add the cucumber, bamboo shoots, red peppers, green peas, and bean shoots and sauté for one minute; then add the *tofu*, soy sauce, chili oil, salt, and pepper. Sauté for one minute.

2. Empty the contents of the wok into a bowl, cover with a lid, and rinse the wok.

3. Heat the wok until dry and hot and add the remaining sesame oil. Sauté the chilled long-grain rice in the hot oil over full heat. Add the vegetables and serve immediately.

Lemon Rice

Lemon rice originates in South India and is flavoured with fresh lemon or lime juice, tasty *urad dal*, mustard seeds, and fresh coconut.

PREPARATION TIME: 5 minutes
COOKING TIME: 25-35 minutes
YIELD: enough for 4 persons

1 cup (250 ml) basmati or other long-grain white rice

2 cups (500 ml) water

1 teaspoon (5 ml) salt

1/2 teaspoon (2 ml) turmeric

3 tablespoons (60 ml) ghee or oil

½ cup (125 ml) raw cashew halves
   or bits

1 teaspoon (5 ml) black
   mustard seeds

1½ teaspoons (7 ml) split urad dal

⅓ cup (85 ml) fresh lemon or
   lime juice

3 tablespoons (60 ml) coarsely
   chopped fresh coriander or
   parsley

¼ cup (60 ml) shredded fresh or
   dried coconut

1. Wash, drain, and dry the rice.
2. Boil the water, salt, and turmeric in a 2-litre/quart saucepan over moderate heat.
3. Heat the *ghee* or oil over moderately low heat in another 2-litre/quart saucepan. Sauté the raw cashew halves or bits in the hot *ghee* until they turn golden brown. Remove them with a slotted spoon and put them aside. Sauté the mustard seeds and *urad dal* in the remaining hot oil until the mustard seeds crackle and the *urad dal* darkens to a rich golden brown.
4. Add the rice and sauté for 1 or 2 minutes, or until the grains are evenly whitish in colour. Add the boiling salted turmeric water. Stir, raise the heat, and bring the water to a full boil. Immediately reduce the heat to low, cover with a tight-fitting lid and gently simmer, without stirring, for 15-20 minutes or until all the water has been absorbed and the rice is tender and flaky.
5. Remove the rice from the heat, leaving the lid on for another 5 minutes to allow the rice to firm.
6. Before you serve the rice, add the cashew nuts, the lemon or lime juice, and the fresh herbs. Mix well and garnish each serving with coconut.

Baked Vegetable Rice
(*Biriyani*)

Biriyani originates in the Moghul period of Indian history. This delightful and colourful vegetarian version, ideal as a festive dish, contains zucchini, lima beans, eggplant, red peppers, cashews, raisins, and spices.

PREPARATION TIME: 5 minutes
COOKING TIME: 25-35 minutes
BAKING TIME: 30 minutes
YIELD: enough for 6-8 persons

2 cups (500 ml) basmati or other
   long-grain white rice

4 cups (1 litre) water

3 teaspoons (15 ml) salt

2½ teaspoons (12 ml) turmeric

4 tablespoons (80 ml) ghee or oil

¼ teaspoon (1 ml) cardamom seeds

1½ teaspoons (7 ml) black
   mustard seeds

2 teaspoons (10 ml) poppy seeds

¼ teaspoon (1 ml) cayenne pepper

1 teaspoon (5 ml) garam masala

1 teaspoon (5 ml) ground coriander

1 large eggplant peeled and diced
   into 1.25 cm (½-inch) cubes

6 ounces (170 g) melted butter

1 large zucchini diced into 1.25 cm
   (½-inch) cubes

1 large red pepper diced into
   1.25 cm (½-inch) cubes

2 cups (500 ml) tomatoes, peeled and
   chopped

1 teaspoon (5 ml) sugar

1 cup (250 ml) cooked lima beans

⅔ cup (165 ml) slivered raw almonds

⅔ cup (165 ml) broken or halved
   raw cashews

⅔ cup (165 ml) raisins

Left: Savoury Cantonese Fried Rice

1. Wash, drain, and dry the rice.
2. Boil the water, 1½ teaspoons (7 ml) salt, and 1½ teaspoons (7 ml) turmeric in a 4-litre/quart saucepan over moderate heat.
3. Heat half the *ghee* or oil in another 2-litre/quart saucepan over moderately-low heat. Sauté the cardamom seeds and the rice in the hot *ghee* for 2 minutes or until the grains turn whitish. Add the boiling water. Stir, raise the heat, and bring the water to a full boil. Immediately reduce the heat to low, cover with a tight-fitting lid, and gently simmer, without stirring, for 15-20 minutes. Remove from the heat, allowing the grains to become firm.
4. Heat the remaining *ghee* or oil in a medium-sized pan or wok over moderately high heat. Sauté the mustard seeds in the hot *ghee* and, when they crackle, add the poppy seeds, the cayenne, *garam masala*, coriander, eggplant pieces, and half the butter. Stir-fry the eggplant for about 3 minutes.
5. Add the zucchini, red pepper, tomato pieces, remaining salt, and sugar. Simmer the vegetables until just tender. Add the lima beans and remove from the heat.
6. Spoon half the rice into a large buttered oven-proof casserole dish and spread evenly. Spread the vegetable mixture on top.
7. Heat the remaining butter in a small pan over moderate heat. Sauté the nuts in the hot butter until they turn pale golden brown. Add the raisins and stir-fry until they swell and the nuts are golden brown.
8. Combine this mixture with the remaining rice and spread on top of the vegetable layer. Place a lid on the casserole dish and bake in a preheated moderate oven (180°C/355°F) for 30 minutes. Serve hot.

15

Rice and Mung Bean Stew
(*Khichari*)

Khichari is a nutritious stew featuring *dal* and rice. There are two main varieties—thin (*geeli khichari*) and thick (*sookha khichari*). Whichever way you prepare *khichari*, it will soon become a delicious favourite. The following recipe is for the thicker variety. *Khichari* is an ideal breakfast food, wonderful when accompanied by yogurt and fresh hot *Puffed Fried Breads* (*Pooris*) or toast. Always serve *khichari* with a wedge of lemon or lime. Not only does this add a delightful nuance of flavour, but it lends nutritional advantage also: there are good sources of iron in the *dal* and vegetables in *khichari*, and the lemon juice, rich in vitamin C, helps your body absorb it. This recipe is mildly spiced. Adjust your own spicing as required.

PREPARATION TIME: 5 minutes
COOKING TIME: 30-40 minutes
YIELD: enough for 6-8 persons

1/3 cup (85 ml) split mung beans

1 cup (250 ml) basmati or other long-grain white rice
3 tablespoons (60 ml) ghee or oil
1/3 cup (85 ml) raw cashew pieces or halves
2 teaspoons (10 ml) cumin seeds
1 tablespoon (20 ml) fresh hot green chili, minced
2 tablespoons (40 ml) minced fresh ginger
1 teaspoon (5 ml) turmeric
1 teaspoon (5 ml) yellow asafoetida powder
1 small cauliflower (about 400 g, or 14 ounces) cut into small flowerets
5-6 cups (1.25-1.5 litres) water
1½ teaspoons (7 ml) salt
1 tablespoon (20 ml) butter
2/3 cup (165 ml) cooked green peas
1 cup (250 ml) tomatoes, peeled and chopped
1/2 cup (125 ml) chopped fresh coriander leaves

1. Wash and drain the *dal* and rice.
2. Heat the *ghee* in a heavy 4-litre/quart non-stick saucepan over moderate heat. Fry the cashews in the hot *ghee* until they turn golden brown and remove them with a slotted spoon. Put them aside. Fry the cumin seeds in the *ghee*. When they turn golden brown add the chilies and ginger. Sauté them for a few seconds; then add the turmeric and asafoetida. Add the cauliflower pieces and stir-fry them for 1 minute. Finally, add the *dal* and rice, stirring with the spices and vegetables for 1 minute.
3. Add the water and bring to a full boil over high heat. Reduce the heat to low, partially cover, and slowly cook, stirring occasionally, for 30-40 minutes or until the *dal* and rice are soft. If the *khichari* dries out too much, add up to one cup (250 ml) warm water. Before removing the *khichari* from the heat, fold in the salt, butter, cooked green peas, chopped tomatoes, toasted cashews, and the chopped fresh coriander leaves, allowing them to warm for one minute. Serve hot.

Spanish Vegetable Rice
(*Paella*)

This is a vegetarian version of the Spanish national dish. It's colourful and delicious and flavoured with pure saffron thread. *Paella* is an ideal choice as a colourful addition to a special dinner or luncheon.

PREPARATION AND COOKING TIME: 40 minutes

YIELD: enough for 6-8 persons

2 cups (500 ml) basmati or other long-grain white rice
1/2 cup (125 ml) olive oil
1/2 teaspoon (2 ml) yellow asafoetida powder
1 large red pepper, pith removed,
seeded and diced
2½ cups (625 ml) Green Vegetable Stock or water
4 large tomatoes, peeled and chopped
1 cup (250 ml) cooked green beans, cut into 2.5 cm (1-inch) sections
3/4 cup (185 ml) cooked fresh green peas or thawed frozen peas
1 stalk celery, chopped
18 black olives, halved and stoned
2 teaspoons (10 ml) salt
1 teaspoon (5 ml) freshly ground black pepper
1/2 teaspoon (2 ml, or about 0.25 g)

crushed saffron threads dissolved in 2 teaspoons (10 ml) hot water
1/2 cup (125 ml) slivered almonds

1. Wash, drain, and dry the rice.
2. Heat the olive oil in a 4-litre/quart saucepan over moderate heat. When the oil is hot, add the asafoetida and red pepper, stirring for about 2 minutes. Add the rice and sauté for about 3 minutes. Meanwhile, heat the vegetable stock until boiling.
3. Add the boiling stock to the rice and increase the heat to full. Add the tomatoes, green beans, peas, celery, olives, salt, pepper, and saffron wa-

ter. When the liquid boils, reduce the heat to very low and simmer the rice, covered, for about 30 minutes or until it is tender. Do not remove the lid during the cooking process.

4. Remove the pan from the heat and turn the *paella* into a warmed serving dish. Garnish with almonds and serve hot.

Indonesian Coconut Rice

The delicate flavour of coconut pervades this simple rice dish. You will need 2 special ingredients: coconut milk (*santan*) and lime leaf. Both are available at Asian specialty stores. The coconut milk can be bought in cans. This recipe requires the liquid variety of coconut milk, not the creamed coconut pulp. The lime leaf can be obtained dried, in packets. The lime leaf can be substituted with a bay leaf.

PREPARATION TIME: 20 minutes
COOKING TIME: 20 minutes
YIELD: enough for 3 or 4 persons

1 cup (250 ml) basmati or other long-grain white rice

1½ cups (375 ml) coconut milk (santan)

½-1 teaspoon (2-5 ml) salt

1 lime leaf (or bay leaf)

1. Wash the rice thoroughly in cold water. Soak it in cold water for 10 minutes, drain, and allow to air-dry for 10 minutes.

2. Boil the coconut milk (*santan*), salt, and lime leaf in a heavy-based 2-litre/quart saucepan. Add the rice. Reduce the heat to very low, allowing the rice to simmer slowly with a tight-fitting lid. After about 15 minutes, the liquid will have evaporated. Carefully stir the grains with a fork and replace the lid. After another 5 minutes, the rice will have completely steamed. Serve immediately.

Tomato Rice with Herbs

This simple combination of rice, herbs, and tomato with an Italian flavour can also be used as an alternative stuffing for baked peppers.

PREPARATION TIME: 5 minutes
COOKING TIME: 25-35 minutes
YIELD: enough for 4 persons

1 cup (250 ml) basmati or other long-grain white rice

1¾ cups (435 ml) water

1 teaspoon (5 ml) salt

1 teaspoon (5 ml) paprika

1 tablespoon (20 ml) tomato paste

2 tablespoons (40 ml) fresh basil leaves, chopped fine

2 tablespoons (40 ml) olive oil

½ teaspoon (2 ml) yellow asafoetida powder

1 cup (250 ml) firm tomatoes, cut into 1.25 cm (½-inch) cubes

2 tablespoons (40 ml) finely chopped fresh parsley

1. Wash, drain, and dry the rice.
2. Bring the water, salt, paprika, tomato paste, and basil slowly to a boil in a 2-litre/quart saucepan over moderate heat.

3. Heat the olive oil in a non-stick 2-litre/quart saucepan over moderately low heat. Sauté the asafoetida in the hot *ghee*. Add the rice and stir-fry for about 2 minutes or until the rice grains turn whitish.

4. Pour in the boiling water. Stir, raise the heat to high, and bring the water to a full boil. Immediately reduce the heat to low, cover with a tight-fitting lid, and gently simmer, without stirring, for 15-20 minutes or until all the water has been absorbed and the rice is tender and flaky.

5. Remove the rice from the heat and allow it to steam for 5 minutes with the lid on. Finally, fold in the tomatoes and fresh parsley and serve immediately.

Above: Tomato Rice with Herbs

SOUPS

Served as a first course or as a complete meal, a side dishe or a refresher, soup is inexpensive and nutritious.

Pictured: Thai Clear Soup with Tofu

Lentil and Tomato Soup

Serve this hearty soup with rice or crusty bread.

PREPARATION TIME: 10 minutes
COOKING TIME: 45-50 minutes
YIELD: enough for 4 persons

1 cup (250 ml) brown lentils

5 cups (1.25 litres) water

2 teaspoons (10 ml) ground coriander

1 tablespoon (20 ml) olive oil

1/4 teaspoon (1 ml) yellow asafoetida powder

1/4 teaspoon (1 ml) freshly ground black pepper

1 teaspoon (5 ml) salt

1 teaspoon (5 ml) brown sugar

1 tablespoon (20 ml) fresh lemon juice

1 cup (250 ml) tomatoes, peeled and chopped

1 tablespoon (20 ml) tomato paste

1 tablespoon (20 ml) chopped fresh parsley

1. Wash and drain the brown lentils.

2. Boil the lentils, water, and ground coriander in a heavy 3-litre/quart saucepan over high heat, stirring occasionally. Reduce the heat to moderately low, cover, and cook for about 45 minutes or until the lentils become soft.

3. Heat the olive oil in a small pan over moderate to moderately high heat. Sauté the asafoetida and black pepper in the hot oil. Add the fried spices to the soup. Add the salt, sugar, lemon juice, and chopped tomatoes. Return the soup to the boil, reduce the heat, and simmer for another 5 minutes. Add the tomato paste and fresh parsley and serve hot.

Above: Minestrone Soup

Minestrone Soup

There are many varieties of this world-famous Italian soup. This one—"*Minestrone alla Milanese*"— is practically a meal in itself. Serve it with fresh bread and salad. For best results, start the soup well in advance of serving time and cook slowly.

PREPARATION AND COOKING TIME : 2 hours 50 minutes
YIELD: enough for 6 to 8 persons

2 tablespoons (40 ml) olive oil

1/2 teaspoon (2 ml) yellow asafoetida powder

1 cup (250 ml) tomatoes, peeled and chopped

1/2 cup (125 ml) dried borlotti beans or kidney beans, soaked overnight in cold water

2 tablespoons (40 ml) chopped fresh basil leaves

1 tablespoon (20 ml) chopped fresh parsley

8 cups (2 litres) water

1 medium carrot, peeled and diced

1 stick of celery, diced

2 medium potatoes, peeled and diced

2 medium zucchinis, sliced

2 cups (500 ml) shredded cabbage

3/4 cup (185 ml) fresh peas

1 1/2 teaspoons (7 ml) salt

1 1/2 teaspoons (7 ml) freshly ground black pepper

1 tablespoon (20 ml) rice-shaped pasta (Risoni) or broken spaghetti

1/2 cup (125 ml) parmesan cheese

1. Heat the olive oil in a large saucepan. Sauté the asafoetida in the hot oil until it becomes aromatic, and then add the tomatoes, drained soaked beans, basil, parsley, and water. Bring to a boil, lower the heat, cover, and simmer for about 1 1/2 hours or until the beans are soft, stirring occasionally.

2. Add the carrots and celery and simmer for another 1/2 hour. Add the potatoes, zucchini, cabbage, peas, salt, and pepper. Ten minutes later add the pasta. After 10 minutes, if the potato, zucchini, cabbage, and peas are tender, turn off the heat. If the soup becomes too thick, add hot water as required. Let the soup sit for 5 minutes; then add the parmesan cheese, reserving some to sprinkle on the individual soup bowls. Serve hot.

Green Split-Pea Dal with Spinach and Coconut Milk

Fresh spinach enhances and enriches the texture of this hearty soup. Serve this soup with *Lemon Rice* for a delightful combination of taste and colour. Soak the *dal* well in advance.

DAL SOAKING TIME: 5 hours
PREPARATION TIME: 10 minutes
COOKING TIME: 1 hour
YIELD: enough for 4 to 6 persons

1 cup (250 ml) green split peas

1 teaspoon (5 ml) minced fresh ginger

1 small hot green chili, seeded and minced

6 cups (1.5 litres) water

1 teaspoon (5 ml) turmeric

2 teaspoons (10 ml) ground coriander

1 small bunch spinach, washed thoroughly and roughly chopped

1½ teaspoons (7 ml) salt

1 cup (250 ml) coconut milk

2 tablespoons (40 ml) ghee or oil

1¼ teaspoons (6 ml) kalonji seeds

¼ teaspoon (1 ml) yellow asafoetida powder

1 teaspoon (5 ml) fresh lemon or lime juice

1. Wash and drain the split peas. Soak in cold water for 5 hours.

2. Boil the ginger, chili, water, turmeric, coriander, and split peas in a heavy 3-litre/quart saucepan over moderate heat. Simmer for about 50 minutes or until the *dal* is soft . Stir occasionally.

3. Add the chopped spinach to the *dal*. When the spinach is soft and the *dal* is smooth, add the salt and coconut milk and return the soup to a simmer.

4. Prepare the final zesty seasoning as follows: heat the *ghee* or oil in a small pan. Sauté the kalonji seeds in the hot *ghee* for 1 minute. Sauté the asafoetida momentarily. Add the spices to the soup, mix well, and allow the spices to blend for a few minutes. Add fresh lemon or lime juice. Serve hot.

Corn Chowder

Select corn with fresh, dark-green husks and plump yellow kernels. Boil the corn in unsalted water for exactly 8 minutes, as excessive cooking toughens the corn.

PREPARATION AND COOKING TIME: 30-40 minutes
YIELD: enough for 6 persons

6 cups (1.5 litres) Root Vegetable Stock or water

2 medium potatoes, peeled and cut into tiny 0.5 cm (¼-inch) cubes

1 bay leaf

2 cups (500 ml) cooked corn kernels (about 3 medium ears of corn)

50 g (1¾ ounces) butter

¼ teaspoon (1 ml) yellow asafoetida powder

¼ teaspoon (1 ml) black pepper

¼ teaspoon (1 ml) nutmeg

2 tablespoons (40 ml) plain flour

1 teaspoon (5 ml) salt, or as desired

½ cup (125 ml) sour cream

2 tablespoons (40 ml) chopped fresh parsley

1. Boil the stock or water over high heat in a heavy 4-litre/quart saucepan. Add the potatoes and bay leaf. Reduce the heat to moderate and semi-cook the potatoes.

2. Whilst the potatoes are cooking, coarsely mince the cooked corn kernels in a food processor or blender until they are half-puréed. Add the puréed corn to the nearly cooked potatoes and simmer for 5 minutes. Remove the saucepan from the heat and transfer the mixture into a bowl. Cover and keep hot.

3. Rinse the saucepan, add the butter and melt over moderate heat. Add the asafoetida, pepper, nutmeg, and the flour. Cook the flour in the butter until it darkens a shade or two. Add the potato-and-corn mixture into the butter and flour whilst stirring with a whisk.

4. Bring the soup to a boil over moderate heat. Remove the saucepan from the heat and add the salt, sour cream, and parsley. Serve in pre-warmed soup bowls with a spoonful of sour cream and garnish with fresh parsley.

Gujarati Yogurt Soup (*Karhi*)

Karhis (or *Kadhis*) are smooth yogurt-based dishes that are served with rice. They are sometimes thick and sauce-like, as in the case of northern Indian *Karhi*. This *Karhi* recipe from Gujarat is traditionally soup-like with a hint of sweetness. Serve with *Boiled Rice* or *Rice and Mung Bean Stew*.

PREPARATION TIME: 5 minutes
COOKING TIME: 20 minutes
YIELD: enough for 5 or 6 persons

3 tablespoons (60 ml) sifted chickpea flour

2 cups (500 ml) water

1½ cups (375 ml) yogurt

½ teaspoon (2 ml) turmeric

1 teaspoon (5 ml) sugar

1 teaspoon (5 ml) salt

2 tablespoons (40 ml) ghee *or* oil

1 teaspoon (5 ml) black mustard seeds

2 hot green chilies, minced

1 teaspoon (5 ml) minced fresh ginger

8-10 curry leaves (fresh if possible)

1 teaspoon (5 ml) fenugreek seeds

¼ teaspoon (1 ml) yellow asafoetida powder

1 tablespoon (20 ml) chopped fresh coriander

1. Place the sifted chickpea flour and ¼ cup (60 ml) of the water into a small bowl and whisk to a smooth paste. Add the rest of the water and whisk again. Carefully whisk in the yogurt, turmeric, sugar and salt.

2. Pour this mixture into a heavy-based 4-litre/quart saucepan and, stirring constantly, bring it to a boil over moderate heat. Reduce the heat and simmer for 10 minutes, stirring often.

3. Heat the *ghee* or oil over moderately-high heat in a small pan. Sauté the mustard seeds in the hot oil. When the seeds crackle, add the chilies, ginger, and curry leaves. Once the curry leaves darken, add the fenugreek. Stir until the fenugreek seeds darken a few shades. Add the asafoetida and stir to mix; then add the contents of the pan to the simmering *karhi*. Stir well, remove from the heat, and cover. Serve hot, garnished with fresh coriander leaves.

South Indian Hot-and-Sour Soup (*Sambar*)

This South Indian soup is traditionally chili-hot. Reduce the chili content for a milder version. Sambar features three main ingredients: *toor dal*, tamarind pulp, and a special spice powder called *sambar masala*. All three ingredients are available at any Indian grocer.

Sambar's delightful hot-and-sour flavour can be made more substantial with the addition of practically any vegetable of your choice. Serve it with plain fluffy rice, with any South Indian selection such as *South Indian Yogurt Rice* or *South Indian Vegetable Combination*, or as an entrée to a special dinner.

DAL SOAKING TIME: 3 hours
PREPARATION TIME: 15 minutes
COOKING TIME: 1 hour
YIELD: enough for 5 persons

1 cup (250 ml) split **toor dal**

6 cups (1.5 litres) water

½ teaspoon (2 ml) turmeric

3 teaspoons (15 ml) butter

1 tablespoon (20 ml) tamarind concentrate

½ cup (125 ml) shredded fresh or dried coconut

½ teaspoon (2 ml) cayenne pepper

2 tablespoons (40 ml) brown sugar

½ cup (125 ml) water for coconut purée

2 tablespoons (40 ml) ghee or oil

1 teaspoon (5 ml) black mustard seeds

2 teaspoons (10 ml) hot green chilies, seeded and minced

¼ teaspoon (1 ml) fenugreek seeds

10 dried curry leaves

¼ teaspoon (1 ml) yellow asafoetida powder

2 teaspoons (10 ml) sambar masala

1½ teaspoons (7 ml) salt

*2 tablespoons (40 ml) chopped fresh
parsley or coriander leaves*

1. Wash and drain the *toor dal*. Soak the *dal* in 4 cups (1 litre) of hot water for 3 hours. Drain.

2. Boil the *dal*, water, turmeric, and butter over high heat in a 4-litre/quart saucepan. Reduce to a simmer. Simmer for 1 hour or until the *dal* becomes soft. Whisk the soup until smooth.

3. Mix the tamarind pulp with a few tablespoons of warm water to form a paste.

4. Blend the fresh or dried coconut, cayenne, sugar, and 1/2 cup (125 ml) water in a blender or food processor until smooth. Pour this mixture into the simmering *dal*. Stir the tamarind purée into the *dal*.

5. Heat the *ghee* or oil in a small pan over moderately high heat. Sauté the mustard seeds in the hot *ghee* until they crackle. Add the green chilies and fenugreek seeds. When the fenugreek seeds turn a darker shade, add the curry leaves, asafoetida, and *sambar masala*. Sauté momentarily; then add to the simmering *dal*. Remove from the heat, season with salt, garnish with the chopped parsley or coriander, and serve hot.

Vegetable Soup

This traditional homestyle soup is a nutritious meal in itself. The whole grains are rich in iron, B vitamins, and protein; the vegetables are rich in A and C vitamins. Serve the soup with bread and salad.

SOAKING TIME: at least 1 hour
PREPARATION TIME: 10 minutes
COOKING TIME: 1 hour
YIELD: enough for 4 to 6 persons

1/4 cup (60 ml) kidney beans

1/4 cup (60 ml) yellow split peas

1/4 cup (60 ml) split mung beans

1/4 cup (60 ml) pearl barley

*3 tablespoons (60 ml) unsalted
butter*

*3/4 teaspoon (3 ml) yellow
asafoetida powder*

1 medium carrot, diced

*1 medium celery stalk (with leaves),
diced*

*1 medium potato, scrubbed
and diced*

1/2 medium turnip, diced

1 medium tomato, peeled and diced

7 cups (1.75 litres) hot water

1/2 teaspoon (2 ml) mixed dried herbs

1/4 teaspoon (1 ml) black pepper

2 teaspoons (10 ml) salt

1/3 cup (85 ml) chopped fresh parsley

1. Soak the beans, split peas and barley in cold water for at least 1 hour.

2. Melt the butter in a 6-litre/quart saucepan over moderate heat. Add the asafoetida and fry momentarily. Add the carrots, celery, potatoes, turnips, and tomatoes and sauté for 5 minutes. Add the water, the drained pre-soaked beans, the herbs, and the pepper and bring to a boil. Simmer for 1 hour or until all ingredients are tender. Season with salt and parsley and serve in pre-warmed soup bowls.

*Left: Gujarati Yogurt Soup shown with
Pappadams (p. 44)*
Above: Vegetable Soup

Cream of Pumpkin Soup

Pumpkin soup is a great winter favourite. Milk and a simple seasoning of black pepper and nutmeg allow the pumpkin flavour to predominate.

PREPARATION AND COOKING TIME: 30 minutes
YIELD: enough for 4 persons

90 g (3 ounces) butter

¼ teaspoon (1 ml) nutmeg

¼ teaspoon (1 ml) freshly ground black pepper

4 cups (or about 1 kg, 2.2 pounds) pumpkin, peeled, seeded, and cubed

3 cups (750 ml) water

1½ cups (375 ml) milk

1 tablespoon (20 ml) plain flour

1 teaspoon (5 ml) salt

1 tablespoon (20 ml) light cream

2 tablespoons (40 ml) chopped fresh parsley

1. Melt half the butter in a 6-litre/quart saucepan over moderate heat. Add the nutmeg, black pepper, and pumpkin cubes and sauté for 10 minutes. Add the water and bring to a boil, cooking until the pumpkin is very tender.

2. Empty the contents of the saucepan into a blender and add half the milk. Purée, being careful to ensure the lid remains on the blender.

3. Rinse the saucepan, add remaining butter and heat gently. Stir the flour into the butter. Return the pumpkin purée to the saucepan along with the remaining milk, stirring constantly until the soup is well-blended. Bring to a boil, simmer for a few minutes, and season with salt. Serve the soup in individual pre-warmed soup bowls, garnished with light cream and chopped parsley. Serve hot.

Mung Bean and Tomato Soup

Whole green mung beans combine wonderfully with tomatoes and cook to a succulent purée in this ever-popular *dal* soup. Mung beans are rich in iron, vitamin B, and protein, and their available protein content increases when combined with bread or rice.

PREPARATION TIME: 10 minutes
COOKING TIME: 45 minutes-1 hour
YIELD: enough for 4 to 6 persons

1 cup (250 ml) whole green mung beans

7¼ cups (1.8 litres) water

½ teaspoon (2 ml) turmeric

1 teaspoon (5 ml) minced fresh ginger

½ teaspoon (2 ml) fresh green chili minced

2 firm, ripe tomatoes, coarsely chopped

2 tablespoons (40 ml) minced chopped parsley

2 teaspoons (10 ml) brown sugar

1½ teaspoons (7 ml) salt

2 tablespoons (40 ml) fresh lemon juice

2 tablespoons (40 ml) mild-tasting olive oil

1½ teaspoons (7 ml) cumin seeds

¼ teaspoon (1 ml) yellow asafoetida powder

1. Wash and drain the mung beans.
2. Boil the beans, water, turmeric, ginger, and chili over high heat in a heavy 3-litre/quart saucepan. Reduce heat to moderately low. Cover with a tight-fitting lid and boil gently for up to 1 hour or until the beans become soft.
3. Add the tomatoes, parsley, sugar, salt, and lemon juice. Continue to simmer for another 5 minutes.
4. Heat the olive oil in a small pan until slightly smoking; add the cumin seeds and sauté until they crackle and turn golden brown. Sauté the asafoetida momentarily; then add the spices to the soup. Allow the seasonings to soak into the soup for 1-2 minutes. Serve hot.

Potato Soup

PREPARATION AND COOKING TIME: 45 minutes
YIELD: enough for 6 persons

5 cups (1.25 litres) water

6 medium baking potatoes, peeled and chopped into 1.5 cm (³⁄₄-inch) cubes

½ cup (125 ml) celery, chopped fine

2 tablespoons (40 ml) butter

¼ teaspoon (1 ml) yellow asafoetida powder

¼ teaspoon (1 ml) coarsely ground black pepper

¼ teaspoon (1 ml) ground celery seeds

1 teaspoon (5 ml) dried dill

1 cup (250 ml) sour cream

1½ teaspoons (7 ml) salt

2 tablespoons (40 ml) chopped fresh parsley

1. Boil the water, diced potatoes, and chopped celery over moderate heat in a 4-litre/quart saucepan. Cover, and simmer until the potatoes are very tender (about 30 minutes). Stir occasionally.
2. Heat the butter in a small pan over low heat. Sauté the asafoetida, black pepper, ground celery seed, and

dried dill momentarily in the hot oil. Add the sour cream, stir to mix, warm for 1 minute, and remove from heat.

3. Blend the potato and celery mixture in a blender or food processor until smooth. Return the puréed potato and celery mixture to the saucepan. Bring the soup almost to a boil over moderate heat, stirring constantly. Add the sour cream mixture, salt, and parsley. Serve immediately.

Above: Chilled Summer Fruit Soup

Chilled Summer Fruit Soup

This cool and refreshing soup can be served as a first course, between courses, or as a dessert. All fruits should be ripe, sweet, and seasonal.

PREPARATION AND COOKING TIME: 30 minutes

YIELD: enough for 6 to 8 persons

1 red apple, peeled and cubed

250g (9 ounces) green seedless grapes

250g (9 ounces) dark sweet cherries, pitted

1 cup (250 ml) water

½ cup (125 ml) dark grape juice

¼ cup (60 ml) pineapple juice

¼ teaspoon (1 ml) grated orange rind

¼ cup (60 ml) diced pitted prunes

1½ cups (375 ml) berries— raspberries, halved strawberries, blueberries, or boysenberries

2 teaspoons (10 ml) arrowroot powder

1 tablespoon (20 ml) apple juice

2 tablespoons (40 ml) maple syrup or honey

2 small seedless oranges, peeled and cut into small segments

sour light cream for topping (optional)

fresh mint sprigs for garnish

1. Boil the apples, grapes, cherries, water, grape juice, pineapple juice, and orange rind in a 4-litre/quart saucepan. Reduce the heat, cover, and simmer for 10 minutes or until the apples are tender. Stir occasionally.

2. Add the prunes and berries. Continue simmering for about 5 minutes or until the prunes are tender.

3. Mix the arrowroot with the apple juice until completely dissolved and stir into the soup. Bring the soup to a boil and stir constantly for 1 minute, or until the soup thickens. Remove from the heat, add maple syrup (or honey) and orange segments. Chill. Serve in large soup bowls with a spoonful of sour cream, garnished with a sprig of fresh mint.

Split-Mung Dal

Used extensively in soups, stews, and sauces in Indian vegetarian cuisine, split mung beans are rich in vegetable protein, iron, and B vitamins. When you combine *dal* with a food that has a complimentary protein (grains, seeds, nuts, or milk products), the usable protein in the *dal* increases dramatically. Serve this simple purée like soup as an entrée to a western-type meal or serve it as part of a traditional Indian meal such as *Sautéed Rice with Poppy Seeds, North Indian Curried Cauliflower and Potatoes, Griddle-Baked Bread, Mixed Vegetable and Yogurt Salad, Creamy Condensed-Milk Rice Pudding,* and *Lemon, Mint, and Whey Nectar.*

PREPARATION TIME: 10 minutes
COOKING TIME: about 1 hour
YIELD: enough for 4 persons

1 cup (250 ml) split mung dal *(without skins)*

6 cups (1.5 litres) water

½ teaspoon (2 ml) turmeric

1 teaspoon (5 ml) ground coriander

2 teaspoons (10 ml) minced fresh ginger

1 teaspoon (5 ml) fresh hot green chili, minced

2 tablespoons (40 ml) ghee or oil

1½ teaspoons (7 ml) cumin seeds

¼ teaspoon (1 ml) yellow asafoetida powder

1 teaspoon (5 ml) salt

2 tablespoons (40 ml) chopped fresh parsley or coriander

1. Wash, and drain the split mung beans.
2. Place the mung beans, water, turmeric, ground coriander, minced ginger, and chili in a heavy 3-litre/quart saucepan and, stirring occasionally, bring to a full boil over high heat. Reduce the heat to moderately low, cover with a lid, and boil for one hour or until the beans become soft.

3. Heat the *ghee* or oil over moderate heat in a small pan. Sauté the cumin seeds in the hot oil until they turn brown; then add the asafoetida powder and sauté momentarily. Pour the seasonings into the *dal*. Add the salt and remove the soup from the heat, allowing the spices to soak for a few minutes. Add the minced fresh herbs and stir well. Serve hot.

Tomato Soup

This light and delicious tomato soup makes the canned variety pale into insignificance. Prepared from fresh ripe tomatoes and served steaming hot with crusty bread, it's a winner!

PREPARATION AND COOKING TIME: 40 minutes
YIELD: enough for 4 persons

3 tablespoons (60 ml) butter

¼ teaspoon (1 ml) yellow asafoetida powder

8-10 medium tomatoes, blanched, peeled and coarsely chopped

½ teaspoon (2 ml) brown sugar

1½ teaspoons (7 ml) salt

½ teaspoon (2 ml) freshly ground black pepper

¼ teaspoon (1 ml) dried basil

2½ cups (625 ml) light vegetable stock or water, heated

1 tablespoon (20 ml) plain flour

1 tablespoon (20 ml) chopped fresh parsley

1. Melt 1 tablespoon (20 ml) butter over low heat in a heavy 3-litre/quart saucepan. When the foam subsides, add the asafoetida, tomatoes, sugar, salt, pepper, and basil. Raise the heat to moderate and sauté for 2 to 3 minutes. Stir in the stock or water, raise the heat, bring to a boil, reduce to a simmer, and cook for 15 minutes or until the tomatoes are fully broken up.

2. Strain the mixture into a large mixing bowl, pressing down on the tomatoes in the strainer to extract as much of the juice as possible. Discard the dry solid residue in the strainer. Set aside the puréed tomatoes.

3. Rinse the saucepan and melt the remaining butter in it over moderate heat. Remove the pan from the heat. With a wooden spoon, stir in the flour to make a smooth paste. Return the pan to the heat and gradually add the strained tomato mixture, stirring constantly. Bring the mixture to the boil, still stirring.

4. Stir in the chopped parsley. Turn the soup into a warmed tureen or individual soup bowls and serve hot.

Left: Cream of Pumpkin Soup (p. 24)

Russian Beetroot Soup (*Borsch*)

Beetroot Soup, *Borsch*, has found its way into numerous Eastern European cuisines.

PREPARATION AND COOKING TIME: 40 minutes
YIELD: enough for 8 to 10 persons

8 cups (2 litres) water

1½ teaspoons (7 ml) salt

2 bay leaves

6 small potatoes, peeled and cut into 2 cm (¾-inch) cubes

3 cups (750 ml) grated cabbage

4 tablespoons (80 ml) ghee or oil

2 medium beetroots, peeled and coarsely shredded

3 tablespoons (60 ml) lemon juice

1 teaspoon (5 ml) ground coriander

1 teaspoon (5 ml) coarsely ground black pepper

½ teaspoon (2 ml) yellow asafoetida powder

1 cup (250 ml) carrots, coarsely grated

2 tablespoons (40 ml) tomato paste

¼ teaspoon (1 ml) clove powder

1 teaspoon (5 ml) brown sugar

2 tablespoons (40 ml) finely chopped fresh parsley

2 cups (500 ml) sour cream

1. Boil 7 cups (1.75 litres) water in a large saucepan over full heat. Add salt, bay leaves, cubed potatoes, and cabbage. Return to a boil, reduce the heat, and allow to simmer, covered, for 20 minutes or until the vegetables are tender.

2. Heat 1 tablespoon (20 ml) *ghee* or oil in a small saucepan over moderate heat. Sauté the grated beetroot for 2-3 minutes; then add 1 cup (250 ml) water. Increase the heat and boil the beetroot. Reduce the heat to low and simmer, covered, for 15 minutes or until the beetroot becomes soft.

3. Add the lemon juice to the beetroot and pour the beetroot into the cooked potato and cabbage. Continue to simmer, covered.

4. Heat 3 tablespoons (60 ml) *ghee* or oil in a small saucepan over low heat. To the hot *ghee* add ground coriander, black pepper, asafoetida, and grated carrots. Increase the heat and sauté for 3-4 minutes or until the carrots become soft. Add the tomato paste and combine this with the soup. Add the clove powder and sugar. Allow the soup to boil for another 2 minutes. Add the parsley. Serve the soup hot in individual soup bowls. Put a tablespoon of sour cream in each serving.

Yellow Split-Pea Soup with Pumpkin

This creamy, smooth *dal* soup with its pleasant lemony taste and chunks of butter-soft pumpkin is ideal as a tasty accompaniment to either a simple or elaborate menu.

DAL SOAKING TIME: 5-6 hours
PREPARATION TIME: 15 minutes
COOKING TIME: 1¾ hours
YIELD: enough for 5 or 6 persons

1 cup (250 ml) yellow split peas

6½ cups (1.625 ml) water

1½ teaspoons (7 ml) minced fresh ginger

2 teaspoons (10 ml) hot green chili, minced

1 bay leaf

½ teaspoon (2 ml) turmeric

2 tablespoons (40 ml) ghee or oil

1 cup or about 250 g (9 ounces) pumpkin, peeled, seeded and diced 1.25 cm (½-inch)

1 teaspoon (5 ml) salt

2 tablespoons (40 ml) fresh lemon or lime juice

1 teaspoon (5 ml) black mustard seeds

1 teaspoon (5 ml) cumin seeds

¼ teaspoon (1 ml) fenugreek seeds

¼ teaspoon (1 ml) yellow asafoetida powder

6 small dried curry leaves

1 tablespoon (20 ml) brown sugar

2 tablespoons (40 ml) chopped fresh parsley or coriander

1. Wash the *dal*. Soak it in 4 cups (1 litre) hot water for 5 hours. Drain.

2. Place the split peas, water, ginger, chili, bay leaf, turmeric, and 2 teaspoons (10 ml) *ghee* or oil in a heavy, 3-litre/quart saucepan. Bring to a full boil over high heat, stirring frequently. Reduce the heat to moderately low, cover with a tight-fitting lid, and boil for 1½ hours or until the split peas become soft. Add the pumpkin and cook for another 10 minutes or until the pumpkin becomes soft. Add the salt and lemon juice.

3. Heat the remaining *ghee* or oil in a small pan over moderately high heat. Sauté the mustard seeds in the hot oil until they crackle. Add the cumin seeds and when the cumin seeds turn dark golden brown, add the fenugreek seeds. When they darken, add the asafoetida and curry leaves, stir once, and empty the contents of the pan into the cooked *dal*. Add the brown sugar and stir well. Let the *dal* sit for 1 or 2 minutes; then add the chopped herbs. Serve hot.

Cream of Asparagus Soup

Select the thin, green-stalked variety (English Asparagus) for this soup.

PREPARATION AND COOKING TIME : 30-40 minutes

YIELD: enough for 5 or 6 persons

500 g (17½ ounces) fresh asparagus

6 cups (1.5 litres) Green Vegetable Stock or water

1 teaspoon (5 ml) salt

¼ teaspoon (1 ml) yellow asafoetida powder

1 stalk of celery, chopped fine

45 g (1½ ounces) butter

2 tablespoons (40 ml) plain flour

½ cup (125 ml) light cream

¼ teaspoon (1 ml) freshly ground black pepper

¼ teaspoon (1 ml) sweet paprika

1. Wash the asparagus well and holding the bunch so the tips are all level, slice off the tips. Place them in a bowl. Cut the stalks into sections and place in a separate bowl.

2. Place 1 cup (250 ml) of the water or stock, one quarter of the salt, and the asparagus tips in a 4-litre/quart saucepan. Simmer for 4-5 minutes or until tender. Remove the tips and place them in a bowl, keeping the cooking water in the saucepan.

3. Place the asparagus stalks, the asafoetida, and the celery in the same saucepan. Covered and simmer over moderate heat for 15-20 minutes or until the vegetables are tender.

4. Remove the saucepan from the heat and pour the contents through a sieve. Keep the reserved liquid and squeeze the vegetables through the sieve, collecting the purée in a separate bowl and discarding the dry residue in the sieve.

5. Melt the butter in a saucepan over moderate heat, add the flour, and slowly add the reserved asparagus stock over low heat. Stir until the soup thickens. Add the vegetable purée, the rest of the salt, the pepper, and the asparagus tips; stir well and heat until almost boiling. Stir in the cream. Serve the soup in pre-warmed soup bowls and garnish each serving with a light sprinkle of paprika.

Above: Cream of Asparagus Soup

Fiery South Indian Toor Dal Soup (*Rasam*)

South India has many regional varieties of *rasam*. This one comes from Bangalore.

The recipe for home-made *rasam* powder, the main seasoning ingredient in this spicy *dal*, appears below. Though you can purchase *rasam* powder at any Asian goods store, home-made is preferable.

PREPARATION TIME: 10 minutes
COOKING TIME: about 1 hour
YIELD: enough for 4 persons

½ cup (125 ml) toor dal

2 teaspoons (10 ml) fresh hot green chili, minced

4 cups (1 litre) water

2 ripe tomatoes, finely chopped

1 tablespoon (20 ml) chopped fresh coriander leaves

1 tablespoon (20 ml) rasam powder (see recipe below)

1 teaspoon (5 ml) salt

¼ teaspoon (1 ml) sugar

½ teaspoon (2 ml) tamarind concentrate

1 tablespoon (20 ml) ghee

1 teaspoon (5 ml) mustard seeds

6 curry leaves

1 teaspoon (5 ml) cumin seeds

¼ teaspoon (1 ml) yellow asafoetida powder

¼ teaspoon (1 ml) turmeric

1. Boil the *toor dal*, water, and chopped green chilies in a heavy saucepan. Reduce the heat and simmer for 45 minutes or until the *dal* becomes soft.

2. Add the tomato, chopped fresh coriander, and *rasam* powder. Continue cooking the soup for another 7-8 minutes, stirring occasionally.

3. Add the salt, sugar, and tamarind concentrate. Continue cooking for another 7-8 minutes.

4. Heat the *ghee* in a small pan. When it becomes very hot, add the mustard seeds and sauté them until they crackle and turn grey. Brown the curry leaves and cumin seeds; then add the asafoetida and turmeric. Add this hot seasoning mixture to the simmering *dal*. Allow the fla-vours to mix and serve hot with plain rice.

Rasam Powder

1 teaspoon (5 ml) oil

1 teaspoon (5 ml) mustard seeds

½ cup (125 ml) whole coriander seeds

6 whole dried hot red chilies

1 teaspoon (5 ml) black peppercorns

1½ teaspoons (7 ml) fenugreek seeds

2 teaspoons (10 ml) cumin seeds

1. Heat the oil in a heavy pan over moderate heat.

2. Sauté the mustard seeds in the hot oil until they crackle. Add all other ingredients. Stir well, reduce the heat to medium, and roast all the spices until they turn brown (about 3 minutes), stirring constantly. Remove the spices from the pan, allow them to cool, and grind them to a powder. This mixture can be stored for some time in a sealed jar.

Mexican Chilled Vegetable Soup (*Gazpacho*)

This chilled soup is very refreshing on a hot day, and requires practically no cooking.

PREPARATION TIME: 10 minutes
CHILLING TIME: 1 hour
YIELD: enough for 4 to 6 persons

1 large peeled cucumber diced into 0.5 cm (¼-inch) cubes (reserve one-third)

1 small green pepper, diced into 0.5 cm (¼-inch) cubes (reserve 1 tablespoon, 20 ml)

2 large fresh ripe tomatoes, diced (reserve half)

2 tablespoons (40 ml) extra virgin olive oil (reserve 1 teaspoon, 5 ml)

1 teaspoon (5 ml) salt

1 tablespoon (20 ml) fresh lemon juice

¼ teaspoon (1 ml) yellow asafoetida powder (reserve)

2 teaspoons (10 ml) honey

½ teaspoon (2 ml) dried dill

¼ teaspoon (1 ml) cayenne pepper

2 tablespoons (40 ml) Eggless Mayonnaise II

2 cups (500 ml) tomato juice

2 tablespoons (40 ml) chopped fresh coriander, as garnish

2 tablespoons (40 ml) chopped fresh parsley, as garnish

1. Blend all the ingredients (except those that are reserved and those for garnish) in a blender or food processor until they are nearly smooth. Empty the contents of the blender into a large bowl.

2. Heat the reserved olive oil in a medium-sized pan over moderate heat. Sauté the asafoetida in the hot oil. Turn off the heat. Add the reserved cucumber, the reserved green pepper, and the reserved tomato pieces to the hot pan. Stir them once and add them to the puréed soup. Mix well. Refrigerate. Serve garnished with the parsley and coriander in chilled soup bowls.

Thai Clear Soup with Tofu

This recipe calls for soft *tofu*, which has a consistency of thick custard, sometimes called "silken *tofu*". The bamboo shoots should be fresh, if possible. Otherwise, canned will do. All special ingredients are available from any Asian grocer.

Serve *Thai Clear Soup* with *Thai Rice, Vegetarian Spring Rolls, Sweet-and-Sour Sesame Sauce, Cantonese Stir-Fried Vegetables with Cashews in Black Bean Sauce,* and *Vietnamese Sweet Mung Bean Cakes* for a delightful South East Asian meal.

PREPARATION AND COOKING TIME: 20 minutes
YIELD: enough for 6 persons

5 cups (1.25 litres) **Chinese Vegetable Stock**

½ cup (125 ml) sliced bamboo shoots

½ teaspoon (2 ml) salt (optional)

1 tablespoon (20 ml) light soy sauce

1 tablespoon (20 ml) vegetable oil

¼ teaspoon (1 ml) yellow asafoetida powder

1 teaspoon (5 ml) Chinese sesame oil

2 teaspoons (10 ml) finely minced fresh ginger

450 g (1 pound) soft tofu cut into 1.25 cm (½-inch) cubes

1 large mild green chili, seeded and cut into 2.5 cm (1-inch) long wafer-thin slices

1. Boil the stock or water in a 4 litre/quart saucepan over high heat. Add the sliced bamboo shoots, salt , and soy sauce. Reduce the heat to moderate and simmer for 5 minutes.

2. Heat the vegetable oil in a small pan over moderate heat. Sauté the asafoetida. Add the sesame oil; then add the contents of the pan into the soup.

3. Add the ginger, *tofu*, and chili. Simmer for 5 more minutes. Serve hot.

Above: Mexican Chilled Vegetable Soup
Left: Fiery South Indian Toor Dal *Soup*

BREADS

The *Bhagavad-gita* states, "All living beings subsist on grains". Breads provide sustaining and nutritious variety to our lives.

Here are a few of the world's most famous breads.

*Pictured: Wholemeal Bread
and soft Bread rolls*

Wholemeal Bread

Breads are delicious, nutritious, and economical to make. They come in a myriad of forms the world over. Here's a recipe for crusty wholemeal bread made especially well-textured with the addition of gluten flour. Obtain the gluten flour from any health food store or specialty grocer.

Follow these tips when making bread: choose the correct flour; add the correct amount of yeast; knead the dough thoroughly; allow the bread to rise before baking, until doubled in bulk; cover the rising dough to prevent a skin forming; and always bake bread in a preheated oven at a high temperature. If you want a soft finish on your bread, rub or brush it with flour. For a crusty finish, brush with salted water. Brush with milk or cream to impart a shiny glaze, and brush with sugar syrup for a sweet glaze.

PREPARATION TIME: 50 minutes
DOUGH RISING TIME: 1½ hours
BAKING TIME: 45 minutes
YIELD: 2 loaves

6 teaspoons (30 ml) fresh yeast
1 tablespoon (20 ml) brown sugar
2½ cups (625 ml) warm water
½ cup (125 ml) gluten flour

2 teaspoons (10 ml) salt
6 cups (1.5 litres) wholemeal flour
1 tablespoon (20 ml) oil
little milk
sesame seeds

1. Combine the yeast, sugar, and warm water in a small bowl, crumbling the yeast and mixing it well. Leave this bowl undisturbed in a warm place for 10 minutes or until frothy.
2. Combine the gluten flour, salt, and half the wholemeal flour in a large bowl. Add the yeast and the oil. Mix with a wooden spoon until well-combined. Let it stand, covered, for 30 minutes.
3. Stir the mixture. Add the flour to make a soft dough. Turn the dough out onto a floured board and knead it for 8-10 minutes or until smooth and elastic.
4. Wash and oil the mixing bowl. Roll the dough into a ball, coat it with oil, and place it in the bowl, covered. Let it rise in a warm spot for 1 hour or until it has doubled in size.
5. Punch down the dough with your fist and knead again lightly. Shape it into 2 loaves. Place the loaves into oiled loaf tins and cover them,

placing them in a warm spot for another 30 minutes or until doubled in size. Meanwhile, preheat the oven to 200°C/390°F.
6. Brush the risen loaves with milk and sprinkle them with sesame seeds. Place them in the hot oven and cook for about 45 minutes or until golden, crisp, and hollow-sounding when tapped. Remove the tins from the oven and let stand for 10 minutes. Now you can carefully invert the bread tins and turn out the loaves, placing them on cooling racks. When the loaves are completely cool, slice and use as required.

Griddle-Baked Bread (*Chapati*)

Chapatis are one of India's most popular breads. They are enjoyed especially in the northern and central regions of India. They are partially cooked on a hot griddle and finished over an open-heat source. *Chapatis* are made from a special wholemeal flour called *atta*, available from Indian grocers. If unavailable, substitute sifted wholemeal flour. You can spread melted butter or *ghee* on the *chapatis* after they are cooked. *Chapatis* are usually served at lunch or dinner and are great whether served with a 5-course dinner or just with a simple *dal* and salad.

PREPARATION TIME: 5-10 minutes
DOUGH RESTING TIME: ½ to 3 hours
COOKING TIME: 25-35 minutes
YIELD: 12 chapatis

2 cups (500 ml) sifted chapati *flour*
½ teaspoon (2 ml) salt (optional)
water
extra flour for dusting

melted butter or ghee *(optional, for spreading over* chapatis *after they've been cooked)*

1. Combine the flour and salt in a mixing bowl. Add up to ²/₃ cup (165 ml) of water, slowly pouring in just enough to form a soft kneadable dough. Turn the dough onto a clean working surface and knead for about 8 minutes or until silky-smooth. Cover with an overturned bowl and leave for ¹/₂ to 3 hours.

2. Knead the dough again for 1 minute. Divide the dough into 1 dozen portions. Roll them into smooth balls and cover with a damp cloth.

3. Preheat a griddle or non-stick heavy frying pan over moderately low heat for 3-4 minutes. Flatten a ball of dough, dredge it in flour, and carefully roll out the ball into a thin, perfectly even, smooth disk of dough about 15 cm (6 inches) in diameter.

4. Carefully pick up the *chapati* and slap it between your hands to remove the excess flour. Slip it onto the hot plate, avoiding any wrinkles. Cook for about 1 minute on the first side. The top of the *chapati* should start to show small bubbles. Turn the *chapati* over with tongs. Cook it until small brown spots appear on the underside (about ¹/₂ minute).

5. If you are using gas, turn a second burner on high, pick up the *chapati* with your tongs, and hold it about 5 cm (2 inches) over the flame. It will swell into a puffy balloon. Continue to cook the *chapati* until it is specked with black flecks. Place the cooked *chapati* in a bowl or basket, cover with a clean tea towel or cloth, and continue cooking the rest of the *chapatis*. When they're all cooked and stacked, you might like to butter them. Serve *chapatis* hot for best results or cover and keep warm in a preheated warm oven for up to ¹/₂ hour.

Left: Griddle-Baked Bread
Above: Italian Fried Corn-Bread

Italian Fried Corn-Bread
(*Polenta*)

Polenta is a yellow maize or cornmeal grown in northern Italy. Regarded there as a staple food, it can be used in many ways after it has been prepared as a rather thick porridge. Plain boiled *polenta* can be grilled, baked, or, as in this recipe, fried. Served with *Tomato Relish* and sprinkled with parmesan cheese, it makes a delicious side dish.

PREPARATION AND COOKING TIME: 40 minutes

POLENTA STANDING TIME: 4 hours

YIELD: enough for 6 to 8 persons

8 cups (2 litres) water

2 teaspoons (10 ml) salt

3¹/₂ cups (875 ml) cornmeal (polenta)

90 g (3 ounces) butter

3 tablespoons (60 ml) olive oil

1. Bring the water and salt to a boil in a 6-litre/quart saucepan over full heat. Gradually sprinkle the cornmeal over the water, stirring constantly with a wire whisk. Make sure that there are no lumps of cornmeal.

2. Reduce the heat to low. Continue to stir the *polenta* mixture until it is very thick (approximately 10 minutes).

3. Leave the *polenta* over low heat for about another 5 minutes, stirring occasionally. It will be ready to remove from the heat when a wooden spoon will stand upright in the centre of the mixture and not drop to the side of the pan.

4. Spoon the mixture into an oiled 28 cm x 18 cm (7-inch x 11-inch) dish. Smooth out the mixture and leave to cool at room temperature for at least 4 hours.

5. Carefully turn the slab of *polenta* out of the tin and cut it in half lengthways. Cut each half into seven slices crossways, each one 4 cm (1¹/₂-inches) wide.

6. Heat the butter and oil together in a heavy frying pan. When hot, add about 6 slabs of *polenta* to the frying pan and reduce the heat to low. Fry gently until the *polenta* is dark golden brown on each side. Place the *polenta* onto a serving dish and serve with *Tomato Relish* and parmesan cheese.

Rajasthani Spicy Dal-Stuffed Bread (*Urad Dal Poori*)

These spicy, fried breads called *Urad Dal Pooris* (and sometimes called *Urad Dal Kachoris*) are a popular roadside snack in Rajasthan. *Urad dal* can be obtained at any Indian grocer. Serve these tasty breads with hot *Pumpkin and Potatoes Marwari Style, Date and Tamarind Sauce*, or as a snack with a dab of fresh yogurt.

DAL SOAKING TIME: 4 hours
PREPARATION TIME: 45 minutes
COOKING TIME: 30 minutes
YIELD: about 20 dal pooris

1 cup (250 ml) urad dal

2 cups (500 ml) sifted chapati flour or half-wholemeal and half-unbleached plain flour

½ cup (125 ml) ghee or oil, warmed

3 teaspoons (10 ml) salt

water

1 tablespoon (20 ml) coriander seeds

1 tablespoon (20 ml) fennel seeds

1 tablespoon (20 ml) cumin seeds

8 whole black peppercorns

4 large dried red chilies

ghee for frying

1. Place the *urad dal* in a bowl, cover with cold water, and leave to soak for 4 hours. Drain, place in a blender or food processor with a sprinkle of cold water, and grind coarsely to a paste. Transfer to a small bowl.

2. In another bowl, combine the flour, 4 tablespoons (80 ml) of warm *ghee*, 2 teaspoons (10 ml) of salt, and enough water to make a stiff but smooth dough. Knead well and put aside, covered with a cloth, for 20 minutes.

3. Sprinkle the coriander seeds, cumin, fennel, black peppercorns, and chilies into a heavy pan and dry-roast them over moderate heat until they darken a few shades and become aromatic (a few minutes). Transfer them to a coffee grinder, or mortar and pestle, and grind them to a powder.

4. Heat the remaining *ghee* or oil in a heavy pan over moderate heat. Add the *dal* paste and stir-fry it, stirring constantly over moderate heat until it starts to stick on the bottom. Remove from the heat, add the powdered spices and 1 teaspoon of the salt, and mix well. Transfer onto a plate or dish to cool.

5. Divide the dough into 20 portions. Roll each portion into a smooth ball. With a rolling pin on a slightly oiled surface, roll out each ball into a thick patty about 5 cm (2-inches) wide. Place 1 tablespoon (20 ml) of cooled filling in the centre of each one, gathering the edges of the dough back over to completely enclose the filling. Pinch the excess dough together and press it back into the centre of the patty. Flatten slightly; then with a rolling pin roll out seam-side down (carefully avoiding puncturing the pastry) into a disk 5-7.5 cm (2-3 inches) wide.

6. When all the *dal pooris* are rolled, heat the *ghee* or oil in a pan or wok to 180°C/355°F and carefully slip in 3 or 4 *dal pooris*. They will immediately sink then rise to the surface. Press them down with a slotted spoon until they inflate. Fry them until lightly browned on one side (about 2 minutes); then turn them over and fry on the second side for another 1 or 2 minutes. Remove with a slotted spoon and drain on a triple-thickness of paper towels. Cook all *dal pooris* and serve hot.

Puffed Fried-Bread (*Poori*)

Popular over all of India, *pooris* are ideal to cook for both small dinner parties and festivals with hundreds of guests. On a number of occasions, I've cooked 500 or more *pooris* in a few hours for big feasts. Once you get the rhythm down, it's effortless and rewarding. *Pooris* are traditionally made with straight wholemeal flour, but you can vary the ingredients. One-half wholemeal or *atta*, and one-half unbleached plain flour makes lighter *pooris*. If you're expert at rolling, try using just plain flour for translucent, gossamer-thin *pooris*.

You can add yeast to your *pooris* for light, bread-like results, as in *Yeasted Puffed Fried-Bread*; you can add spices to your *poori* dough; you can sprinkle sugar on top of *pooris* for a sweet snack; or you can stuff them with various sweet and savoury fillings, as in *Stuffed Puffed-Bread*.

The dough for this *poori* recipe differs from *chapati* dough in that butter or *ghee* is rubbed into the flour and less water is added, to form a drier dough. No flour is used on the rolling surface.

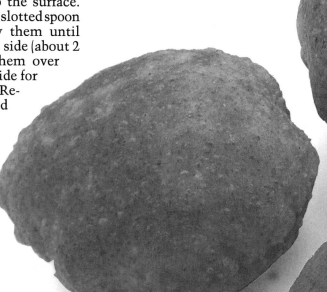

Pooris are traditionally eaten hot, straight out of the *ghee* or oil, but cold *pooris* are great for picnics or snacks when travelling. Serve *pooris* with practically any menu at any time.

PREPARATION TIME: 15 minutes
DOUGH RESTING TIME: 1/2-3 hours
COOKING TIME: 15 minutes
YIELD: 16 medium-sized pooris

2 cups (500 ml) sifted chapati *flour* or half-wholemeal and half-unbleached plain flour

1/2 teaspoon (2 ml) salt

2 tablespoons (40 ml) melted butter or ghee

2/3 cup (165 ml) warm water, or as needed

ghee *or* oil for deep-frying

1. Combine the flour and salt in a mixing bowl. Rub in the butter or *ghee* until the mixture resembles a coarse meal. Add up to 2/3 cup (165 ml) of water, slowly pouring in just enough to form a medium-soft kneadable dough. Turn the dough onto a clean working surface and knead for 5-8 minutes or until silky smooth. Cover with an overturned bowl and leave for 1/2 to 3 hours.

2. Knead the dough again for 1 minute. Divide the dough into 16 portions, roll them into smooth balls, and cover them with a damp cloth.

3. Preheat the *ghee* or oil in a wok or deep pan over low heat. Meanwhile, with a rolling pin roll all your balls of dough into smooth disks about 11.5-12.5 cm (4 1/2-5 inches) wide. Increase the *ghee* or oil temperature until it reaches about 185°C/365°F. Lift up a rolled *poori* and slip it into the hot oil, making sure it doesn't fold over. It will sink to the bottom then immediately rise to the surface. Hold it under the surface with a slotted spoon until it puffs up into a balloon. After a few seconds, when it is browned to a light-golden colour, turn it over and cook the other side to an even golden colour. Lift out the *poori* with the slotted spoon and carefully drain it in a large colander. Repeat for all the *pooris*. Serve immediately, if possible, or leave in a preheated, slightly warm oven for up to 2 hours.

Pictured: Puffed Fried-Bread

Savoury Wholemeal Pancakes
(*Dosa*)

Each country of the world has many varieties of pancakes, and India is no exception. Each region has its favourite versions. *Dosas* are a favourite in South India. Whereas traditional *dosas* are quite large, this recipe presents smaller pancakes to fit a household pan. And whereas traditional *dosas* are prepared from varieties of *dal* and rice combinations, these are prepared from basically just *chapati* flour, spices, and fresh herbs. Serve these slightly crisp pancakes with *Tomato Chutney*, *Coconut Chutney*, or plain yogurt.

PREPARATION TIME: 25 minutes
BATTER RESTING
  TIME: 15 minutes
COOKING TIME: about 45 minutes
  to 1 hour
YIELD: about 1 dozen dosas

2 cups (500 ml) sifted chapati *flour*
  or wholemeal flour

1 teaspoon (5 ml) yellow
  asafoetida powder

1½ teaspoons (7 ml) salt

¼ teaspoon (1 ml) baking powder

3 hot green chilies, finely chopped

1 tablespoon (20 ml) finely chopped
  fresh coriander leaves

melted ghee *or oil*

1. Combine the flour, asafoetida, salt, and baking powder in a large bowl and mix well. Add enough cold water to form a smooth, pouring-consistency batter. Fold in the chilies and chopped coriander leaves. Transfer the batter to a pouring jug or large measuring cup with a spout and set aside for 15 minutes before cooking.
2. Brush a 20 cm (8-inch) cast-iron frying pan with a film of melted *ghee* or oil and warm it over moderate heat. When hot, pour in about ¼ cup (60 ml) of the batter, or enough to cover the base of the pan, and immediately tilt it to spread the batter into

a thin 20 cm (8-inch) pancake. Drizzling a little *ghee* or oil around the edges of the *dosa* cook until the edges brown and the bottom turns golden brown in patches (about 3 minutes). Flip the *dosa* over, sprinkle with more oil, and cook it for another 1½-2 minutes. Slide the cooked *dosa* onto a clean plate and serve it either flat or folded in half. Make all the *dosas* in the same way, stirring the batter occasionally. Serve hot.

Stuffed Pan-Fried Bread
(*Paratha*)

This is a delicious Singapore version of the famous Indian stuffed bread, *paratha*. These flaky, soft breads are pan-fried slowly with *ghee* or oil until golden brown. They're great served at any time with a chutney or sauce.

PREPARATION TIME: 20 minutes
COOKING TIME: approximately
  40 minutes
YIELD: 10 parathas

For filling

2 tablespoons (40 ml) peanut or
  safflower oil

½ teaspoon (2 ml) yellow
  asafoetida powder

2 cups (500 ml) grated cabbage

1½ cups (375 ml) carrots, peeled
  and grated

1 cup (250 ml) mung bean shoots

1 teaspoon (5 ml) soy sauce

½ teaspoon (2 ml) sugar

½ teaspoon (2 ml) salt

½ teaspoon (2 ml) cornflour

ghee *or oil to cook the* parathas

For pastry

1 tablespoon (20 ml) peanut or
  safflower oil

½ teaspoon (2 ml) salt

2 cups (500 ml) plain flour

1. To prepare the filling: heat the oil in a wok or large pan over moderate heat. When hot, add the asafoetida and fry momentarily. Increase the heat to full, add the vegetables, and stir-fry briskly for 4-5 minutes. Add soy sauce, salt, and sugar, stir-frying for another minute. Mix a little liquid from the wok (or water if the vegetables are dry) with the cornflour and pour this thickening paste into the vegetables. Sauté for another ½ minute. Set aside to cool.
2. To make the pastry: mix the oil and salt with the plain flour and rub in the oil until the mixture resembles a coarse meal. Add enough cold water (a little over ½ cup [125 ml]) to form a soft dough. Knead well for about 5 minutes. Divide into 10 balls.

Pictured: Savoury Wholemeal Pancakes

3. On a lightly floured surface, roll out each ball with a rolling pin into paper-thin disks 25 cm (10-inches) wide.

4. Divide the filling into 10 portions. Place 1 portion of filling in the centre of each disk of pastry, spreading it out about 5 cm (2-inches) wide.

5. Fold in each side so the filling is completely covered, the pastry overlaps in the centre, and you end up with a square *paratha*. To seal, use water to moisten the areas where the pastry overlaps. Roll gently to seal and flatten.

6. Place one or two *parathas* on a griddle, hotplate, or heavy frying pan brushed with *ghee* or oil over moderate heat. Turn occasionally until the *paratha* displays golden-brown marbled spots on the surface of both sides (about 3-4 minutes). Repeat with all *parathas*, brushing them with *ghee* or oil when required. Serve hot.

Middle Eastern Round Bread (*Pita*)

No Middle Eastern meal is complete without these traditional slightly leavened, round, soft breads. Sometimes called *Khobz*, or pocket breads, they are becoming increasingly popular in the west. Try baking them yourself.

Distinct from traditional breads, these breads rise only once and are then baked at a very high temperature for a short time. During the process the dough separates to form the pouch or hollow, enabling the bread to be later split in half and stuffed. Traditionally, this bread is made with strong white flour, but if you wish you can substitute wholemeal flour or a softer white flour (you might then need to adjust baking time). *Pita* breads can be served with a traditional Middle Eastern meal (see section on menu planning), filled with your favourite salad along with *Falafel*, or used as a base for *Asparagus and Pinenut Pizza*.

PREPARATION TIME: 1 hour
BAKING TIME: 5 minutes per batch
YIELD: 24 small pitas or 12 large pitas

3 teaspoons (15 ml) dried yeast

1½ cups plus 5 tablespoons (475 ml) warm water

½ teaspoon (2 ml) brown sugar

6 cups (1.5 litres) strong white flour

2 teaspoons (10 ml) salt

extra flour for kneading and dusting

1. Combine the yeast, warm water, and sugar in a large bowl. Stir thoroughly to dissolve the yeast.

2. Stir in the flour and salt and knead for about 5 minutes to form a smooth dough, sprinkling on a little extra flour if required.

3. Shape the dough into a cylinder. Divide the dough into 24 portions for small *pitas* or into 12 for large *pitas*. Shape each portion into a smooth ball. Place the balls on a floured surface and cover them with a cloth.

4. Carefully form a ball into a smooth, crease-free disk and roll out on a floured board with a rolling pin to form a 0.5 cm (¼-inch) thick bread. Repeat until all the breads are rolled. Small breads should be about 12.5 cm (5 inches) in diameter, and large ones about 20 cm (8-inches).

5. Preheat the oven to 240°C/465°F. Place the loaves on a floured bench top in a draught-free area, covered with clean, dry tea towels. Do not allow the breads to dry out. The breads should rise for 30-45 minutes.

6. Place 1 large or 4 small *pitas* on an ungreased baking sheet and bake on the bottom of the hot oven for 3-4 minutes. When cooked, the bottoms should be golden and the tops cream coloured. Remove and wrap the *pitas* in dry tea towels. Repeat until all the breads are done.

Note: Take care not to leave the oven door open between batches, and don't allow the breads to go crisp or brittle. They should be soft and flexible when they come out of the oven. If you're not going to use the breads straight away, allow them to cool and store them in plastic bags until required.

Mozzarella and Tomato Pizza

This is a crisp-based pizza holding a filling of herb-flavoured tomatoes, with a topping of sliced black olives, peppers, and golden, melting mozzarella cheese. To save time, prepare the filling whilst the dough is rising.

PREPARATION TIME: 20 minutes
DOUGH RISING TIME: 30 minutes
ROLLING AND TOPPING
  TIME: 10 minutes
BAKING TIME: 15-20 minutes
YIELD: one 25 cm (10-inch) pizza

Base

3 teaspoons (15 ml) fresh yeast
½ teaspoon (2 ml) sugar
½ cup (125 ml) lukewarm water
1½ cups (375 ml) plain flour
¼ teaspoon (1 ml) salt
2 tablespoons (40 ml) olive oil

Filling

2 teaspoons (10 ml) olive oil
¼ teaspoon (1 ml) yellow asafoetida powder
one 400 g (14-ounce) can whole Italian tomatoes, chopped and undrained, or 1½ cups (375 ml) fresh tomato purée
1 tablespoon (20 ml) tomato paste
½ teaspoon (2 ml) dried oregano
½ teaspoon (2 ml) dried basil
1 teaspoon (5 ml) sugar
1 teaspoon (5 ml) salt
¼ teaspoon (1 ml) freshly ground black pepper

Topping

125 g (4½ ounces) grated mozzarella cheese
2 tablespoons (40 ml) grated parmesan cheese
1 cup (250 ml) thin strips of eggplant, deep-fried until dark golden-brown, then salted
1 small red pepper, diced
60 g (2 ounces) black olives, pitted and halved

1. Cream the yeast with the sugar in a bowl, add lukewarm water, and let it stand for 10 minutes or until bubbles appear on the surface. Sift the flour and salt into a bowl, make a well in the centre, and add the oil and yeast mixture. Mix to a firm dough.

Pictured: Mozzarella and Tomato Pizza

2. Turn the dough onto a floured surface and knead it for 10 minutes or until the dough is smooth and elastic. Place it in a lightly oiled bowl, cover, and leave in a warm place for 30 minutes or until the dough has doubled in size.

3. Knock the dough down with your fist and knead into a small ball. Flatten out the dough with a rolling pin and roll it into a circular sheet of pastry that will just fit in a 25 cm (10-inch) pizza pan. Place the dough carefully in the pan.

4. Meanwhile make your filling: heat the olive oil in a large frying pan over moderate heat. When hot, add the asafoetida and sauté momentarily. Add the undrained canned tomatoes or tomato purée, tomato paste, oregano, basil, sugar, salt, and pepper. Bring the sauce to a boil; then reduce the heat and, stirring occasionally, simmer uncovered for 10 to 15 minutes or until the sauce is thick and smooth.

Allow the filling to cool somewhat.

5. Spread the cooled filling over the pizza base, leaving a little border uncovered. Combine half the grated mozzarella cheese with the parmesan and sprinkle it over the tomato filling. Top with the eggplant strips, chopped peppers, and olives. Sprinkle on the remaining cheese and bake in a pre-heated hot oven (220°C/430°F) for 15-20 minutes or until the crust is golden brown.

Stuffed Puffed-Bread
(Stuffed Poori)

These tasty treats have been a great favourite at the Hare Krishna Sunday Feasts for decades. Fried puffed-breads (pooris) are stuffed with layers of potato, beans, yogurt, crunchy chickpea pearls, sweet-and-sour tamarind sauce, and finally a sprinkle of hot and sweet spices. Irresistible!

PREPARATION AND COOKING TIME: 1½ hours
YIELD: 16 stuffed pooris

Pooris
1 cup (250 ml) unbleached plain flour

1 cup (250 ml) chapati flour or wholemeal flour

½ teaspoon (2 ml) salt

2 tablespoons (40 ml) ghee or oil

⅔ cup (165 ml) warm water, or as needed

ghee or oil for deep-frying

Potato filling
2 medium potatoes, cut into 0.5 cm (¼-inch) cubes

¼ teaspoon (1 ml) salt

Mung bean filling
¼ cup (60 ml) whole green mung beans, raw

4 cups (1 litre) water

¼ teaspoon (1 ml) salt

Tamarind sauce
1 tablespoon (20 ml) tamarind concentrate

1 tablespoon (20 ml) water

2 tablespoons (40 ml) brown sugar

pinch salt

¼ teaspoon (1 ml) cayenne pepper

Chickpea flour batter pearls
¼ cup (60 ml) chickpea flour

¼ teaspoon (1 ml) salt

¼ teaspoon (1 ml) cayenne pepper

¼ teaspoon (1 ml) ground cumin

water

ghee or oil for deep frying

Other ingredients
1¼ cups (310 ml) yogurt

½ teaspoon (2 ml) garam masala

ghee or oil for deep-frying

1. Prepare pooris (see Puffed Fried-Bread). Set them aside.

2. Boil the potato cubes in slightly salted water in a small saucepan, until soft. Drain and set aside.

3. Boil the mung beans in 4 cups (1 litre) unsalted water until they are soft but not broken up. Drain, toss with salt, and set aside.

4. Combine all the ingredients for the tamarind sauce in a bowl. Whisk until smooth. Set aside.

5. Heat a small quantity of ghee or oil (about 2.5 cm, or 1-inch) in a small pan or wok. Mix all the dry ingredients for the chickpea-flour-batter pearls in a bowl. Pour in sufficient cold water to form a thick batter. When the oil reaches 180°C/355°F, pour some of the batter through the holes of a colander into the hot oil. Fry the little pearls of batter for a few minutes or until they are golden brown and crisp, remove them with a slotted spoon, and set them aside. Repeat until all the batter is used.

6. To assemble the stuffed pooris: place all the pooris on a tray with the pooris' thick side down. Puncture a small hole in the top of each poori. Drop in a few pieces of potato, followed by a small spoon of soft mung beans. On top of that, spoon a good sized spoon of yogurt; sprinkle-in some chickpea pearls, a spoon of tamarind sauce, and finally a sprinkle of garam masala. Serve immediately.

Mexican Oatmeal Corn and Cheese Bread

This is an unusual but tasty bread which requires minimum fuss in preparation. It is best baked in a well-oiled 23 cm (9-inch) cast-iron frying pan, enabling it to be "pan-fried" in the oven.

Serve *Mexican Oatmeal Corn and Cheese Bread* warm, as a cold snack or as part of a summer luncheon or buffet with a light tomato sauce and a fresh salad.

PREPARATION TIME: 5 minutes

BATTER STANDING TIME: at least 30 minutes

BAKING TIME: 20-30 minutes

YIELD: enough for 6 persons

3/4 cup (185 ml) oatmeal

1/4 cup (60 ml) yellow cornmeal (polenta)

1 1/2 teaspoons (7 ml) baking powder

1/2 teaspoon (2 ml) bicarbonate of soda

1/2 teaspoon (2 ml) salt

1 cup (250 ml) cultured buttermilk or sour milk

1 teaspoon (5 ml) lemon juice

1 1/2 cups (375 ml) grated tasty cheese (not parmesan)

2 tablespoons (40 ml) finely chopped fresh parsley or coriander

2 tablespoons (40 ml) oil

1. Combine the oatmeal, cornmeal, baking powder, bicarbonate of soda, salt, and buttermilk in a bowl. Mix well and set aside to stand for at least 30 minutes.
2. Add the remaining ingredients (except the oil) and combine the mixture well.
3. Heat 1 tablespoon (20 ml) of the oil in a heavy, pre-oiled, cast-iron frying pan or cake tin and spoon in the bread batter, spreading it evenly. Drizzle the remaining oil over the batter and bake it in a preheated hot oven (200°C/390°F) for 20-30 minutes or until golden brown on top.
4. Whilst the bread is still warm, slice into 6 pieces. Serve warm or at room temperature.

Bagels

These famous doughnut-shaped rolls are a distinctive part of Jewish cuisine. They are first cooked in water, then baked, giving the bagel its characteristic hard, glazed crust.

PREPARATION TIME: 30 minutes

DOUGH RISING TIME: 1 hour 10 minutes

BOILING TIME: 10 minutes

BAKING TIME: about 30 minutes

YIELD: 18 bagels

2 cups (500 ml) warm water

2 teaspoons (10 ml) dry yeast

1 teaspoon (5 ml) brown sugar

1/4 cup (60 ml) olive oil

5 cups (1.25 litres) plain baking flour

1 tablespoon (20 ml) salt

4 litres/quarts water for boiling

2 tablespoons (40 ml) brown sugar

2 tablespoons (40 ml) milk for glazing

poppy seeds for decoration

1. Mix 3/4 cup (185 ml) water, yeast, and 1 teaspoon (5 ml) brown sugar in a bowl and let sit covered in a warm place for 10 minutes or until bubbles appear.
2. Add this mixture, along with the oil and the rest of the water, to the flour and salt in a large mixing bowl. Mix well to a stiff dough and knead for 10 minutes on a lightly floured board.
3. Let the dough rise for 1 hour or until doubled in size in a warm, undisturbed place. Punch the dough with your fist and knead for a few minutes.
4. Divide the dough into 18 portions; then with your hands roll each one into a rope shape, approximately 15 cm (6-inches) long. Moisten the ends and overlap them, squeezing them together to seal, forming rings. Allow all the bagels to stand in a warm place for 10 minutes on an oiled tray.
5. Bring the water to a rolling boil in a large pan. Add the 2 tablespoons (40 ml) of brown sugar and drop 5 or 6 of the bagels into the water. Allow the bagels to boil for 3 minutes, turning once, not allowing them to overlap.
6. With a slotted spoon, remove the bagels from the water and place them onto an oiled oven tray. When all bagels have been boiled and placed on trays, brush them with milk and sprinkle poppy seeds on them. Finally, bake in a hot oven (230°C/450°F) until the bagels are golden brown. Serve hot or cold.

Pictured: Fruity Bran Muffins

Yeasted, Puffed Fried-Bread
(Khamiri Poori)

Here's another delicious variety of Indian bread. Yeasted *pooris* traditionally contain a home-made yeast mixture called *Khamir* made by natural fermentation. I have adapted the recipe using fresh yeast. These lovely *pooris* taste and smell like hot baked bread and are great served at tea time. Serve with either a sweet or savoury accompaniment.

PREPARATION TIME: 25 minutes
DOUGH RISING TIME: 1 hour 10 minutes
COOKING TIME: ½ hour
YIELD: 16 medium pooris

3 teaspoons (15 ml) fresh yeast

3 teaspoons (15 ml) sugar

¾ cup (185 ml) warm water, or as required

1 cup (250 ml) plain flour

1 cup (250 ml) sifted chapati flour or fine wholemeal flour

1 teaspoon (5 ml) salt

2 tablespoons (40 ml) ghee or butter

ghee or oil for frying

1. Combine the yeast, sugar, and a little warm water in a bowl. Cover and leave the mixture in a warm place for 10 minutes or until it becomes frothy.

2. Sift the flours together and combine with the salt in a mixing bowl. Rub in the butter or *ghee* until the mixture resembles a coarse meal. Add the yeast mixture and gradually pour in the rest of the warm water to form a firm, kneadable dough. Turn the dough onto a clean working surface and knead it for about 8 minutes or until silky-smooth. Rub a little *ghee* or butter on the dough and place it in an oiled bowl. Cover with a cloth and leave in a warm spot for at least 1 hour or until it doubles in size.

3. Punch down the risen dough with your fist and knead again for 1 minute. Divide the dough into 16 portions and roll them into smooth balls. Press the balls into little patties and with a rolling pin roll each patty into a disk 11.5-12.5 cm (4½-5 inches). Place the disks carefully on oiled baking trays and leave them in a warm spot to rise again.

4. Heat the *ghee* or oil over moderate heat until it reaches about 185°C/365°F. Lift up a rolled *poori* and slip it into the hot oil, making sure it doesn't fold over. It will sink to the bottom then immediately bob up to the surface. Hold it under the surface with a slotted spoon until it puffs up into a balloon. After a few seconds, when it is browned to a light golden colour, turn it over and cook the other side to an even golden colour. Lift out the *poori* with a slotted spoon and carefully drain it on paper towels. Repeat for all the *pooris*. Serve them immediately, if possible, or leave in a preheated, slightly warm oven for up to 2 hours.

Fruity Bran Muffins

Muffins are light and quick to prepare. These little breads are baked in special deep, round muffin tins and served hot for breakfast. This recipe comes from Govinda's Bakery in Los Angeles.

Mix the ingredients swiftly, as overmixing will produce tough, coarse muffins.

PREPARATION TIME: 10 minutes
BAKING TIME: 20 minutes
YIELD: 6 muffins

½ cup (125 ml) raw sugar

1½ cups (375 ml) wholemeal flour

1 cup (250 ml) mixed dried fruit

2 cups (500 ml) wheat bran

at least 1 cup (250 ml) cold milk

1 tablespoon (20 ml) melted butter

1 tablespoon (20 ml) golden syrup (or dark corn syrup)

1 tablespoon (20 ml) water

1½ teaspoons (7 ml) baking soda

1. Combine the sugar, flour, fruit, and bran in a bowl and set aside.

2. Reserve 1 tablespoon (20 ml) milk. Combine the rest of the milk with the melted butter in a small bowl. Add the golden syrup, combine, and add to the bran mixture.

3. Heat the water and the reserved milk in a small saucepan. When hot, add the baking soda. When the mixture froths, pour it into the bran mixture. Mix in quickly and thoroughly. The mixture should be fairly moist. (Some additional milk may be required.)

4. Spoon into a greased muffin tray and bake at 180°C/355°F for 20 minutes or until the muffins are golden brown. Serve hot.

Soft Breadrolls

Sprinkled with poppy seeds before baking for an extra taste dimension, these are an excellent all-purpose bread roll. Try serving them with *Tomato Soup* or cut them and fill with *Gopal's Famous Vegie-Nut Burgers* topped with your choice of salads and sauce

PREPARATION TIME: 20 minutes
DOUGH RISING TIME: 1 hour 10 minutes
BAKING TIME: 15-20 minutes
YIELD: 12 large breadrolls

6 cups (1.5 litres) plain flour
2 teaspoons (10 ml) salt
3 teaspoons (15 ml) fresh yeast
1 teaspoon (5 ml) brown sugar
1 cup (250 ml) warm water
3 teaspoons (15 ml) oil
1 cup (250 ml) warm milk
milk and poppy seeds for glazing

1. Sift the flour with the salt into a mixing bowl.

2. Combine the fresh yeast and brown sugar with the warm water and leave in a warm, undisturbed place for 10 minutes or until frothy.

3. Add the oil and frothy yeast mixture to the sifted flour. Mix and add sufficient warm milk to produce a soft dough. Turn out onto a floured board and knead for 10 minutes or until the dough is soft and pliable.

4. Place the dough in an oiled bowl, rub the dough with oil, cover, and leave in a warm spot for 1 hour or until the dough has doubled in size.

5. Punch down the dough, knead lightly, and form into a long cylinder. Cut into 12 pieces and shape them into rounds. Place them carefully onto floured baking sheets, leaving enough room for expansion. Cover them loosely with plastic wrap and place in a warm spot for another 15-20 minutes or until they have again doubled in size. Meanwhile, preheat the oven to 230°C/450°F.

6. Brush the rolls lightly with milk, sprinkle with poppy seeds, and place them in the preheated oven. Bake for 15 to 20 minutes or until golden brown and hollow-sounding when tapped. Place on a cooling rack and allow to cool before serving.

Corn Flat-Bread
(*Tortilla*)

Tortillas are the national bread of Mexico. They are thin and round and made from a white cornmeal called *masa*. *Tortillas* are cooked on a griddle without browning, so they are quite soft and may be eaten as they are or fried briefly in oil to crisp them. *Masa* is hard to get outside of Mexico, so I have suggested *polenta* mixed with fine wholemeal flour as a substitute. *Tortillas* may be used as a plate or scoop for other foods, such as *Tacos*, or rolled and stuffed, as in *Enchiladas*.

PREPARATION AND COOKING TIME: 30 minutes
YIELD: 8 tortillas

1/4 cup (60 ml) cornmeal (polenta)
1/4 cup (60 ml) cold water
1/2 cup (125 ml) boiling water
1/2 teaspoon (2 ml) salt
1 tablespoon (20 ml) oil
1 cup (250 ml) fine wholemeal flour

1. Combine the cornmeal and cold water in a bowl.

2. Stir the cornmeal mixture into the boiling salted water in a saucepan over full heat. Stir until the mixture is thick, drawing away from the sides of the pan.

3. Remove the thickened mixture from the heat and place it in a bowl.

4. Add the oil and mix thoroughly. Stir in the wholemeal flour to make a soft dough and knead on a lightly floured board until smooth (about 10 minutes), adding more flour if necessary.

5. Divide the dough into 8 equal portions and shape them into balls. Flatten the balls and roll them out to 0.125 cm (1/16-inch) thickness.

6. Heat an un-oiled, heavy cast-iron pan over moderate heat and, one at a time, bake the *tortillas*, flipping them over several times until they are lightly golden on both sides. Cool. Serve as suggested above.

Crispy Dal Wafers
(*Pappadams*)

Crispy dal-wafers (*pappadams* or *paparh*) are often served as part of a full Indian dinner menu, usually at the beginning or as a closing item. They can be deep-fried or toasted over a flame. Although they are technically not breads, they are eaten like breads. They're also great for party snacks. Raw *pappadams* can be purchased at any Asian grocer shop, and come, plain or spiced, in all sizes.

COOKING TIME: a few seconds per wafer if deep-fried; a few minutes if toasted over a flame.

Pictured: Asparagus and Pinenut Pizza

To deep-fry

1. Heat *ghee* or oil in a wok or large frying pan over moderately high heat. When hot (185°C/365°F), gently slip in a *pappadam*. It will immediately sizzle and expand. When it crinkles on the edges, turn it over with tongs and after 2-3 seconds remove it and place it on paper towels or in a colander to drain. Serve hot or cold.

To toast over a flame

1. Place a raw *pappadam* on a cake rack and hold it about 5 cm (2 inches) above a heat source set on high. Move the wafer around, until the whole surface is lightened in colour, expanded, and flecked with brown. Turn it over and cook the other side. Remove and stack. Serve hot or cold. Dry-roasted *pappadams* are great for persons on a low-fat diet.

Asparagus and Pinenut Pizza

These pizzas are quick and easy because they're made not with the traditional yeasted pizza dough but with Middle Eastern breads. If you prefer, try making your own *Pita* breads. The recipe for *Middle Eastern Round Bread (Pita)* yields delicious pizza bases. Topped with homemade pinenut sauce, asparagus, and melting mozzarella cheese, they're sure to please.

PREPARATION AND COOKING TIME: 30-40 minutes

YIELD: four 13 cm (5-inch) pizzas or two 25 cm (10-inch) pizzas

1 tablespoon (20 ml) olive oil

1 tablespoon (20 ml) pinenuts

1 tablespoon (20 ml) olive oil, extra.

1 cup (250 ml) fresh basil leaves, packed

¼ teaspoon (1 ml) yellow asafoetida powder

1 teaspoon (5 ml) salt

2 tablespoons (40 ml) grated parmesan cheese

1 bunch asparagus (250 grams, or about 9 ounces)

2 large or 4 small Middle Eastern breads

1 small red pepper, chopped

250 g (about 9 ounces) grated mozzarella cheese

¼ cup (60 ml) grated parmesan cheese

1. Heat 1 tablespoon (20 ml) of olive oil in a small saucepan over moderate heat. When hot, stir in the pinenuts and sauté them until they're lightly browned. Remove them undrained from the pan and empty them into a blender or food processor along with the extra oil, the basil leaves, asafoetida, salt, and 2 tablespoons (40 ml) of parmesan cheese. Process until smooth.

2. Cut the asparagus into 2.5 cm (1-inch) lengths and boil or steam until tender. Drain, rinse under cold water, and drain again.

3. Spread the breads with the pinenut sauce and top with asparagus, diced pepper, and cheeses. Place the pizzas on oven trays and bake in a moderate (180°C/355°F) oven until the pizzas are golden brown.

VEGETABLE DISHES

If you are tired of seeing vegetables relegated to soggy mounds on the side of your plate, this chapter is for you—a selection of tastefully herbed and spiced dishes prepared in every way imaginable.

*Pictured: French Braised
Summer Vegetables*

North Indian Curried Cauliflower and Potatoes

This is a popular North Indian vegetable dish. Combined with hot *Puffed Fried Breads (Pooris)*, *dal*, and salad, it can be served any time of the day and on any occasion.

PREPARATION AND COOKING TIME: 15-20 minutes

YIELD: enough for 4-5 persons

1/4 cup (60 ml) ghee or oil

1/2 teaspoon (2 ml) black mustard seeds

1 teaspoon (5 ml) cumin seeds

1 teaspoon (5 ml) minced fresh ginger

2 hot green chilies, seeded and chopped

3 medium potatoes, cut into 1.25 cm (1/2-inch) cubes

1 medium cauliflower, cut into small flowerets

2 medium tomatoes blanched, peeled, and diced

1/2 teaspoon (2 ml) turmeric

1/2 teaspoon (2 ml) garam masala

2 teaspoons (10 ml) ground coriander

1 teaspoon (5 ml) brown sugar

2 teaspoons (10 ml) salt

2 tablespoons (40 ml) coarsely chopped fresh coriander or parsley

1 tablespoon (20 ml) fresh lemon juice

1. Heat the *ghee* or oil in a large, heavy saucepan over moderate heat. When the *ghee* is hot, add the mustard seeds. When they crackle, add the cumin and sauté them until they darken a few shades. Add the ginger and chilies, sauté for a few moments, and then add the potato and cauliflower pieces. Stir-fry the vegetables for 4 or 5 minutes or until the vegetables start to stick to the bottom of the pan.

2. Add the tomatoes, turmeric, *garam masala*, ground coriander, sugar, and salt.

3. Mix well, reduce the heat to low, cover the saucepan, and, stirring occasionally, cook for 10 to 15 minutes or until the vegetables are tender. Add water if necessary during this time but don't over-stir the vegetables. When the vegetables are cooked, add the fresh coriander and the lemon juice. Serve hot.

Vegetarian Shepherd's Pie

Those of you of "Anglo-Saxon" background, like myself, will perhaps be familar with the non-vegetarian origins of this dish.

PREPARATION AND COOKING TIME: 1 1/2 hours

YIELD: enough for 6 to 8 persons

For base of pie

1 1/4 cups (310 ml) brown lentils

2 litres/quarts water

2 tablespoons (40 ml) olive oil

1 teaspoon (5 ml) yellow asafoetida powder

1/4 teaspoon (1 ml) freshly ground black pepper

1 cup (250 ml) celery, diced

home-made curd cheese (panir) from 8 cups (2 litres) milk and pressed for 1/2 hour

5 tablespoons (100 ml) soy sauce

For potato topping

6 large baking potatoes, peeled and cubed

2 tablespoons (40 ml) butter

1/2 cup (125 ml) milk

1 teaspoon (5 ml) salt

2 tablespoons (40 ml) sour cream

*3 tablespoons (60 ml) chopped
fresh parsley*

1. Boil the brown lentils and water in a heavy 6-litre/quart saucepan. Reduce to a simmer and cook until they become soft. Strain through a colander. Put the lentils aside and retain the liquid for use as a soup stock at a later date.

2. Meanwhile, boil the potato cubes in slightly salted water until they become soft. Drain and mash them until smooth. Add the butter, milk, salt, and sour cream and mix well.

3. Heat the olive oil in a small, heavy pan until very hot. Add the asafoetida and pepper and sauté momentarily. Add the celery bits and stir well; reduce the heat and braise the celery until soft, stirring occasionally. Remove from the heat.

4. Mash the drained lentils until smooth.

5. Crumble the curd cheese in a bowl and add the soy sauce. Mix well. Combine this mixture with the mashed lentils and the braised seasoned celery bits. Spread this pie filling evenly in the bottom of an ovenproof casserole dish. Cover this with the mashed potatoes. Smooth the mashed potatoes and use a fork to mark the top with lines. Bake in a very hot oven (230°C/450°F) until the top is browned. Remove from the oven, sprinkle with fresh parsley, and serve hot.

Baked Stuffed Avocados

In this succulent and unusual entrée, avocados are stuffed with *tofu* and green peas, smothered in a lemon-chili-coconut sauce, and baked.

PREPARATION TIME: 10 minutes
COOKING TIME: 10 minutes
BAKING TIME: 10 minutes
YIELD: enough for 4 persons

2 large, firm but ripe avocados

Pictured: Baked Stuffed Avocados

2 tablespoons (40 ml) olive oil

*¼ teaspoon (1 ml) yellow
asafoetida powder*

*1 teaspoon (5 ml) chopped
fresh ginger*

*1 cup (250 ml) firm tofu, diced to
1.25 cm (½-inch) cubes*

1 teaspoon (5 ml) Chinese sesame oil

*1 tablespoon (20 ml) chili sauce
(without garlic or onions)*

1 tablespoon (20 ml) sweet soy sauce

*1 match-box size chunk of creamed
coconut, chopped*

½ cup (125 ml) cooked green peas

*1 tablespoon (20 ml) fresh
lemon juice*

1 teaspoon (5 ml) salt

*1 tablespoon (20 ml) minced fresh
coriander leaves*

1. Carefully run a knife from the stem end downwards and right around the avocados. Twist to separate the two halves. Remove the seeds.

2. With a spoon, scoop out the avocado flesh leaving a 1.25 cm (½-inch) border. Chop the avocado flesh into large rough chunks.

3. Heat the olive oil in a heavy non-stick frying pan over medium heat. Add the asafoetida and sauté for a few seconds. Add the ginger and sauté for 1 minute. Add the *tofu* and stir-fry carefully. When the *tofu* is browned, drizzle on the sesame oil, chili sauce, and soy sauce. Fold in the creamed coconut, stirring until it melts.

4. Add the peas, lemon juice, salt, minced fresh coriander, and stir well. Finally, add the avocado pieces, stir to mix, and remove from the heat. Place the avocado halves carefully on a flame-proof *gratin* dish and add the stuffing. Bake in a preheated oven at 180°C/355°F for 10 minutes and serve immediately.

Spinach, Tomato, Eggplant, and Chickpea Stew

This well-known and succulent vegetable combination from North India is a popular addition to many Hare Krishna Sunday Feast menus. Cooked until the spinach softens, it is a textured, juicy dish. If you prefer a purée like dish, cook it further until the spinach and eggplant cook right down. Either way, it's delicious served with *Puffed Fried Breads* or *Lemon Rice*.

PREPARATION TIME: 30 to 45 minutes
YIELD: enough for 6 to 8 persons

¹/₄ cup (60 ml) ghee or oil

1 tablespoon (20 ml) minced fresh ginger

2 hot green chilies, seeded and minced

1 teaspoon (5 ml) cumin seeds

¹/₂ teaspoon (2 ml) black mustard seeds

10 dried curry leaves

¹/₄ teaspoon (1 ml) yellow asafoetida powder

1 medium eggplant washed and cut into 1.25 cm (¹/₂-inch) cubes

4 medium tomatoes, peeled and cut into 1.25 cm (¹/₂-inch) cubes

450 g (1 pound) fresh spinach, washed and roughly chopped

1 teaspoon (5 ml) turmeric

1¹/₂ teaspoons (7 ml) salt

2 cups (500 ml) cooked and drained chickpeas

1¹/₂ teaspoons (7 ml) brown sugar

1 teaspoon (5 ml) fresh lemon juice

1. Heat the *ghee* or oil in a heavy 4-litre/quart saucepan or large wok over moderate heat. When the *ghee* is hot, add the ginger, chilies, cumin seeds,

Above: Baked Tomatoes Stuffed with Rice and Green Peas

and mustard seeds. When the mustard seeds crackle, add the curry leaves, asafoetida powder, and eggplant cubes. Stir-fry the eggplant for 8 to 10 minutes or until the eggplant is a little softened.

2. Stir in the tomatoes, spinach, turmeric, and salt. Partially cover and reduce the heat to moderately low. Cook until the eggplant is soft and the spinach is reduced in size, stirring when required. Add the cooked chickpeas and cook for another 5 minutes. If you would like the dish to be moist and textured, add the sugar and lemon juice now. Otherwise, cook until the vegetables become purée-like. Remove from the heat and serve hot.

Peppers Stuffed with Herbed Potatoes and Cheese

Select medium-sized green, red, or yellow peppers for this baked side-dish or entrée.

PREPARATION TIME: 15 minutes
COOKING TIME: 30 to 40 minutes
YIELD: 6 stuffed peppers

6 medium, square shaped peppers

boiling water

1/2 cup (125 ml) melted butter

1 teaspoon (1 ml) yellow
*   asafoetida powder*

1 teaspoon (5 ml) dried dill

1 teaspoon (5 ml) sweet paprika

1 1/2 teaspoons (7 ml) salt

1 teaspoon (5 ml) dried basil

3 tablespoons (60 ml) minced
*   fresh coriander*

3 cups (750 ml) hot mashed potatoes

1 cup (250 ml) grated cheddar cheese

1. Carefully slice a lid off each pepper and with a small serrated knife cut away the centre piece of each lid, leaving only edible flesh. Put the lids aside. Scoop out all the fibre and seeds and wash the peppers thoroughly. Plunge them into boiling water for 2 to 3 minutes, remove, and drain upside down.

2. Pour 4 tablespoons (80 ml) of the melted butter into a saucepan and over low heat; sauté the asafoetida

for a few moments. Add the dill, paprika, salt, basil, and fresh coriander. Stir and remove from the heat.

3. Place the mashed potatoes, three-quarters of the grated cheese, and the herbed butter in a bowl and mix until smooth.

4. Stuff all the peppers with the herbed potato and sprinkle the reserved cheese on top. Replace the cored lids. Place in a baking dish, brush with the reserved butter and bake in a preheated oven at 180°C/355°F for 30 to 40 minutes or until the peppers are tender and lightly browned.

Baked Tomatoes Stuffed with Rice and Green Peas

Lightly-seasoned fluffy *basmati* rice makes the best filling for stuffed tomatoes. Be sure to select firm, ripe tomatoes.

PREPARATION AND COOKING
*   TIME: 25 to 35 minutes*
BAKING TIME: 10 to 15 minutes
YIELD: enough for 6 persons

1 cup (250 ml) basmati or other
*   long-grain white rice*

5 tablespoons (100 ml) ghee or oil

6 whole cloves

one 3.75 cm (1 1/2-inch) cinnamon
*   stick*

2 whole cardamom pods, bruised

1/3 cup (85 ml) slivered almonds

2 cups (500 ml) water

1 cup (250 ml) fresh green peas

1 1/2 teaspoons (7 ml) salt

6 large or 12 small firm,
*   ripe tomatoes*

1 1/2 teaspoons (7 ml) minced
*   fresh ginger*

1/2 teaspoon (2 ml) turmeric

Rice filling

1. Clean, wash, and drain the rice.

2. Heat 4 tablespoons (80 ml) of *ghee* or oil in a heavy 2-litre/quart saucepan over moderate heat. When the *ghee* is hot, add the whole cloves, cinnamon stick, bruised cardamom pods, and almonds. Stir-fry for 30 seconds or until the almonds are golden. Bring the water to a boil in another pan.

3. Add the rice to the spice and nut mixture and stir-fry for about 2 minutes or until the rice is whitish.

4. Add the boiling water to the rice and nut mixture; add the peas and 1 teaspoon (5 ml) of salt. Stir, raising the heat to high and bringing the water to a full boil.

Immediately reduce the heat to low, cover with a tight-fitting lid and, without stirring, simmer for 15 to 20 minutes or until the rice is dry and tender. Fluff the rice with a fork and (if desired) remove the whole spices.

Stuffed tomatoes

1. Preheat the oven to 180°C/355°F.

2. Cut a thin slice off the top of each tomato and set the slices aside. With a teaspoon, scoop out the seeds and pulp, leaving a 0.5 cm (1/4-inch) thick case, and set them aside. Chop or blend the tomato pulp and force it through a strainer. Collect the pulp and discard the seeds.

3. Heat 1 tablespoon (20 ml) of *ghee* or oil in a 1-litre/quart saucepan over medium heat. When hot, drop in the minced ginger and fry until brown. Add the tomato pulp, 1/2 teaspoon (2 ml) salt, and turmeric and cook for 5 minutes or until the pulp is reduced to a thick purée.

4. Stuff the tomatoes with the savoury rice-filling and pour a teaspoon of the thick tomato sauce into the opening of each tomato. Replace the tops of the tomatoes.

5. Set the tomatoes in a glass casserole dish and bake them in the oven at 180°C/360°F for 10 or 15 minutes. Serve hot.

Gauranga Potatoes

In this dish, slices of potato are folded with herbs, butter, and sour cream and baked to a golden brown. It is irresistibly rich and delicious, yet effortless to prepare.

PREPARATION AND COOKING TIME: 50 minutes to 1 hour

YIELD: enough for 4 to 6 persons

8 medium potatoes, peeled and sliced into 0.5 cm (1/4-inch) disks

water

1 tablespoon (20 ml) olive oil

3/4 teaspoon (3 ml) yellow asafoetida powder

1/2 teaspoon (2 ml) ground dried rosemary

1/4 teaspoon (1 ml) freshly ground black pepper

1/2 teaspoon (2 ml) turmeric

3 cups (750 ml) sour cream

1 tablespoon (20 ml) melted butter

2 teaspoons (10 ml) salt

1/2 cup (125 ml) water

1 teaspoon (5 ml) sweet paprika

2 tablespoons (40 ml) chopped fresh parsley

1. Boil the potato slices in lightly salted water in a 4-litre/quart saucepan until they are cooked but firm. Remove and drain.

2. Add the olive oil to a medium saucepan, over moderate heat and when hot, add the asafoetida. Sauté momentarily; add the rosemary, black pepper, and turmeric and stir briefly. Add the sour cream, melted butter, salt, and water. Whisk it into a smooth sauce and remove from the heat.

3. Combine the potato slices and sour cream sauce in a mixing bowl. Pour the mixture into a casserole dish, sprinkle with paprika, and place in the top of a preheated (200°C/390°F) oven. Bake for 30 minutes or until the top is golden brown. Garnish with fresh parsley and serve hot.

French Braised Summer Vegetables
(*Ratatouille*)

This is my version of the famous French vegetable medley of eggplants, zucchinis, red and green peppers, and tomatoes so popular in Provence. The eggplants are first rubbed in salt to remove their bitterness (*dégorging*). Serve *Ratatouille* cold with crusty soft sesame bread rolls, or hot with fluffy yellow rice.

EGGPLANT DÉGORGING TIME: 30 minutes

PREPARATION AND COOKING TIME: 30 minutes

YIELD: enough for 4 to 6 persons

2 medium eggplants, cut into 2.5 cm (1-inch) cubes

salt for dégorging

1/2 cup (125 ml) olive oil

1/2 teaspoon (2 ml) yellow asafoetida powder

1 large red pepper and 1 large green pepper, cored, seeded, and cut into long strips about 1.25 cm (1/2-inch) wide

4 medium zucchinis, cut into 0.5 cm (1/4-inch) slices at an angle (bias cut)

1/4 teaspoon (1 ml) freshly ground black pepper

4 medium tomatoes, peeled and cut into eighths

1 teaspoon (5 ml) salt

2 tablespoons (40 ml) chopped fresh parsley

1. To *dégorge* the eggplants: place the eggplant cubes in a colander, sprinkle with salt, and let sit for about 30 minutes. Rinse thoroughly. Drain and pat the eggplants dry with paper towels.

2. Heat the olive oil in a large saucepan over moderate heat. When the oil is hot, add the asafoetida and fry momentarily. Add the eggplant cubes and sauté, stirring often, for 3 minutes. Add the peppers, zucchini, and black pepper; cover and cook gently without any water for about 15 minutes or until the zucchinis, peppers, and eggplants are tender (if the vegetables stick, add a little water). Add the tomatoes and cook only until they warm through. Add the salt and parsley and mix well. Serve hot or cold.

Thai Vegetable Curry

Here's a tasty and unusual combination of potatoes and *tofu* simmered in a spicy lemon-peanut-coconut sauce. Serve alongside *Thai Rice* for a light meal.

***PREPARATION AND COOKING TIME:** 45 minutes*

***YIELD:** enough for 4 persons*

2 whole cloves

1 tablespoon (20 ml) coriander seeds

1 teaspoon (5 ml) cumin seeds

5 dried chilies

3 black peppercorns

one 2.5 cm (1-inch) cinnamon stick, broken into pieces

3 tablespoons (60 ml) vegetable oil

½ teaspoon (2 ml) yellow asafoetida powder

2 small fresh hot green chilies, seeded and sliced into thin strips

1 teaspoon (5 ml) lemongrass powder

½ teaspoon (2 ml) galangal (laos) powder

2 cups (500 ml) coconut milk

1 teaspoon (5 ml) salt

1 tablespoon (20 ml) instant tamarind concentrate

2 tablespoons (40 ml) warm water

400 g (14 ounces) firm tofu cut into 1.25 cm (½-inch) cubes

4 tablespoons (80 ml) roasted peanuts

½ teaspoon (2 ml) cardamom seeds

4 medium potatoes parboiled, peeled, and cut into 1.25 cm (½-inch) cubes

2 tablespoons (40 ml) brown sugar

3 tablespoons (60 ml) light soy sauce

3 tablespoons (60 ml) fresh lemon juice

1. Dry-roast the cloves, coriander seeds, cumin seeds, chilies, peppercorns, and cinnamon in a small pan over moderate heat until the spices become aromatic (2-3 minutes). Remove the pan from the heat and transfer the spices to a coffee mill. Grind the spices to a powder; transfer to a small bowl.

2. Heat the vegetable oil in a 6-litre/quart saucepan over moderate heat. When the oil becomes hot, add the asafoetida, green chilies, lemongrass powder, *galangal* (*laos*) powder, and dry-roasted spices. Stir momentarily, add the coconut milk and salt, and stir until warm. Remove from the heat.

3. Combine the tamarind concentrate with the warm water. Whisk until smooth. Add the cubed *tofu* to the coconut milk mixture along with the peanuts, cardamom seeds, parboiled potatoes, brown sugar, light soy sauce, tamarind water, and lemon juice. Return to a very low heat and, stirring occasionally, simmer uncovered for 25 to 30 minutes or until the sauce thickens and the potatoes are tender. Serve hot.

Pictured: Gauranga *Potatoes*

South Indian Vegetable Combination
(*Aviyal*)

A famous dish from the Malabar coast of Kerala, South India, *Aviyal* is much loved on festive menus. Practically any combination of vegetables can be used, as long as they are cut in such a way that they all cook in about the same amount of time. In Kerala, local vegetables would be used. However, I have suggested a combination of potato, sweet potato, peas, pumpkin, beans, carrot, and zucchini. This version is flavoured in the traditional way with fresh coconut, yogurt, and green chilies. Serve hot with *Boiled Rice*.

*PREPARATION AND COOKING
   TIME: 20 to 30 minutes*

YIELD: enough for 6 to 8 persons

*4 tablespoons (80 ml) coconut oil
   or ghee*

6-8 fresh (or dried) curry leaves

*1 cup (250 ml) sweet potato cut into
   1.5 cm (³/4-inch) cubes*

*1 cup (250 ml) green beans cut into
   1.5 cm (³/4-inch) lengths*

*1 cup (250 ml) pumpkin cut into
   1.5 cm (³/4-inch) cubes*

*1 cup (250 ml) carrots cut into
   batons 3.75 cm x 1.25 cm x
   1.25 cm (1¹/2 inches x ¹/2 inch x
   ¹/2 inch)*

*1 cup (250 ml) zucchini cut into
   1.5 cm (³/4-inch) cubes*

¹/2 cup (125 ml) fresh green peas

*1 cup (250 ml) potato cut into
   1.5 cm (³/4-inch) cubes*

²/3 cup (165 ml) water

1 teaspoon (5 ml) turmeric

1 teaspoon (5 ml) ground coriander

3 hot green chilies, minced

Pumpkin and Potatoes, Marwari-Style

This popular vegetable dish from Rajasthan, northern India, is quick and easy to prepare and full-bodied in flavour with varieties of hot and sweet spicy flavours. Serve it with hot *Rajasthani Spicy Dal-Stuffed Breads* or *Puffed Fried Breads*.

*PREPARATION AND COOKING
   TIME: 20 to 30 minutes*

YIELD: enough for 6 to 8 persons

3 tablespoons (60 ml) ghee or oil

*¹/2 teaspoon (2 ml) black
   mustard seeds*

*1 teaspoon (5 ml) kalonji
   (nigella) seeds if available*

one 5 cm (2-inch) cinnamon stick

seeds from 2 cardamom pods

2 whole cloves

2 bay leaves

¹/2 teaspoon (2 ml) fenugreek seeds

2 tablespoons (40 ml) yogurt

*¹/4 teaspoon (1 ml) yellow
   asafoetida powder*

1 teaspoon (5 ml) ground coriander

1 teaspoon (5 ml) ground cumin

1 teaspoon (5 ml) chili powder

¹/2 teaspoon (2 ml) turmeric

*450 g (1 pound) potatoes (about 4
   cups), peeled and cut into 1.25 cm
   (¹/2-inch) cubes*

*450 g (1 pound) pumpkin (about 4
   cups), peeled and cut into 1.5 cm
   (³/4-inch) cubes*

²/3 cup (165 ml) water

1 teaspoon (5 ml) lemon juice

¹/2 teaspoon (2 ml) sugar

1¹/2 teaspoons (7 ml) salt

1. Heat the *ghee* or oil in a heavy 4-litre/quart saucepan over moderate heat. When the *ghee* is hot, add the mustard seeds, *kalonji* seeds, cinnamon stick, cardamom seeds, cloves, and bay leaves. Sauté the spices until the mustard seeds crackle. Add the fenugreek seeds and sauté until they darken a few shades.

2. Add the yogurt, asafoetida, coriander, cumin, chili, and turmeric and stir-fry for 1 minute. Add the potatoes, pumpkin, and water. Cover and cook on a medium heat for 15 minutes or until the vegetables are tender. Add a little hot water if the vegetables start to stick. Add the lemon juice, sugar, and salt and serve hot.

*Above: Scrambled Curd
Right: Green Beans served with Mashed
Potato Puffs*

½ cup (125 ml) plain yogurt

⅔ cup (165 ml) shredded
 fresh coconut

2 teaspoons (10 ml) salt

1. Heat the oil or *ghee* in a large heavy-based non-stick pan over moderate heat. Sauté the curry leaves until they darken a few shades. Add all the vegetables, sauté them for 2 or 3 minutes, and add the water, turmeric, and coriander, stirring well. Bring the liquid to a boil.

2. Reduce the heat to low, cover, and simmer, stirring occasionally for about 15 minutes or until the vegetables are tender. Add the chilies, yogurt, coconut, and salt. Serve hot.

Scrambled Curd

This is the vegetarian counterpart to scrambled eggs.

Fresh curd cheese (*panir*) is scrambled with sour cream and sprinkled with black salt (which has a distinct sulphur-like flavour), spices, and fresh herbs to produce a stunning result. Serve at breakfast with hot toast or *Puffed Fried Breads* (*Pooris*), and *Tomato Chutney*.

**PREPARATION AND COOKING
 TIME: 40 to 50 minutes**

YIELD: enough for 4 to 6 persons

6 litres (10½ pints) full-cream milk

7 tablespoons (140 ml) lemon juice

2 tablespoons (40 ml) ghee or butter

½ teaspoon (2 ml) yellow
 asafoetida powder

¼ teaspoon (1 ml) turmeric

½ teaspoon (2 ml) sweet paprika

1 teaspoon (5 ml) salt

¼ teaspoon (1 ml) coarsely ground
 black pepper

¾ cup (185 ml) cream or sour cream

2 tablespoons (40 ml) coarsely
 chopped fresh coriander leaves,

1 teaspoon (5 ml) Indian black salt
 (kala namak), finely ground

1. Boil the milk in a heavy-based 8-10 litre/quart saucepan, stirring constantly. When the foam rises, gradually add the lemon juice and reduce the heat to low. Stir very slowly until the solid curd cheese separates from the yellowish whey. (If separation does not occur after 1 minute, add a little more lemon juice.)

2. Pour the curds and whey into a colander lined with a triple-thickness of cheesecloth. Press under a heavy weight for 10 to 15 minutes.

3. Unwrap the curd cheese and break it into 2.5 cm (1-inch) chunks.

4. Heat the *ghee* or butter in a large pan or wok over moderate heat. Sauté the asafoetida and turmeric in the hot *ghee*. Add the pieces of curd cheese and stir gently until the turmeric-coloured *ghee* is well distributed. Increase the heat and add the paprika, salt, and pepper. When the curd cheese is well mixed, remove from the heat.

5. Add the cream or sour cream and the black salt, stirring carefully. Add the fresh herbs, mix well, and serve hot.

Green Beans

Here's a delicious way to serve seasonal French stringless green beans. Serve as an entrée or part of a multi-course dinner.

**PREPARATION AND COOKING
 TIME: 15 minutes**

YIELD: enough for 4 or 5 persons

2 tablespoons (40 ml) ghee or oil

½ teaspoon (2 ml) black
 mustard seeds

one 1.25 cm (½-inch) cube of ginger
 sliced into paper-thin julienne
 strips

450 g (1 pound) fresh green
 stringless beans, "topped and
 tailed" and cut into 2.5 cm
 (1-inch) diagonal slices

¼ cup (60 ml) water

½ teaspoon (2 ml) ground cumin

¼ teaspoon (1 ml) turmeric

1 teaspoon (5 ml) salt

2 tablespoons (40 ml) minced fresh
 coriander leaves

1 teaspoon (5 ml) fresh lemon juice

1. Sauté the mustard seeds and ginger strips in *ghee* or oil in a 3-litre/quart saucepan over moderate heat until the mustard seeds crackle.

2. Add the beans and stir-fry over moderate heat for about 5 to 7 minutes. Add the water, cover securely, and boil gently for 5 minutes. Remove the lid and when most of the water has evaporated, add the remaining ingredients except the lemon juice. Cook until the beans are tender-crisp and the water has evaporated. Add the lemon juice and serve hot.

Cabbage, Potato, and Yogurt with Anise

The combination of yogurt, lemon juice, and brown sugar creates a delicious sweet-and-sour glaze for the vegetables. Serve with hot fluffy rice or a crusty bread, and a soup or *dal*.

PREPARATION AND COOKING TIME: 45 minutes

YIELD: enough for 4 to 6 persons

2 tablespoons (40 ml) ghee or oil

1½ teaspoons (7 ml) cumin seeds

1½ teaspoons (7 ml) anise seeds

1 small cabbage, cored and sliced very thin

1 teaspoon (5 ml) turmeric

½ teaspoon (2 ml) hot paprika or cayenne

6 medium potatoes, peeled and cut into 2.5 cm (1-inch) cubes

1 cup (250 ml) yogurt

1 tablespoon (20 ml) fresh lemon juice

2 teaspoons (10 ml) salt

1 tablespoon (20 ml) brown sugar

1. Heat the *ghee* or oil in a heavy 6-litre/quart non-stick saucepan over moderate heat. Sauté the cumin and anise seeds until golden brown. Add the cabbage and stir-fry for about 2 minutes. Cover the pan and, reducing the heat, cook the cabbage until it shrinks.

2. Add the turmeric, paprika, and the potato cubes. Mix well and replace the lid. Cook, stirring occasionally until the potatoes are tender. (You may need to add a little water.)

3. Remove the pan from the heat and fold in the yogurt, lemon juice, salt, and brown sugar. Stir to mix and serve hot.

Vegetables au Gratin

Delightfully simple to make, *Vegetables au Gratin* is a great favourite on the wintertime menu at Gopal's Restaurant.

Consisting of lightly steamed vegetables in a mornay sauce, topped with grated cheese, and baked in the oven until golden brown, it combines wonderfully with a light soup and bread accompaniment, such as *Vegetable Soup* and *Wholemeal Bread*.

PREPARATION AND COOKING TIME: 40 minutes.

YIELD: enough for 6 to 8 persons

8 cups (2 litres) assorted vegetables cut into large bite-sized chunks (try a selection from the following: cauliflower, broccoli, carrots, French beans, green peas, baby potatoes, asparagus, squash, pumpkin, sweet potato)

⅔ cup (165 ml) butter

¼ teaspoon (1 ml) yellow asafoetida powder

¼ teaspoon (1 ml) nutmeg

⅔ cup (165 ml) plain flour

5 cups (1.25 litres) warm milk

2 teaspoons (10 ml) salt

¾ teaspoon (3 ml) ground white pepper

250 g (about 9 ounces) grated cheddar cheese

1 tablespoon (20 ml) extra butter

2 tablespoons (40 ml) chopped fresh parsley

1. Lightly steam all the vegetables until they're cooked but still a little firm.

2. Melt the butter in a medium-sized saucepan over moderate heat. Remove the pan from the heat. Add the asafoetida powder and nutmeg. Stir in the flour with a wooden spoon to make a smooth paste. Gradually add the milk, stirring constantly.

3. Return the pan to the heat and bring the sauce to a boil, still stirring. Reduce the heat to low and simmer, stirring constantly, for 1 minute or until the sauce is thick and smooth. Add the salt, pepper, and half of the grated cheese. Add the steamed vegetables and mix well.

4. Spoon the vegetables into a buttered baking dish. Cover them with the remaining grated cheese and dot with little pieces of butter. Bake in a preheated hot oven (205°C/400°F) for 25 minutes or until the top is golden brown. Garnish with chopped fresh parsley.

Right: Vegetables au Gratin

Cauliflower and Potato Supreme
(*Gobi Aloo Bhaji*)

For best results with this North Indian favourite, use pure *ghee* as the frying medium. Serve this rich vegetable dish for special occasions.

PREPARATION AND COOKING TIME: 35 minutes
YIELD: enough for 5 or 6 persons

2 large baking potatoes peeled and cut into 2.5 cm (1-inch) cubes

ghee or oil for deep frying

1 medium cauliflower cut into flowerets

¹/₄ teaspoon (1 ml) coarsely ground black pepper,

¹/₂ teaspoon (2 ml) ginger powder

¹/₂ teaspoon (2 ml) turmeric

¹/₄ teaspoon (1 ml) cayenne pepper

1 teaspoon (5 ml) salt

1 cup (250 ml) plain yogurt or sour cream at room temperature

1 tablespoon (20 ml) chopped fresh coriander or parsley

1. Rinse the potato cubes in cold water. Drain and pat them dry.

2. Place enough *ghee* in a deep wok or pan that will well-cover the quantity of potatoes. Heat the *ghee* to 190°C/375°F. Fry the potatoes until golden brown (8 to 10 minutes). (You might need to fry in 2 batches.) Remove and drain the potatoes. Deep-fry the cauliflowers until they're cooked but slightly firm. Remove and drain them.

3. When all the vegetables are deep-fried, drained, and still warm, place them in a large bowl, add the spices, salt, and yogurt or sour cream. Add the fresh herbs and serve immediately. If not serving immediately, when you are ready to serve, warm the spiced vegetables in a low-heat oven and add the yogurt or sour cream.

Zucchini, Green Peppers, and Tomato

Here's a succulent combination of young zucchinis, green peppers, and juicy tomato pieces braised together that's quick and easy to prepare. For a simple summer lunch, combine this dish with *Chapatis* or *Rice with Green Peas and Almonds* and a crisp salad.

PREPARATION TIME: 20 to 30 minutes
YIELD: enough for 4 to 6 persons

2 tablespoons (40 ml) ghee or oil

1 teaspoon (5 ml) cumin seeds

1¹/₂ teaspoons (7 ml) fresh green chilies, seeded and minced

¹/₄ teaspoon (1 ml) yellow asafoetida powder

1 teaspoon (5 ml) turmeric

2 small green peppers, diced into 1.25 cm (¹/₂-inch) squares

6 medium zucchinis cut into 1.25 cm (¹/₂-inch) cubes

1 teaspoon (5 ml) ground coriander

6 medium tomatoes blanched, peeled, and cut into eighths

1¹/₂ teaspoons (7 ml) salt

1 teaspoon (5 ml) brown sugar

1 tablespoon (20 ml) chopped fresh parsley or coriander

Pictured: Zucchini, Green Peppers, and Tomato served with Yellow Rice (p.10)

1. Sauté the cumin seeds in *ghee* or oil in a large, heavy, non-stick saucepan or wok over moderate heat until the seeds darken a few shades. Add the green chilies, asafoetida, and turmeric and stir momentarily. Add the green peppers and stir-fry for 2 to 3 minutes.

2. Add the zucchini and ground coriander and, stirring occasionally, cook the vegetables for an additional 2 minutes. Add the tomato pieces, mix well, and reduce the heat to moderately low, stirring occasionally. Cook until the zucchini becomes translucent and soft but not mushy. Add the salt, sugar, and herbs. Stir to mix, remove from the heat, and serve hot.

Pictured: Eggplant, Potato, and Curd Cheese

Eggplant, Potato, and Curd Cheese

Our spiritual master, Srila Prabhupada, taught Dipak, my old friend and culinary guide, how to prepare this vegetable dish in 1972 giving it the unusual sub-title of 'Meat-eaters Delight'. Because the *panir* cheese is cut into large uneven chunks and deep-fried in *ghee* until dark, then slowly stewed in spiced whcy, it develops a very "meaty" texture and appearance. Serve this rich and juicy vegetable dish with plain boiled rice, a simple dal, crisp salad, and flat bread.

Note: Save the whey when you make the *panir* cheese.

PREPARATION AND COOKING TIME: 1 hour

YIELD: enough for 4 or 5 persons

ghee *for deep-frying*

2 large baking potatoes, peeled and cut into 2.5 cm (1-inch) cubes

2 large eggplants, cut into 2.5 cm (1-inch) cubes

home-made curd cheese (panir), plus the whey, made from 8 cups (2 litres) milk, pressed for ½-hour, and cut into 2.5 cm (1-inch) cubes

1 tablespoon (20 ml) ghee

2 teaspoons (10 ml) cumin seeds

1 teaspoon (5 ml) crushed dried red chilies

½ teaspoon (2 ml) yellow asafoetida powder

½ teaspoon (2 ml) turmeric

2 cups (500 ml) whey

½ teaspoon (2 ml) ground coriander

1½ teaspoons (7 ml) salt

1. Add enough *ghee* to half-fill a wok or deep-frying pan. Place over moderate heat and allow it to reach 190°C/375°F. If you use a large wok or pan, you can fry all of the potatoes simultaneously. Otherwise, add half the potatoes and deep-fry them until golden brown (8 to 10 minutes). Remove and drain them. When the potatoes are all fried, allow the *ghee* to return to the required temperature.

2. Add half the eggplant pieces and deep-fry them until they are golden brown. Remove and drain them. Allow the *ghee* to return to the frying temperature; then fry the remaining eggplants and drain them.

3. Deep-fry the *panir* cubes until they are dark golden brown. Remove and drain. Turn off the heat under the *ghee*.

4. Heat 1 tablespoon (20 ml) *ghee* over moderate heat in a heavy 3 litre/quart saucepan. Sauté the cumin seeds until golden brown. Add the chilies, asafoetida, and turmeric. Stir momentarily; then carefully add the whey, salt, and ground coriander. Raise the heat until the whey boils.

5. Add the potatoes, eggplant cubes, and pieces of fried *panir*. Combine the vegetables with the whey, taking care not to crush the eggplant. Boil, reduce the heat to low, and simmer the vegetables for about 20 minutes. Cook until the potatoes become glazed and light golden. The eggplant should be soft but not mushy, and the *panir* cubes should be juicy. Serve hot.

Indonesian Vegetable Stew (*Sayur Asam*)

Indonesian vegetable stews (*Sayurs*) are actually half-way between stews and soups. They are traditionally served with rice and a *sambal* (chili relish). This dish features four special Indonesian ingredients, all available at good Asian grocers: *laos* (Indonesian ginger), lime leaf, lemongrass, and coconut milk (*santan*). It also contains a Chinese green vegetable called *bok choy*.

PREPARATION TIME: 10 minutes
COOKING TIME: 15 minutes
YIELD: enough for 4 persons

2 small slices fresh **laos** *(Indonesian ginger) or the common variety of fresh ginger or 1 teaspoon (5 ml)* **laos** *powder*

½ teaspoon (2 ml) ground coriander

1 fresh hot green chili, seeded and chopped

2 cups (500 ml) **Chinese Vegetable Stock** *or water*

1 tablespoon (20 ml) corn oil

½ teaspoon (2 ml) yellow asafoetida powder

½ cup (125 ml) French stringless green beans, "topped and tailed" and cut into 5 cm (2-inch) lengths

1 lime leaf (substitute with bay leaf if unavailable)

½ teaspoon (2 ml) lemongrass flakes or powder

½ cup (125 ml) **Chinese bok choy** *leaves, cut into thin strips*

450 g (1 pound) zucchinis, cut into 2.5 cm (1-inch) wedges

1 cup (250 ml) coconut milk (santan)

1 teaspoon (5 ml) salt

1 teaspoon (5 ml) sugar

1. Place the *laos* or ginger, ground coriander, and chili in a blender. Add vegetable stock or water and blend. Empty into a bowl.

2. Fry the asafoetida and green beans in oil in a wok for 1 minute. Add the stock and spice mixture, lime leaf or bay leaf, and lemongrass and simmer covered for 8 to 10 minutes. Add the *bok choy* and zucchini and cook covered for another 3 minutes or until the zucchini is tender. Add the coconut milk (*santan*), salt, and sugar and simmer for another minute. Serve hot.

Vegetarian Stroganoff

This delicious combination of vegetables with herbs and sour cream is enhanced by the addition of *tofu* cubes that have been frozen and thawed. The texture of *tofu* changes dramatically after it has been frozen and thawed. It becomes firmer and chewy, much resembling the texture of meat. You can freeze an entire block of *tofu* or cut it into strips or cubes and then freeze it. If you freeze it and let it thaw naturally, you get a crumbly textured *tofu*, resembling Textured Vegetable Protein (TVP). If you quick-thaw the frozen *tofu* in boiling water, it will retain its shape. You can wring out the *tofu* like a sponge and season it as required. This *stroganoff* recipe calls for frozen, quick-thawed cubes of *tofu* that have been seasoned and marinated. Serve with hot noodles or rice for a complete main meal.

TOFU *FREEZING TIME: 2 days*
SEASONING AND MARINATING
  TIME: 15 minutes
PREPARATION AND COOKING
  TIME: 40 minutes

YIELD: enough for 4 persons (when served with rice or noodles)

450 g (1 pound) firm **tofu** *cut into 2.5 cm (1-inch) cubes, placed on a plate, and frozen for 2 days*

2 tablespoons (40 ml) vegetable oil

½ teaspoon (2 ml) yellow asafoetida powder

½ teaspoon (2 ml) black pepper

2 tablespoons (40 ml) Japanese **tamari** *or soy sauce*

¼ cup (60 ml) dry white grape juice

30 g (1 ounce) butter

3 large zucchinis, cubed

1 medium red or green pepper, diced

3 large tomatoes, blanched, peeled, and chopped

1 teaspoon (5 ml) dried dill

1 tablespoon (20 ml) sweet paprika

1½ teaspoons (7 ml) salt

1 cup (250 ml) sour cream

1. Remove the *tofu* from the freezer, separate the pieces from the plate by rinsing under hot water, and plunge them into boiling water. When the *tofu* pieces soften and float, re-move them from the heat and drain them. Rinse them under cold water; then squeeze them between your palms until they're completely dry.

2. Heat the oil in a heavy frying pan over moderate heat. Sprinkle in half the asafoetida, stir momentarily, and then add half the black pepper and the dry *tofu* pieces. Sauté for 1 minute; then add the *tamari* or soy sauce and grape juice, bring to the boil and simmer for another 2 minutes. Remove from the heat and allow to marinate for 15 minutes.

3. In a heavy 4-litre/quart saucepan or wok, melt the butter over moderate heat. Add the asafoetida, zucchini, and peppers, stir-frying for 2 to 3 minutes. Add the tomatoes, dill, paprika, salt and pepper, and cook until the zucchini and peppers become soft, adding water if necessary. Add the *tofu* and marinade and simmer for 5 minutes more. Serve hot over rice or noodles topped with sour cream.

Asparagus with Oil and Lemon Sauce

This is a typical dish from the Veneto region of northern Italy. Its beauty lies in its simplicity. Serve this dish as *antipasto (entrée)*.

PREPARATION AND COOKING TIME: 20 minutes

YIELD: enough for 4 persons

2 bunches of fresh asparagus (500 g, a little over 1 pound)

juice of 1 lemon

3 tablespoons (60 ml) olive oil

½ teaspoon (2 ml) salt

¼ teaspoon (1 ml) freshly ground black pepper

¼ teaspoon (1 ml) freshly grated nutmeg

2-4 tablespoons (40-80 ml) grated parmesan cheese

1. Wash the asparagus. Cut off the woody part at the base. Peel the lower section to reveal the tender edible flesh. Tie the asparagus in a bundle and stand it in a tall pot in 5 cm (2 inches) of water. Cover the pot and allow the asparagus to boil gently over moderate heat until the stems are cooked but still a little firm (about 5-10 minutes). Alternatively, place the asparagus in a steamer.

2. Place the asparagus on a warmed serving dish. Mix the lemon juice, oil, salt, pepper, and nutmeg, pour this sauce over the hot asparagus, and sprinkle with cheese. Serve immediately.

Pictured: Asparagus with Oil and Lemon Sauce

Cantonese Stir-Fried Vegetables with Cashews in Black Bean Sauce

This is a delicious mèlange of tasty vegetables and cashew nuts. All special ingredients are available at Chinese grocers. Shop-bought salty black bean sauce however is not a reliable item for strict vegetarians since it sometimes contains other ingredients not listed on the label. Better to use home-made *Cantonese Black-Bean Sauce*. Serve with *Boiled Rice* or as part of a multi-course Chinese dinner.

PREPARATION AND COOKING TIME: 30 minutes

YIELD: enough for 6 to 8 persons

½ cup (125 ml) cashew nuts

warm water for soaking

oil for deep-frying

450 g (1 pound) firm tofu cut into 1.25 cm (½-inch) cubes

2 small eggplants cut into 2.5 cm (1-inch) cubes

½ large carrot, thinly sliced

Left: Cantonese Stir-Fried Vegetables

2 medium green peppers and 1 medium red pepper cut into 1.5 cm (¾-inch) chunks

2 medium cucumbers, unpeeled, cut into 1.5 cm (¾-inch) cubes

10 water chestnuts, slit through the centre

2 tablespoons (40 ml) Chinese Vegetable Stock or water

½ teaspoon (2 ml) Chinese sesame oil

1 teaspoon (5 ml) thick soy sauce

1 teaspoon (5 ml) sugar

2 tablespoons (40 ml) Cantonese Black Bean Sauce

1 teaspoon (5 ml) cornflour blended with 2 teaspoons (10 ml) cold water to form a paste

1. Soak the cashews in warm water for 10 minutes. Drain and pat them dry.

2. Heat the oil in a wok or pan until hot (185°C/365°F). Deep-fry the cashews until golden brown. Remove, drain, and set them aside. Deep-fry the *tofu* cubes in batches until golden. Remove, drain, and set them aside. Deep-fry the eggplant pieces in batches until dark golden brown. Remove, drain, and set them aside.

3. Meanwhile, bring water to the boil in a small saucepan. Add the carrots and boil until just tender. Remove, rinse under cold water, and drain.

4. Heat 1 tablespoon (20 ml) deep-frying oil in a wok over high heat. When the oil is hot, add the chopped red and green peppers and stir-fry briskly until crisp-tender (about 1-2 minutes). Remove and set them aside.

5. Heat another 1 tablespoon (20 ml) frying oil in the wok over high heat. When hot, add the cucumbers, carrots, and water chestnuts and stir-fry briskly for 1 minute. Add the peppers, *tofu*, eggplants, water or stock, sesame oil, soy sauce, sugar, and black-bean sauce. Stir the cornflour paste into the vegetable mixture, add the cashew nuts, stir for another 30 seconds and serve hot.

Creamed Spinach with Curd Cheese (*Palak Panir*)

Spinach with home-made curd cheese and cream is one of North India's favourite vegetable dishes. There are dozens of regional varieties. Here's a simple, quick-cooking version. Serve with *Yellow Rice* or hot buttered *Chapatis*.

PREPARATION TIME: 5 minutes

COOKING TIME: 30 minutes

YIELD: enough for 5 or 6 persons

1 teaspoon (5 ml) chopped fresh ginger

1 fresh hot green chili, seeded and minced

1 teaspoon (5 ml) ground coriander

½ teaspoon (2 ml) sweet paprika

½ teaspoon (2 ml) ground cumin

½ teaspoon (2 ml) turmeric

1 tablespoon (20 ml) ghee or oil

2 large bunches of spinach, washed, trimmed and finely chopped

4 tablespoons (80 ml) cream

fresh homemade curd cheese (panir) made from 8 cups (2 litres) of milk, cut into 1.25 cm (½-inch) cubes

½ teaspoon (2 ml) garam masala

1 teaspoon (5 ml) salt

1. Place the ginger and chili in a food processor or blender and process with a few spoons of cold water. Add the coriander, paprika, cumin, and turmeric and blend to form a smooth paste. Scrape the paste into a bowl.

2. Heat the *ghee* in a large saucepan over moderate heat. When the *ghee* is hot, add the spice paste and chopped spinach. Fold in the spinach, combining it with the spices. Cook over full heat until the spinach reduces in volume. Reduce the heat slightly and, stirring often, cook the spinach for another 15 minutes or until it becomes soft.

3. Fold in the cream; add the cubes of *panir*, the *garam masala*, and the salt. Cook for an additional 5 minutes and serve hot.

Hungarian Vegetarian Ghoulash

Here's a simple but hearty combination of potatoes, tomato, and chunks of fried curd cheese simmered in a tasty gravy flavoured with Hungarian paprika. Serve *Hungarian Vegetarian Ghoulash* hot with fresh *Wholemeal Bread* for a tasty wintertime meal.

PREPARATION AND COOKING TIME: 30-40 minutes

YIELD: enough for 6 to 8 persons

ghee or oil for deep-frying

fresh homemade curd cheese from 12 cups (3 litres) milk, pressed until very firm and cut into 2.5 cm (1-inch) chunks

3 or 4 whole dried red chilies

1 teaspoon (5 ml) yellow asafoetida powder

5 medium tomatoes, peeled and quartered

2 tablespoons (40 ml) Hungarian sweet paprika

1¹/₂ teaspoons (7 ml) salt

8 medium potatoes, cut into 2.5 cm (1-inch) cubes

4 cups (1 litre) warm water

1. Deep-fry the chunks of *panir* cheese in oil or *ghee* in a deep-frying pan or wok over moderate heat until they become dark golden brown. Remove and drain.

2. Heat 1 tablespoon (20 ml) of *ghee* or oil over moderate heat in a heavy 6-litre/quart saucepan or large wok. When hot, add the red chilies and sprinkle in the asafoetida. Sauté momentarily and add the tomato pieces, paprika, salt, potato, and deep-fried curd chunks. Pour in the warm water and raise the heat to full. When the water boils, reduce the heat slightly and cook, uncovered, for 20 minutes or until the potatoes are soft. Serve hot.

Italian Eggplant and Tomato Appetizer

In the realm of Italian Cuisine, *antipasto* (appetizers) come in varied forms, much like the Middle Eastern equivalent, *mezze*. Savoury breads (*crostini*), vegetable salads, miniature pizzas (*pizzette*), and assorted simple vegetable entrées would feature as vegetarian *antipasto*. Here is my version of *Antipasto di Melanzane*, from Naples. Serve it at the outset of a main meal.

PREPARATION AND COOKING TIME: 30 minutes

YIELD: enough for 4 to 6 appetizer-sized portions

2 medium eggplants, washed

1 cup (250 ml) oil (not olive oil)

¹/₄ cup (60 ml) olive oil

¹/₄ teaspoon (1 ml) yellow asafoetida powder

3 ripe tomatoes, peeled, seeded, and chopped

1 tablespoon (20 ml) tomato paste

¹/₂ cup (125 ml) water

1 teaspoon (5 ml) salt

¹/₂ teaspoon (1 ml) freshly ground black pepper

1. Cut the eggplants into 0.5 cm (¹/₄-inch) slices. Cut each slice into strips 6 cm (2¹/₂ inches) long and 0.5 cm (¹/₄-inch) wide.

2. Heat the oil in a frying pan over moderately high heat. When the oil is hot, add enough eggplant strips to fill the frying pan. Shallow-fry the eggplant until it becomes soft. Remove the eggplant from the pan with a slotted spoon and drain.

3. Heat the olive oil in another frying pan over moderate heat. When the oil is hot, add asafoetida, tomatoes, tomato paste, and water. Cook uncovered for 10 minutes or until the sauce is thick.

4. Add the salt and pepper, mix well, and carefully add the eggplant. Serve either hot or cold.

Tomato, Peas, and Home-made Curd
(*Matar Panir*)

This dish originates in Punjab, northern India. However, it is well-known all over India, and there are hundreds of variations of the same dish. But the same main ingredients are always there: peas and *panir* cheese in a spiced, minted tomato sauce. Here's a delicious version that can be served with any meal, anytime. It especially lends itself to special feasts and dinners and can be kept warm for some time, actually improving the flavour of the dish.

PREPARATION AND COOKING TIME: 45 minutes

YIELD: enough for 5 or 6

2 tablespoons (40 ml) ghee or oil

1/2 teaspoon (2 ml) black mustard seeds

5 teaspoons (25 ml) cumin seeds

3 teaspoons (15 ml) minced fresh ginger

1 or 2 hot green chilies, minced

8 large ripe tomatoes, peeled and diced fine

1 tablespoon (20 ml) ground coriander

1 teaspoon (5 ml) turmeric

1/2 teaspoon (2 ml) ground fennel

1/2 teaspoon (2 ml) garam masala

1 teaspoon (5 ml) brown sugar

3 tablespoons (60 ml) chopped fresh coriander leaves or parsley

1 tablespoon (20 ml) chopped fresh mint leaves

homemade curd cheese (panir) made from 8 cups (2 litres) milk, pressed until firm and cut into 1.5 cm (1/2-inch) cubes

ghee or oil for deep-frying

2 cups (500 ml) cooked fresh or frozen peas

2 cups (500 ml) whey or water

2 tablespoons (40 ml) tomato paste

1 1/2 teaspoons (7 ml) salt

1. Heat 2 tablespoons (40 ml) *ghee* or oil in a 5-litre/quart saucepan over moderate heat. Sauté the mustard seeds until they crackle. Add the cumin seeds and stir until they darken a few shades. Add the ginger and green chilies and sauté momentarily. Add the chopped tomatoes, powdered spices, sugar, and half the herbs. Partially cover and, stirring occasionally, simmer for about 15 minutes or until the tomatoes break down and turn pulpy.

2. Heat the *ghee* or oil in a pan or wok over moderately high heat. When hot (185°C/365°F), deep-fry the cubes of *panir* cheese a batch at a time until golden brown. Remove and drain.

3. Add the peas and water or whey to the tomato and spice mixture. Boil, reduce to a simmer, and cook uncovered for 5 minutes. Add the tomato paste and salt and mix well; then add the *panir* cubes and simmer for 5 more minutes. Before serving, add the remaining herbs. Serve hot.

Okra in Tomato Sauce

Okra releases a glutinous sap when cut, and sweats when salted, so dry it thoroughly before cooking and add salt after the cooking is completed. Okra is a summer vegetable. When selecting okra look for small pods. If the pointed end snaps off, it is fresh. Serve this dish, which originates in Trinidad, as an entrée or side dish.

PREPARATION TIME: 10 minutes
COOKING TIME: 20 to 30 minutes
YIELD: enough for 6 persons

500 g (a little over 1 pound) young okra pods

3 tablespoons (60 ml) olive oil

1/4 teaspoon (1 ml) yellow asafoetida powder

1 small green pepper, seeded and chopped into small cubes

1 medium hot green chili, seeded and chopped

3 medium tomatoes, peeled and chopped

1/2 teaspoon (2 ml) brown sugar

1 teaspoon (5 ml) salt

1. Wash the okra, dry them with paper towels, and cut off the stem ends. Heat the oil in a heavy pan and sauté the okra until lightly browned all over, (about 10 minutes). Lift out the okra with a slotted spoon, and transfer to a saucepan.

2. Sauté the asafoetida in the oil remaining in the pan, add the peppers and chili, and stir-fry until they become soft.

3. Add the tomatoes and sugar and simmer for 4 to 5 minutes or until the tomatoes break down.

4. Pour the tomato mixture over the okra, stir to mix, and cook covered until the okra is tender (about 5 minutes). Sprinkle in the salt and serve hot.

Pictured above left: Tomato, Peas, and Home-made Curd served with Puffed Fried-Breads (p.36).

SALADS

Here's an interesting collection of crisp, colourful international salads.

Pictured: Italian Market Salad

Mediterranean Salad (*Salata*)

This crisp, tossed salad from Tunisia is a blend of lettuce, tomatoes, cucumbers, radishes, green peppers, parsley, lemon juice, oil, and mint. Serve *Salata* with *Middle Eastern Round Bread* (*Pita*), *Falafel*, *Tahini Sauce*, and *Syrian Yogurt Cheese* (*Labneh*) for a Middle Eastern feast!

PREPARATION TIME: 15 minutes
YIELD: enough for 6 to 8 persons

1 medium Cos lettuce, torn into bite-sized pieces

3 small, firm tomatoes, cut into wedges

1 medium continental cucumber, sliced

6 small radishes, sliced into thin rings

1 small green pepper cored, seeded, and thinly sliced

1 small fresh green chili, seeded and sliced into wafer-thin strips

2 or 3 inner leaves of Iceberg lettuce rolled up and shredded into wafer-thin strips (chiffonade)

½ cup (125 ml) chopped fresh parsley, packed

4 tablespoons (80 ml) olive oil

4 tablespoons (80 ml) fresh lemon juice

¼ teaspoon (1 ml) yellow asafoetida powder

1 teaspoon (5 ml) salt

½ teaspoon (2 ml) freshly ground black pepper

1 teaspoon (5 ml) dried mint leaves

1. Toss the lettuce, tomatoes, cucumber, radishes, pepper, green chili, shredded lettuce strips, and parsley in a large salad bowl.

2. Blend the olive oil, lemon juice, asafoetida, salt, pepper, and mint in a small bowl.

3. Pour the dressing over the salad when ready to serve, and toss gently to coat. Serve immediately.

Greek Salad

A Greek Salad is not tossed but carefully constructed, making an attractive centrepiece at a buffet lunch or dinner. This stunning salad features feta cheese and Greek black olives, both available from continental grocers. This salad is not served on individual plates but, following Greek style, is dismantled piece by piece, smorgasbord style, by the guests.

PREPARATION TIME: 20 minutes
YIELD: enough for 6 to 8 persons

1 medium crisp Cos or Iceberg lettuce

⅔ cup (165 ml) olive oil

½ cup (125 ml) fresh lemon juice

1 teaspoon (5 ml) salt

½ teaspoon (2 ml) freshly ground black pepper

500 g (a little over 1 pound) feta cheese cut into 1.25 cm (½-inch) cubes

1 tablespoon (20 ml) dried oregano

1 medium cucumber, unpeeled, sliced into 0.5 cm (¼-inch) rings

500 g (a little over 1 pound) whole cherry tomatoes

250 g (9 ounces) Greek black olives (try Kalamata)

1 small green pepper, seeded and sliced into 0.5 cm (¼ inch) rings

1. Line a large oblong platter with the outer leaves of a crisp head of lettuce. Tear the remaining leaves into small pieces; season them with a quarter of the olive oil, half the lemon juice, and half of the salt and pepper. Arrange the lettuce on the platter.

2. Pour another quarter of the olive oil and half the oregano on the *feta* cheese cubes.

3. Salt and pepper the cucumber slices. Place the cucumbers in an overlapping ring around the outer perimeter of the platter.

4. Arrange three-quarters of the cherry tomatoes among the cucumber slices.

5. Place a ring of *feta* cheese and half the olives inside the ring of cucumber. Pile the remaining cherry tomatoes in the centre along with the remaining black olives.

6. Decorate the centrepiece with the slices of pepper and pour the remaining lemon and oil on the salad, garnishing it with the remaining salt, pepper, and oregano.

North Indian Cabbage and Peanut Salad (*Kobi Pachadi*)

A *pachadi* is a raw vegetable salad with finely cut pieces of vegetables, lemon juice and oil dressing, nuts, and freshly grated coconut. This attractive salad, a sort of 'Indian coleslaw', originates in the Maharashtra state on the west coast of India. This salad can be made in advance, for the taste improves as it marinates.

PREPARATION TIME: 10 minutes
YIELD: enough for 6 to 8 persons

1/2 a medium cabbage (inner leaves only), finely shredded (about 6 cups, or 1.5 litres)

4 medium tomatoes, finely chopped

1/2 cup (125 ml) ground, roasted peanuts

2/3 cup (165 ml) grated fresh coconut

1 teaspoon (5 ml) salt

1 teaspoon (5 ml) brown sugar

6 teaspoons (30 ml) fresh lemon juice

2 tablespoons (40 ml) light corn oil

1/2 teaspoon (2 ml) brown mustard seeds

1/2 teaspoon (2 ml) cumin seeds

1/4 teaspoon (1 ml) turmeric

1/2 teaspoon (2 ml) yellow asafoetida powder

1 tablespoon (20 ml) hot green chili, seeded and minced

4 tablespoons (80 ml) coarsely chopped, fresh coriander leaves

1. Place the cabbage, tomato, peanut powder, coconut, salt, sugar, and lemon juice in a large bowl. Mix well and set aside.
2. Fry the mustard seeds in oil in a small pan over moderate heat until they crackle. Add the cumin seeds, turmeric, asafoetida, and green chili. Fry until the cumin seeds turn a darker shade. Remove from the heat.
3. Add the spices to the cabbage. Toss the salad thoroughly and garnish with the coriander leaves. Chill and serve cold.

French Steamed Vegetable Salad

This salad served with soup and crusty fresh bread makes a delightful summer meal.

PREPARATION TIME: 10 minutes
COOKING TIME: 10 minutes
CHILLING TIME: 2 hours
YIELD: enough for 6 to 8 persons

2 large new potatoes, washed, peeled, and cut into 1.25 cm (1/2-inch) cubes

3 large carrots, washed, peeled, and cut into 1.25 cm (1/2-inch) cubes

2 cups (500 ml) fresh green French beans, cut into 2 cm (3/4-inch) lengths

2 cups (500 ml) freshly shelled peas

1/2 small cauliflower, broken into tiny flowerets

1 large cucumber peeled, seeded, and diced into quarter-rounds

1/2 teaspoon (2 ml) salt

11/4 cups (310 ml) French Salad Dressing

2 tablespoons (40 ml) chopped fresh parsley for garnish

1. Cook the potatoes, carrots, beans, and peas in boiling salted water for 6 or 7 minutes or until the vegetables are just barely tender. Remove the vegetables and drain them, saving the water. Place the cauliflower pieces in the same water and cook until they are just tender. Drain.
2. Allow the cooked vegetables to cool. Toss them in a salad bowl with the diced cucumbers and salt; season well with *French Salad Dressing*. Chill the salad for 2 hours. Toss again and serve with a garnish of chopped fresh parsley.

Left: Greek Salad
Above left: Mediterranean Salad served with Eggplant Rings with Cheese.

North Indian Potato Salad

Here's another sample from the wonderful world of potato salads. This recipe is very simply dressed in yogurt and sour cream with a lemon-mustard-mint flavour and a hint of chili.

*PREPARATION TIME: a few
   minutes*
COOKING TIME: 15 minutes
COOLING TIME: ¹/₂ hour
YIELD: enough for 6 persons

8 medium potatoes, unpeeled

*1 tablespoon (20 ml) fresh
   lemon juice*

1¹/₂ teaspoons (7 ml) salt

2 tablespoons (40 ml) yogurt

3 tablespoons (60 ml) sour cream

*¹/₂ teaspoon (2 ml) green chilies,
   seeded and minced*

1 tablespoon (20 ml) safflower oil

*1 teaspoon (5 ml) black
   mustard seeds*

*1 tablespoon (20 ml) chopped fresh
   mint leaves*

lettuce leaves for decoration

1. Boil the potatoes whole in lightly salted water until soft. Peel and cut them into 2.5 cm (1-inch) cubes.
2. While the potatoes are still warm, place them in a bowl and add the lemon juice, salt, yogurt, sour cream, and chilies.
3. Fry the mustard seeds in oil in a small pan over moderate heat until the seeds crackle. Toss the oil and mustard into the salad; add three-quarters of the mint leaves. Allow the salad to cool for ¹/₂ hour. Serve it on a bed of lettuce leaves garnished with the remaining mint leaves.

Pictured: North Indian Potato Salad

New York Potato Salad

Cooking the potatoes in half-water and half-whey will help the potatoes retain their shape. This rich potato salad is best prepared whilst the potatoes are still warm.

PREPARATION TIME: 15 minutes
COOKING TIME: 15 minutes
REFRIGERATION TIME: 1 hour
YIELD: enough for 4 to 6 persons

Potatoes

*1 kg (2.2 pounds) peeled, sliced
   potatoes cooked in half-whey,
   half-water until soft*

²/₃ cup (165 ml) dry white grape juice

¹/₂ teaspoon (2 ml) sweet paprika

Mustard dressing

4 tablespoons (80 ml) lemon juice

*2 teaspoons (10 ml) dry mustard,
   soaked for 10 minutes in
   1 tablespoon (20 ml) warm water*

¹/₄ teaspoon (1 ml) salt

¹/₂ cup (125 ml) olive oil

¹/₄ teaspoon (1 ml) black pepper

*1 cup (250 ml) finely chopped fresh
parsley*

Mayonnaise dressing

³/₄ cup (185 ml) evaporated milk

¹/₂ teaspoon (2 ml) salt

*³/₄ teaspoon (3 ml) yellow
   asafoetida powder*

³/₄ cup (185 ml) safflower oil

*2 tablespoons (40 ml) fresh
   lemon juice*

1¹/₂ teaspoons (7 ml) dried dill

2 tablespoons (40 ml) sour cream

1. Marinate the still warm, cooked potatoes in grape juice.
2. Whisk the ingredients for the mustard dressing.
3. Whisk the ingredients for the mayonnaise dressing.
4. Pour both dressings over the marinated potatoes and gently fold until well combined. Sprinkle the paprika over the salad and refrigerate. Serve cold.

Fettuccine, Pepper and Cream Cheese Salad

Fettuccine pasta with its delightful "bird's-nest" appearance is the basis for this tasty salad. Combined with cream cheese and roasted peppers, it's great served cold with a main savoury dish.

PREPARATION AND COOKING TIME: 25 minutes

CHILLING TIME: at least one hour

YIELD: enough for 4 persons

250 g (9 ounces) fettuccine noodles

2 large red peppers, halved, cored, and seeded

125 g (4½ ounces) firm cream cheese, diced into little cubes

6 to 8 walnuts, chopped

Dressing

4 tablespoons (80 ml) olive oil

1 tablespoon (20 ml) walnut oil, if available

1 tablespoon (20 ml) lemon juice

1 teaspoon (5 ml) mustard powder

1 teaspoon (5 ml) salt

¼ teaspoon (1 ml) freshly cracked black pepper

1. Cook the *fettuccine* in lightly salted water for 8 to 10 minutes or until it is tender but still a little firm (*al dente*). Drain the pasta.

2. Grill the peppers with the cut-side down under a griller on high heat (or hold them over a flame) until the skins blacken and blister. When the peppers are cool, skin them and cut them into long, thin, even strips.

3. Add the pepper strips to the cheese and walnuts in a salad bowl. Combine all dressing ingredients and add to the noodles. Toss the noodles, dressing, peppers, cheese, and nuts. Chill the salad for at least 1 hour before serving

Pictured: Fettuccine, Pepper and Cream Cheese Salad

Lebanese Bulgur-Wheat Salad
(*Tabbouleh*)

This Lebanese salad is probably the most famous of all Middle Eastern *mezze* (hors d'oeuvres). Bulgur wheat (parched, ground, par-boiled wheat grains) is not only tasty and substantial but also very nutritious. It is rich in protein, calcium, phosphorus, iron, potassium, niacin, and vitamins B1 and B2. Bulgur wheat salad is easy to prepare and is characterised by its fresh lemon-mint-parsley flavour. Traditional Middle Eastern cooks sometimes use an extra ingredient in their salads: a tart seasoning made from the ground seeds of a Mediterranean flowering plant called *sumac*, which adds a special lemony taste. I have included this as optional. It is available from any well-stocked Middle Eastern grocer, as is the bulgur wheat which, incidentally, is sometimes referred to as *bourghul* or cracked wheat. *Tabbouleh* is traditionally served in fresh, crisp lettuce leaves. Add more lemon juice if necessary, to assure the authentic fresh-lemon taste.

WHEAT SOAKING TIME: 1½ hours

PREPARATION TIME: 10 minutes

YIELD: enough for 6 persons

250 g (9 ounces) fine bulgur wheat

½ teaspoon (2 ml) yellow asafoetida powder

at least ½ cup (125 ml) fresh lemon juice

½ cup (125 ml) olive oil

1½ teaspoons (7 ml) salt

¼ teaspoon (1 ml) coarsely ground black pepper

3 cups (750 ml) finely chopped parsley

3 tablespoons (60 ml) fresh mint

2 teaspoons (10 ml) sumac (optional)

1 cup (250 ml) seeded, unpeeled cucumber, diced into 1 cm (³/₈-inch) cubes

2 medium tomatoes, diced

lettuce leaves for decoration

1. Soak the bulgur wheat for 1½ hours in warm water. Drain it and squeeze out the moisture. Dry it further by spreading it on a cloth and patting it dry.

2. Place the soaked wheat, asafoetida, lemon juice, olive oil, salt, pepper, parsley, mint, and *sumac* in a large bowl and mix well. Add the cucumber and tomatoes and toss. Chill and serve with lettuce leaves.

Hawaiian Brown-Rice Salad

In this salad, plump long-grain brown rice is combined with fresh salad vegetables and pineapple, tossed in an herbed Italian dressing, and served on a bed of crisp lettuce leaves.

PREPARATION TIME: 10 minutes
YIELD: enough for 8 to 10 persons

6 cups (1.5 litres) salted long-grain brown rice, cooked and chilled

1 small cucumber, peeled, seeded, and diced

4 crisp radishes, finely sliced

3 slices of fresh pineapple, diced

2 firm, ripe tomatoes, diced

1/2 small red pepper, diced

1/2 small green pepper, diced

1/4 cup (60 ml) cooked green peas

1/4 cup (60 ml) cooked corn niblets

1/2 stalk celery, finely chopped

2 inner leaves of lettuce rolled up and cut into long, wafer-thin slices (chiffonade)

1 teaspoon (5 ml) olive oil

2 fresh hot green chilies, seeded and cut into long, wafer-thin strips

1/4 teaspoon (1 ml) yellow asafoetida powder

1/2 cup (125 ml) finely chopped fresh parsley,

1 cup (250 ml) Italian Salad Dressing

lettuce leaves for decoration

1. Place all the ingredients (except the dressing, 1 teaspoon (5 ml) olive oil, and the asafoetida) in a large bowl.

2. Sauté the asafoetida in olive oil in a small pan. Pour the oil and asafoetida into the bowl of rice and vegetables. Mix well.

3. Toss the salad with the dressing. Serve the salad on a bed of crisp lettuce leaves.

Indonesian Gado Gado Salad

This version of the exotic *Gado Gado* salad, popular throughout Indonesia, can be served as a side salad to accompany a main meal for four persons, or as a main dish for two persons. Obtain the Chinese *bok choy*, coconut milk (*santan*), and the *tofu* (bean curd) from any well-stocked Chinese or Asian grocer. This salad is served with a steaming-hot peanut dressing.

PREPARATION TIME: 15 minutes
COOKING TIME: 25 minutes
YIELD: enough for 2 to 4 persons

250 g (9 ounces) Chinese bok choy leaves washed and cut into bite-sized pieces

water for boiling and blanching

125 g (4 1/2 ounces) mung bean shoots

2 or 3 small new potatoes

1 cup (250 ml) French beans, "topped and tailed" and cut into 3.75 cm (1 1/2-inch) lengths

oil for deep-frying

450 g (1 pound) firm tofu, cut into 1.5 cm (3/4-inch) cubes

3/4 cup (185 ml) raw peanuts

4 Brazil nuts

1 teaspoon (5 ml) chili powder, or more for a hotter sauce

1/2 teaspoon (2 ml) yellow asafoetida powder

1 teaspoon (5 ml) salt

1 teaspoon (5 ml) brown sugar

1/2 cup (125 ml) coconut milk (santan)

1/2 medium cucumber, unpeeled and cut into batons. (To cut into batons, cut cucumber into slices 1 cm [3/8 inch] thick and 5 cm [2 inches] long. Cut each slice again into 1 cm [3/8 inch] strips.)

1 small bunch watercress, washed and separated

1 tablespoon (20 ml) fresh lime or lemon juice

1 cup (250 ml) cold water

1. Blanch the *bok choy* leaves in boiling water for about 1 minute. Rinse in cold water and drain well.

2. Wash and blanch the bean shoots in a similar fashion, but for just 30 seconds. Rinse and drain.

3. Cook the potatoes whole in lightly salted boiling water until soft; then peel them and cut them into bite-sized pieces.

4. Cook the beans in lightly salted boiling water for five minutes; then drain and allow to cool.

5. Place the oil over moderate heat. When fairly hot (185°C/365°F), deep-fry the cubes of *tofu* until slightly golden. Remove them with a slotted spoon and drain in a colander.

6. Reduce the oil temperature to about 180°C/355°F and deep-fry the peanuts until golden (2 to 3 minutes). Remove and drain.

7. Deep-fry the Brazil nuts until golden (about 3 minutes) and drain.

8. Place the chili powder, asafoetida, fried nuts, salt, and sugar in a food processor and blend to a smooth powder. Add 1 cup (250 ml) cold water to the blended ingredients.

9. Transfer the contents of the blender to a heavy pan, bring to the boil, and simmer for 5 minutes. Add the coconut milk (*santan*) and remove from the heat.

10. Pile the Chinese *bok choy* leaves, bean shoots, potatoes, beans, *tofu*, cucumber, and watercress in individual neat piles on a large plate. Boil the dressing, add the lime juice, and immediately pour the dressing over the salad. Serve immediately. The dressing may be served separately.

Right: Indonesian Gado Gado Salad

Waldorf Salad

This famous gourmet dish is an ideal light accompaniment to a heavy meal. Tart, firm, green apples are preferable, adding a refreshing tang to this sweet, fruity salad.

PREPARATION TIME: 10 minutes
YIELD: enough for 6 to 8 persons

3 green apples, unpeeled, cored, and diced into 1.25 cm (½-inch) cubes

1 cup (250 ml) diced celery

1 teaspoon (5 ml) fresh lemon juice

¼ cup (60 ml) Eggless Mayonnaise II

½ cup (125 ml) full-fat sour cream

½ teaspoon (2 ml) salt

¼ teaspoon (1 ml) freshly ground black pepper

½ cup (125 ml) walnut pieces

Mix the apples and celery in a bowl. Add the lemon juice, mayonnaise, sour cream, salt, pepper, and walnuts. Chill and serve.

Gujarati Green-Bean and Coconut Salad

With the addition of grated fresh coconut and peanut powder, French beans are transformed into this elegant salad from Gujarat.

PREPARATION AND COOKING TIME: 20 minutes
YIELD: enough for 4 persons

375 g (13 ounces) French stringless beans, cut into 7.5 cm (3-inch) lengths

2 tablespoons (40 ml) vegetable oil

½ teaspoon (2 ml) black mustard seeds

¼ teaspoon (1 ml) yellow asafoetida powder

1 teaspoon (5 ml) fresh green chili, seeded and finely chopped

½ teaspoon (2 ml) salt

½ teaspoon (2 ml) sugar

¼ cup (60 ml) roasted peanut powder

½ cup (125 ml) grated fresh coconut

1. Boil the French beans in lightly salted water until they are cooked but still green and firm. Drain, rinse with cold water, drain again, and allow to cool in a bowl.

2. Sauté the mustard seeds in hot oil in a heavy pan over moderate heat until the seeds crackle. Add the asafoetida and sauté momentarily. Add the spices to the French beans.

3. Toss the green chili, salt, sugar, peanut powder, and grated fresh coconut with the beans. Serve at room temperature.

Steamed Cauliflower Salad with Green Mayonnaise

This colourful and fresh-tasting salad is a great patio salad on a hot summer's day. Select a fresh cauliflower with firm tight buds.

PREPARATION AND COOKING TIME: 15 minutes

YIELD: enough for 4 to 6 persons

1 large cauliflower, cut into medium flowerets

1 large bunch watercress

2 spinach leaves

¼ cup (60 ml) fresh tarragon, chervil, or parsley, chopped

1 teaspoon (5 ml) lemon juice

1 cup (250 ml) Eggless Mayonnaise II

1. Boil the cauliflower pieces in a large pan of lightly salted water for a few minutes; then remove. The cauliflower pieces should be cooked but firm. Rinse them under cold water and drain.

2. Simmer the watercress and spinach in the boiling water for 2 minutes. Remove, drain, and rinse. Purée the spinach, watercress, and chopped herbs in a food processor or blender. Add the lemon juice and mayonnaise. Arrange the cauliflower pieces on a serving platter and pour the green mayonnaise over when ready to serve.

Pictured: Asparagus, Green Bean and Broccoli Salad (p.75)

Bombay Cauliflower Salad

This type of salad is called a *koshimbir*. It is popular on the tropical west coast of India. The cauliflower is cooked just slightly, so it remains crunchy. Serve this salad with a bowl of fresh yogurt and Indian bread like *chapati, poori,* or *paratha.*

PREPARATION TIME: 5 minutes
COOKING TIME: 5 minutes
YIELD: enough for 4 to 6 persons

½ medium cauliflower, cut into very small flowerets

¼ cup (60 ml) dry-roasted peanut powder

⅓ cup (85 ml) grated fresh coconut

1 tablespoon (20 ml) fresh green chili, seeded and finely chopped

½ teaspoon (2 ml) salt

½ teaspoon (2 ml) brown sugar

2 teaspoons (10 ml) fresh lemon juice

2 tablespoons (40 ml) chopped fresh coriander

1. Blanch the cauliflower pieces in boiling water for one minute.

2. Rinse the cauliflower under cold running water until it cools to room temperature. Drain it thoroughly and place in a bowl. Add the peanut powder, coconut, chili, salt, sugar, and lemon juice. Mix well. Garnish with chopped fresh coriander and serve immediately.

Sicilian Radicchio and Fennel Salad

Radicchio lettuce, with its beautiful red and purple leaves and pleasantly bitter taste, is actually Italian wild chicory and is also sometimes known as corn lettuce. This simple salad from Sicily, *"Insalata di Radicchio e Finocchio"*, can be made in a few minutes.

PREPARATION TIME: 10 minutes
YIELD: enough for 4 to 6 persons

Salad

3 small radicchio lettuces (about 350 g, 12 ounces)

3 small fennel bulbs

60 g (2 ounces) black olives

Dressing

1/4 cup (60 ml) olive oil

3 tablespoons (60 ml) fresh lemon juice

6 black olives, pitted

1/2 teaspoon (2 ml) salt

pinch of black pepper

1 teaspoon (5 ml) raw sugar

1. Separate and wash the leaves of the lettuce.

2. Remove the tops of the fennel bulbs, cut the bulbs in half, and trim the ends. Cut the fennel into 1.25 cm (1/2-inch) strips. Arrange the lettuce, fennel, and olives decoratively on a serving plate.

3. To make the dressing: blend the oil, lemon juice, and pitted olives in a food processor or blender. Add the salt, pepper, and raw sugar. Spoon the dressing over the salad and serve immediately.

Asparagus, Green Bean and Broccoli Salad

This cooked green vegetable salad can be prepared in advance. It's great served as a side dish with bread, soup, and a main-course savoury dish like *Vegetarian Lasagna* or *Spaghetti Alla Napoletana*. Select crisp, fresh beans; tight, dark broccoli; and thin, fresh asparagus for outstanding results.

PREPARATION TIME: 10 minutes
COOKING TIME: 5 minutes
YIELD: enough for 6 persons

250 g (9 ounces) broccoli, cut into flowerets

250 g (9 ounces) green beans, cut into 3 cm (1 1/4-inch) sections

250 g (9 ounces) asparagus, cut into 3 cm (1 1/4-inch) sections

water for boiling

Dressing

2 tablespoons (40 ml) olive oil

1/4 teaspoon (1 ml) yellow asafoetida powder

2 tablespoons (40 ml) fresh lemon juice

1/4 teaspoon (1 ml) dry mustard powder

1 teaspoon (5 ml) grated fresh ginger

1 teaspoon (5 ml) soy sauce

1. Boil the water in a large pan.

2. Plunge the broccoli, green beans, and asparagus into the water and boil for 3 minutes or until the vegetables are bright green and tender-crisp. Drain, and refresh under cold water. Drain again thoroughly, and place in a serving bowl and refrigerate. Toss the dressing with the salad just before serving.

Mixed Vegetable and Yogurt Salad (*Raita*)

A *raita* is an Indian raw vegetable salad, generally featuring one or two main ingredients that float in lightly seasoned creamy fresh yogurt. *Raitas* are simple to prepare and provide a light, cooling contrast to an elaborate meal. Serve this salad with a meal that contains little or no yogurt.

PREPARATION TIME: 10 minutes
YIELD: enough for 5 or 6 persons

2 cups (500 ml) plain yogurt

1/3 cup (85 ml) tomatoes, cut into 1 cm (3/8-inch) cubes

1/3 cup (85 ml) raw peas

1/3 cup (85 ml) radishes, cut into 1 cm (3/8-inch) cubes

1/3 cup (85 ml) red peppers, cut into 1 cm (3/8-inch) cubes

1/3 cup (85 ml) cucumber, cut into 1 cm (3/8-inch) cubes

1/3 cup (85 ml) celery, cut into 1 cm (3/8-inch) cubes

1 tablespoon (20 ml) cumin seeds

1 teaspoon (5 ml) fennel seeds

1/2 teaspoon (2 ml) salt

1/4 teaspoon (1 ml) cracked black pepper

2 tablespoons (40 ml) chopped fresh coriander or parsley

1. Whisk the yogurt until smooth. Add all the vegetables.

2. Dry-roast the cumin and fennel seeds in a small frying pan over low heat until they turn dark brown. Remove the seeds from the pan and grind them coarsely in a coffee mill. Add them to the salad and toss with the salt, pepper, and chopped fresh herbs. Chill before serving. Serve the chilled *raita* in small bowls, allowing 1/2 cup (125 ml) per serving.

Avocado and Bean Salad

Avocados combine well with cheese and beans. Dressed and served in lettuce leaves, this salad is substantial and tasty.

PREPARATION TIME: 10 minutes
YIELD: enough for 8 persons

2 large ripe avocados, peeled and cut into 1.5 cm (³/₄-inch) cubes

1 cup (250 ml) cooked and chilled green beans chopped into 2.5 cm (1-inch) sections

1 cup (250 ml) cooked and chilled kidney beans

1 cup (250 ml) cooked and chilled chickpeas

1 cup (250 ml) cubed cheddar cheese

¹/₂ cup (125 ml) chopped green pepper

¹/₄ cup (60 ml) chopped pimiento (baby red peppers in brine or oil)

²/₃ cup (165 ml) olive oil

²/₃ cup (165 ml) fresh lemon juice

3 tablespoons (60 ml) honey

2 teaspoons (10 ml) chopped fresh parsley

2 teaspoons (10 ml) chopped fresh coriander leaves

¹/₂ teaspoon (1 ml) black pepper

1 teaspoon (5 ml) salt

1 large Iceberg, Cos, or Mignonette lettuce

1. Combine the avocados, beans, chickpeas, cheese, green pepper, and pimientos in a bowl.
2. Mix the olive oil, lemon juice, honey, half the parsley, coriander, black pepper, and salt.
3. Fold the dressing carefully into the bean and avocado mixture. Serve individual portions of salad on lettuce leaves and garnish with the remaining chopped parsley.

Italian Market Salad

This delicious combination of fresh greens, steamed vegetables, and cottage cheese marinated in a delicious lemon and oil dressing should be served with crusty bread rolls.

PREPARATION TIME: 15 minutes
COOKING TIME: 5 minutes
YIELD: enough for 6 persons

1 medium zucchini, cut into long wedges

2 medium carrots, peeled and cut into long wedges

2 stalks celery, cut into 2.5 cm (1-inch) strips

125 g (4¹/₂ ounces) snow peas, tips and strings removed

one 400 g (14-ounce) can artichoke hearts marinated in brine, drained, and quartered

1 cup (250 ml) firm cottage cheese, cubed

3 radishes, sliced

2 or 3 inner lettuce leaves, sliced into paper-thin strips

2 medium green chilies, seeded and sliced into long paper-thin strips

125 g (4¹/₂ ounces) cherry tomatoes, halved

¹/₂ cup (185 ml) olive oil

¹/₂ teaspoon (2 ml) yellow asafoetida powder

¹/₂ cup (125 ml) fresh lemon juice

1 tablespoon (20 ml) chopped fresh basil

1 teaspoon (5 ml) dry mustard, mixed with 2 teaspoons (10 ml) cold water

1 teaspoon (5 ml) salt

¹/₂ teaspoon (2 ml) freshly ground black pepper

crisp lettuce leaves for serving

fresh basil leaves for garnish

125 g (4¹/₂ ounces) pitted black olives, for garnish

1. Boil the zucchini, carrots, and celery in lightly salted water in a large pan until the vegetables are crisp but tender (about 2 minutes). Before draining, add the snow peas to the water. Remove the pan from the heat and blanch the snow peas for 1 minute. Drain all the vegetables, refresh under cold water, and drain again. Allow the vegetables to thoroughly cool.
2. Combine the artichoke hearts,

cottage cheese, radishes, sliced lettuce, green chilies, tomatoes, and steamed vegetables in a large bowl.

3. Blend the olive oil, asafoetida, lemon juice, basil, mustard paste, salt, and pepper in a bowl.

4. Toss the vegetables and the dressing. Cover and marinate in the refrigerator for at least one hour.

5. Serve on individual lettuce leaves garnished with fresh whole basil leaves and black olives.

Pasta Salad

This is a sophisticated salad with a distinctly Middle Eastern flavour. The combination of the lemon-oil dressing and *tahini* creates a unique taste which blends wonderfully with firm, tender broccoli and cauliflower florets, crisp lettuce, and strips of red peppers. Serve as an accompaniment to a summer brunch or as a tasty picnic or patio-salad with *Middle Eastern Round Bread, Tomato and Asparagus Quiche, Crispy Flat Rice and Cashews (Gujarati Chidwa), Mango Ice Cream,* and *Middle Eastern Lemonade.*

PREPARATION
TIME: 20 minutes

YIELD: enough for 8 persons

300 g (11 ounces) broccoli flowerets, par-boiled, drained, and chilled

300 g (11 ounces) cauliflower (about half a small one), cut into flowerets, par-boiled, drained, and chilled

2 small red peppers, cored, seeded, and thinly sliced

1 cup (250 ml) cooked but firm (al dente) conchiglie or small penne rigate pasta, cooled

1/4 teaspoon (1 ml) yellow asafoetida powder

4 tablespoons (80 ml) tahini

1 teaspoon (5 ml) salt

1/2 teaspoon (2 ml) freshly ground black pepper

1 tablespoon (20 ml) olive oil

5 tablespoons (100 ml) fresh lemon juice

1/2 small Cos or Iceberg lettuce, torn into bite-sized pieces

3 tablespoons (60 ml) chopped fresh parsley

1. Place the cooked broccoli, cauliflower, peppers, and pasta in a medium-sized bowl.

2. Whisk the asafoetida, *tahini*, salt, pepper, olive oil, and lemon juice in a small bowl. If the dressing is too thick, add water.

3. Pour the dressing over the salad and toss gently to coat. Refrigerate, covered, to chill. Just before serving, add the lettuce and garnish with the chopped fresh parsley.

Above Left: Avocado and Bean Salad
Right: Sicilian Radicchio and Fennel Salad (p.74)

CHUTNEYS, JAMS AND PICKLES

Chutneys, both cooked and fresh, serve as accents to other dishes. This piquant selection will tease the palate and add colour, flavour, and variety to any meal.

This chapter also includes pickles and jams. So prepare to have both your imagination and your digestion stimulated!

Pictured: Tamarillo Chutney

Pineapple Chutney

Pineapple chutney should be "too hot to bear, but too sweet to resist".

PREPARATION AND COOKING TIME: about 1 hour
YIELD: about 2 cups (500 ml)

3 tablespoons (60 ml) ghee

2 teaspoons (10 ml) cumin seeds

4 broken dried red chilies, or as desired

1 large ripe pineapple, peeled, cored, and cut into 1.25 cm (1/2-inch) cubes

1/2 teaspoon (2 ml) ground cinnamon

1/2 teaspoon (2 ml) ground cloves

2/3 cup (165 ml) brown sugar

1/3 cup (85 ml) raisins

1. Heat the *ghee* in a 2-quart/litre heavy-based saucepan over moderate heat until it is hot but not smoking. Sauté the cumin seeds in the hot *ghee* until they slightly darken. Add the chilies and cook until golden brown. Add the pineapple pieces, ground cinnamon, and cloves. Gently boil the chutney, stirring occasionally, over moderate heat until the pineapple becomes soft and the juice evaporates. Stir constantly as the preparation nears completion.

2. When the saucepan is dry and the pineapple starts to stick on the bottom, add the sugar and raisins and cook until thick and jam-like. Serve at room temperature.

Tomato Chutney

Cooked chutneys act as piquant relishes that accent other dishes with which they are served. This North Indian-style tomato chutney is hot, spicy, and sweet. It can be either eaten immediately or refrigerated for up to a week.

PREPARATION AND COOKING TIME: 15-30 minutes
YIELD: 2 - 2 1/2 cups (500-625 ml)

3 tablespoons (60 ml) ghee or oil

1/2 teaspoon (2 ml) black mustard seeds

1/2 teaspoon (2 ml) cumin seeds

one 5 cm (2-inch) piece of cinnamon stick

3-4 whole dried red chilies, broken

1/2 teaspoon (2 ml) turmeric

3 1/2 cups (875 ml) firm, ripe tomatoes, peeled and coarsely chopped

2/3 cup (165 ml) sugar

1/2 cup (125 ml) sultanas (optional)

1/2 teaspoon (2 ml) salt

1. Heat the *ghee* or oil in a large, heavy frying pan over moderate heat. Sauté the mustard seeds in the hot *ghee* until they begin to crackle. Add the cumin and cinnamon. When the cinnamon darkens, add the chili bits and the turmeric. Immediately add the chopped tomatoes and, stirring to mix, cook over moderate heat for 10 minutes.

2. Add the sugar, sultanas, and salt. For moist chutney, continue to cook for another 5 minutes. For a thick jam-like chutney, cook for another 15 minutes or until the chutney appears thick and glazed. Serve warm or cold.

Peach Chutney

This is actually more of a pickle or relish than a chutney. It can be kept in sterilized jars for up to 3 months and is delicious served as a condiment with a main meal. It makes a great gift when presented in attractive jars.

PREPARATION AND COOKING TIME: 50 minutes
YIELD: about 5 cups (1.25 litres)

2 tablespoons (40 ml) corn oil or light vegetable oil

1 tablespoon (20 ml) yellow mustard seeds

2 small fresh red chilies, finely chopped

1/2 teaspoon (2 ml) yellow asafoetida powder

2 medium red peppers, chopped into 1.25 cm (1/2-inch) cubes

2 medium green peppers, chopped into 1.25 cm (1/2-inch) cubes

2 kg (4 1/2 pounds) peaches, peeled and cut into 1.25 cm (1/2-inch) cubes

1 1/2 cups (375 ml) fresh lemon juice

2 cups (500 ml) lightly packed brown sugar

1. Heat the oil in a heavy 4-litre/quart saucepan over moderate heat. Sauté the mustard seeds in the hot oil until they crackle, then add the chilies and asafoetida and stir until the chilies darken.

2. Add the peppers and cook one minute. Add the peaches, lemon juice, and brown sugar, stirring constantly without boiling until the sugar is dissolved. Bring to a boil, reduce the heat, and simmer uncovered, without stirring, for 45 minutes or until the relish is thick. (Towards the end it might require minimal stirring to avoid sticking.) Pour into hot, sterilized jars and seal when cold.

"Radha Red" Plum Chutney

This is a version of the famous "Radha Red" plum chutney that has been a favourite at many Hare Krishna multi-course feasts throughout Australia for decades. It features the subtle and exotic flavour of pure camphor, sometimes available at Chinese and Indian grocery stores. The plums should, if possible, be the Damson variety or the red plums referred to as "blood plums".

PREPARATION TIME: about 1 hour
YIELD: about 3 cups (750 ml)

4 tablespoons (80 ml) butter

1 1/2 teaspoons (7 ml) ground coriander

1/4 teaspoon (1 ml) powdered cardamom seeds

3 tablespoons (60 ml) finely-shredded fresh coconut

1.4 kg (3 pounds) ripe red plums, pitted and cut into eighths

2 cups (500 ml) sugar

a pinch of raw camphor crystals

1. Heat the butter over low heat in a heavy 5-litre/quart saucepan until it froths. Add the coriander, cardamom, and coconut, sauté for one minute, and add the plums. Raise the heat and bring the chutney to a boil; then reduce the heat and simmer covered for about 15 minutes or until the plums lose their shape.

2. Add the sugar and continue to simmer uncovered for another 40-45 minutes or until the chutney is fairly thick and glazed, stirring occasionally. Add the camphor crystals and mix well. Serve at room temperature or refrigerate covered for up to 4 days.

Left: Tomato, Plum and Pineapple chutneys.

Tamarillo Chutney

Tamarillos, or tree tomatoes, are glossy, plum-red fruits the size and shape of large eggs. Though tamarillos are native to South America, they also grow plentifully in New Zealand. They have juicy, slightly acidic flesh. Serve this piquant relish with fried savoury dishes.

PREPARATION AND COOKING TIME: 1 1/2-2 hours
YIELD: 6 cups (1.5 litres)

1/4 cup (60 ml) ghee or oil

1/4 teaspoon (1 ml) cumin seeds

1/4 teaspoon (1 ml) ground dried red chilies

8 cups (2 litres) ripe tamarillos, blanched, peeled and chopped

1/4 teaspoon (1 ml) ground cloves

1/2 teaspoon (2 ml) turmeric

1/2 teaspoon (2 ml) yellow asafoetida powder

1/2 teaspoon (2 ml) minced fresh ginger

1 teaspoon (5 ml) ground cinnamon

1 teaspoon (5 ml) ground coriander

1 teaspoon (5 ml) ground nutmeg

3/4-1 cup (185-250 ml) sugar

1 cup (250 ml) sultanas

1. Heat the *ghee* in a heavy non-stick saucepan. Sauté the cumin seeds in the hot *ghee* until they brown. Add the chili and chopped tamarillos. Bring to a boil, reduce the heat, and simmer until soft.

2. Add all the remaining ingredients and return to the boil. Reduce the heat and simmer for about 1 1/2-2 hours, stirring occasionally, until the chutney is thick and glazed. Pour into hot, sterilized jars and seal when cold.

Apple Chutney

Chutney varies immensely according to the kind of apples used, but invariably sour Granny Smiths seem to produce the best results. This chutney is hot yet sweet and can be served as an accompaniment to a great variety of savoury dishes. Allow 1-4 spoonfuls per serving. Apple chutney can be refrigerated in a sealed container.

**PREPARATION AND COOKING
   TIME: 1 hour**
YIELD: enough for 10 persons

2 tablespoons (40 ml) ghee or oil
1½ teaspoons (7 ml) cumin seeds

**2 fresh hot green chilies,
   cut into thin rings**
**2 teaspoons (10 ml) minced
   fresh ginger**
1 teaspoon (5 ml) turmeric
**500 g (about 1 pound) tangy green
   apples, peeled, cored and sliced**
¼ cup (60 ml) water
**1¼ teaspoons (6 ml) ground
   cinnamon**
¾ teaspoon (3 ml) ground nutmeg
1 cup (250 ml) sugar

1. Heat the *ghee* or oil in a heavy 2-litre/quart saucepan over medium heat. Sauté the cumin seeds in the hot *ghee* until golden brown. Add the green chilies and minced ginger and sauté for 1 minute; then add the turmeric and the sliced apples. Stir-fry for 2-3 minutes.

2. Reduce the heat to low and add the water, cinnamon, and nutmeg. Cook, stirring occasionally, for about 15-20 minutes or until the apples become soft. Add the sugar and continue to cook the chutney until it becomes jam-like. Serve at room temperature or cover and refrigerate for up to a week.

Fig and Apple Relish

If you have a fig tree in your garden, or have access to one, then here's something to do with the enormous quantity of figs that are yielded when these luxurious fruits come into season. This delicious chutney-like relish goes wonderfully well as an accompanying condiment to a heavy meal and keeps for 6 weeks if refrigerated.

**PREPARATION AND COOKING
   TIME: 1½ hours**
YIELD: about 6 cups (1.5 litres)

10 medium fresh ripe figs, chopped
3 medium apples, peeled, cored, and
chopped into 1.25 cm
(½-inch) cubes
2 cups (500 ml) brown sugar, packed
1 cup (250 ml) sultanas
**½ cup (125 ml) dried apricots,
   chopped**
1 cup (250 ml) fresh lemon juice
2 cups (500 ml) white grape juice
¼ cup (60 ml) tomato paste
**1 tablespoon (20 ml) yellow
   mustard seeds**
**½ teaspoon (2 ml) yellow
   asafoetida powder**
½ teaspoon (2 ml) ground cinnamon

½ teaspoon (2 ml) ground cardamom

1. Combine all the ingredients in a heavy 4-litre/quart saucepan. Cook over low heat, stirring constantly until the sugar dissolves.

2. Bring the relish to the boil, reduce the heat, and simmer uncovered for about 1½ hours or until the relish is as thick as desired. Stir the mixture towards the end of cooking time to prevent it from sticking.

3. Pour the relish into hot, sterilized jars and seal when cold.

Fresh Coconut Chutney

This tasty, cream-textured chutney is not cooked but is prepared by combining all fresh ingredients. Coconut chutney plays an integral part in South Indian cuisine. Serve this chutney to accompany *Savoury Wholemeal Pancakes* (*Dosa*) and *Mashed Potato Puffs* (*Alu Vadas*).

PREPARATION TIME: 10 minutes
YIELD: about 2½ cups (625 ml)

1½ cups (375 ml) shredded
  fresh coconut

1½ cups (375 ml) yogurt or 1 cup
  (250 ml) yogurt and ½ cup
  (125 ml) buttermilk

½ cup (125 ml) cold water

1 tablespoon (20 ml) minced
  fresh ginger

2 teaspoons (10 ml) hot green chilies,
  seeded and minced

¼ teaspoon (1 ml) freshly ground
  black pepper

½ teaspoon (2 ml) salt

2 tablespoons (40 ml) ghee or light
  vegetable oil

1 teaspoon (5 ml) black
  mustard seeds

1½ teaspoons (7 ml) split urad dal

10 or 12 curry leaves, fresh or dried

¼ teaspoon (1 ml) yellow
  asafoetida powder

1. Combine the coconut, yogurt, water, fresh ginger, chilies, pepper, and salt in a mixing bowl.

2. Heat the *ghee* in a small pan over moderately high heat until it is almost smoking. Sauté the mustard seeds in the hot *ghee* until they crackle. Add the *urad dal* and sauté until it turns golden brown. Add the curry leaves and stir until they soften; add the asafoetida and then immediately remove the pan from the heat and mix the spices into the bowl of yogurt and coconut. Serve at room temperature. This chutney can be refrigerated for up to 2 days.

Mint Chutney

Fresh mint chutney, which requires no cooking, is great to make when you have an abundance of mint. The round-leaved varieties of *Mentha rotundifolia*, such as apple mint, Bowles mint, or pineapple mint, lend themselves especially well to this condiment. Serve mint chutney with *Cauliflower and Pea Samosas*, or *Potato and Pea Croquettes*.

PREPARATION TIME: 10 minutes
YIELD: about 1 cup (250 ml)

1¾ cups (435 ml) trimmed fresh
  mint, packed

3 tablespoons (60 ml) water

2 tablespoons (40 ml) caster sugar

2 tablespoons (40 ml) fresh lime
  or lemon juice

2 hot green chilies, seeded
  and chopped

¼ cup (60 ml) shredded
  fresh coconut

1 teaspoon (5 ml) salt

Blend all the ingredients in a food processor or blender until smooth. If required, add a little cold water to achieve a runny consistency. Transfer the chutney to a bowl and serve. It will keep refrigerated for 1 or 2 days.

Lime and Ginger Marmalade

After you add the sugar to the marmalade, the depth of the sugar, lime, and water mixture should not exceed 5 cm (2 inches). This bittersweet marmalade can be refrigerated for months.

STANDING TIME: overnight
PREPARATION AND COOKING
   TIME: about 1¼ hours
YIELD: 4 cups (1 litre)
3 large ripe limes
3 cups (750 ml) water
about 3½ cups (875 ml) white sugar
1½ teaspoons (7 ml) minced
   fresh ginger

1. Cut the limes into 0.25 cm (¹/₈-inch) rings and remove the seeds. Combine the limes and water in a bowl and leave to stand overnight.

2. Place the lime and water mixture in a non-stick 3-litre/quart saucepan and bring to a boil over high heat. Reduce the heat and simmer, covered, for about 1 hour. By this time the rind should be tender. Remove from the heat.

3. Pour the mixture into a bowl and measure exactly how much lime and water there is. Add an equal quantity of sugar and return the lime and sugar mixture to the saucepan.

4. Stirring over low heat, allow the sugar to dissolve. Return the mixture to a boil and cook without stirring for 10-15 minutes or until a spoon of the marmalade sets on a cold plate.

5. Remove the saucepan from the heat and add the minced ginger. When the marmalade cools, pour it into hot, sterilized jam jars. When the marmalade has cooled, seal the jars.

Above: Raspberry Jam with Lime and Ginger Marmalade

Sweet Lime Pickle

Indian-style pickles are best made in hot climates because they are traditionally made slowly in jars that are exposed to sunlight. Sunlight is an antiseptic; it also expedites the pickling process, and acts to prevent fermentation. Pickles are generally preserved in salt, oil, or lemon juice. (Mustard oil is an excellent choice.) This lime pickle is simultaneously sweet, spicy, and hot.

PREPARATION TIME: 20 minutes
PICKLING TIME: 5-6 weeks
YIELD: 2 cups (500 ml)

4 or 5 small limes
2 tablespoons (40 ml) salt
1 teaspoon (5 ml) powdered black mustard seeds
1 teaspoon (5 ml) cayenne pepper
1 teaspoon (5 ml) turmeric
1 cup (250 ml) brown sugar
1/3 cup (85 ml) fresh lime or lemon juice

1. Wash and dry the limes thoroughly. In a completely dry spot (any water will spoil the pickle), slice each lime lengthwise into 8 pieces (retain any juice).
2. Mix the salt, mustard seed powder, cayenne, and turmeric in a bowl.
3. Bring the sugar and the lime juice to a boil in a small saucepan over high heat. Boil for 2 minutes and set aside.
4. Arrange a layer of lime slices, cut-side-up, alternated with a sprinkled layer of the salt and spice mixture in the glass jar until the jar is filled.
5. When the lime and sugar liquid is cooled to lukewarm, pour it into the jar, covering the lime and spice layers. Cool the jar; then tightly screw on a non-metallic lid.
6. Place the jar of pickle in the sun, bringing it inside every night. Shake the jar two or three times a day. After 5-6 weeks, the pickle is ready to use, although the longer you wait, the better the pickle.

Peanut and Coriander Chutney

This chutney is popular in Northern India and is a delightful combination of hot, sour, sweet, and astringent flavours. Traditionally, this chutney is prepared using dried tamarind pulp. Here, we use "instant tamarind" and reduce the preparation time of this chutney to only 10 minutes. Serve this excellent uncooked chutney as a dip for *Cauliflower and Pea Samosas* or *Rajasthani Spicy Dal-Stuffed Bread*.

PREPARATION TIME: 10 minutes
YIELD: 1 1/2 cups (375 ml)

1 tablespoon (20 ml) tamarind concentrate
1/4 cup (60 ml) hot water
1 tablespoon (20 ml) ghee or peanut oil

Raspberry Jam

Try this jam when you have an abundance of ripe, juicy raspberries.

PREPARATION AND COOKING TIME: 15 minutes
YIELD: about 4 cups (1 litre)

1 kg (2.2 pounds) fresh ripe raspberries
4 cups (1 litre) sugar
3 cups (750 ml) water
1 teaspoon (5 ml) lemon rind, finely grated

1. Combine all the ingredients in a large heavy non-stick saucepan. At this stage the mixture should be no more than 5 cm (2-inches) deep. Heat slowly to dissolve the sugar. Increase the heat, bring to a boil, and boil the jam rapidly, uncovered, without stirring for about 15 minutes or until a teaspoon of jam jells on a cold plate. You might have to stir the jam occasionally towards the end. When a little cooler, pour the jam into hot, sterilized glass jars and seal.

1/2 cup (125 ml) raw peanuts, skinned
1/3 cup (85 ml) shredded fresh coconut
1 teaspoon (5 ml) salt
1-2 hot green chilies, seeded and chopped
1 tablespoon (20 ml) brown sugar
1/4 cup (60 ml) cold water
1 cup (250 ml) fresh coriander leaves, packed

1. Combine the tamarind concentrate with the hot water until it becomes a smooth paste.
2. Place the *ghee* in a heavy frying pan over low heat. When the *ghee* is hot, add the peanuts and, stirring often, roast them for 3 or 4 minutes or until the peanuts turn pale golden brown. Add the coconut and stir for another minute.
3. Combine the peanuts, coconut, tamarind purée, salt, chilies, sugar, cold water, and fresh coriander leaves in a blender or food processor. Process until creamy and smooth. (You might need to add a little more water.) Transfer to a bowl and serve at room temperature. This chutney is best served immediately but can be refrigerated for 2-3 days.

SAVOURIES

Here's a mouth-watering selection of vegetable puffs, savoury pastries, crispy snacks, and rich extravaganzas. There's a savoury here for every occasion—breakfast or brunch, picnic or patio, snack or banquet.

Pictured: Ricotta Cheese-filled Pastries

Baked Stuffed Cheesy Corn Breads *(Enchiladas)*

Enchiladas are a Mexican dish made of soft, flat tortillas that are dipped in sauce and rolled around a filling, then topped with more sauce, sprinkled with cheese, baked, and served with sour cream. Richly indulgent and delicious, they're great for party catering.

PREPARATION TIME: 1 hour
BAKING TIME: 15 minutes
YIELD: 1 dozen large or 2 dozen small enchiladas

Sauce
3 tablespoons (60 ml) olive oil

1 small hot green chili, minced

1/4 teaspoon (1 ml) yellow asafoetida powder

4 teaspoons (20 ml) ground cumin

1 tablespoon (20 ml) ground coriander

3 cups (750 ml) tomato purée

1 cup (250 ml) tomato paste

2 teaspoons (10 ml) salt

2 teaspoons (10 ml) sugar

Filling
3 cups (750 ml) ricotta cheese

3 cups (750 ml) grated mozzarella cheese

1 medium bunch spinach, chopped, steamed until tender, and drained

2 cups (500 ml) cooked corn kernels

1/2 teaspoon (2 ml) yellow asafoetida powder

1 teaspoon (5 ml) black pepper

2 teaspoons (10 ml) brown sugar

1/4 teaspoon (1 ml) freshly ground nutmeg

1 teaspoon (5 ml) salt

oil or ghee *for deep frying*

1 dozen large or 2 dozen small tortillas

1 cup (250 ml) sour cream

To prepare the sauce
1. Heat the olive oil in a medium-sized saucepan over moderate heat. Sauté the minced chili in the hot oil for a few seconds. Add the asafoetida, cumin, and coriander; then add the tomato purée and tomato paste. Reduce the heat and simmer for 30 minutes. Add the salt and sugar and remove the sauce from the heat. Set aside.

To prepare the filling
1. Combine the ricotta cheese, 2 cups (500 ml) of grated cheese, spinach, corn, asafoetida, pepper, sugar, nutmeg, and salt in a large bowl and mix well.

To assemble the *enchiladas*
1. Heat the oil or *ghee* in a frying pan over high heat. When the *ghee* is hot (185°C/365°F), fry the *tortillas* individually for about 10 seconds on each side. Use smooth-tipped tongs to flip the *tortillas* in the oil. Remove and drain them on paper towels. The *tortillas* should be pliable.

2. Spread enough sauce on each *tortilla* to cover. If small *tortillas* are being used, spoon 1 heaped tablespoon of filling into the centre of each *tortilla* and fold in half. If large *tortillas* are being used, spoon 2 heaped tablespoons of filling into the center of each *tortilla*, spread into a strip and roll up the *tortilla*.

3. When all the *tortillas* are stuffed and laid out, pour over all the sauce. Sprinkle with the remaining grated cheese, place in a preheated moderate oven (180°C/355°F), and bake for 15 minutes or until the cheese is hot and bubbly.

Serve each *enchilada* hot with a spoonful of sour cream.

Eggplant Parmigiana

Eggplants lend a certain richness to this classic Mediterranean baked savoury dish: layers of crumbed and battered eggplant fillets baked with herbed tomato sauce and parmesan cheese. *Dégorge* the eggplants before using them; that is, the eggplants are treated with salt to remove excess bitterness, also allowing them to soak up less oil when they are fried. Try serving *Eggplant Parmigiana* with *Mediterranean Salad*, *Minestrone Soup*, and *Breadrolls* for a delightful summer luncheon.

DÉGORGING TIME: 30 minutes (optional)
PREPARATION AND COOKING TIME: 40 minutes
BAKING TIME: 40 minutes
YIELD: enough for 8 to 10 persons

Sauce
1/4 cup (60 ml) olive oil

3/4 teaspoon (7 ml) yellow asafoetida powder

2 medium red peppers, finely diced

1/2 stalk celery, finely diced

6 cups (1.5 litres) tomato purée

2 teaspoons (10 ml) dried oregano

1 teaspoon (5 ml) dried marjoram

2 tablespoons (40 ml) fresh basil

1/4 teaspoon (1 ml) ground cloves

2 tablespoons (40 ml) brown sugar

2 teaspoons (10 ml) salt

2 cups (500 ml) grated parmesan cheese

For fried eggplant
ghee *or* oil *for deep-frying*

2 cups (500 ml) wholemeal flour

2 teaspoons (10 ml) salt

1 teaspoon (5 ml) black pepper

water *for batter*

3 large eggplants, sliced into 1.25 cm (1/2-inch) fillets (approximately 12 slices)

1 cup (250 ml) cultured buttermilk

2 cups (500 ml) breadcrumbs

To *dégorge* the eggplants (optional)

1. Rub salt on the eggplant slices and let them sit for half an hour. Rinse the eggplant slices thoroughly with cold water and dry them with paper towels.

To make the sauce

1. Heat the olive oil over high heat in a heavy saucepan. Sauté the asafoetida; then add the minced red peppers and celery. Stir-fry for a few minutes. Add the tomato purée, herbs, spices, sugar, and salt. Bring the mixture to the boil, reduce the heat, and simmer the sauce, stirring occasionally, for about 15 minutes. Remove from the heat.

To batter and fry the eggplant

1. Heat the *ghee* or oil for deep-frying until it reaches about 185°C/365°F. Combine the flour, salt, pepper, and cold water to form a medium-thick batter. Dip a few slices of eggplant in the buttermilk, roll them in breadcrumbs, and dip them into the batter. Fry them in the hot *ghee* or oil until golden brown on both sides. Remove and drain. Repeat this procedure until all the eggplants are cooked.

To assemble the casserole

1. Preheat the oven to 180°C/355°F. Spread one-third of the tomato sauce in a deep casserole dish (about 25 cm x 30 cm [10 inches x 12 inches]). Place half of the eggplant slices on top. Carefully pour and spread another one third of the tomato sauce on top and sprinkle on half the parmesan cheese. Layer the rest of the eggplant in the dish; then pour on the rest of the tomato sauce. Sprinkle on the remaining cheese. Bake for 40 minutes. Serve hot or warm.

Note: As an alternative, serve the fried, crumbed, and battered eggplant fillets hot, on individual platters, with a generous spoonful of sauce and parmesan cheese.

Eggplant Rings with Cheese

Rings of eggplant are sandwiched together with a ring of mozzarella cheese and fried in a herbed batter for these tasty, cheesy savouries. They're ideal served piping hot for special party catering.

PREPARATION TIME: 5 minutes
BATTER STANDING
   TIME: 30 minutes
COOKING TIME: 10 minutes
YIELD: 6 to 8 pieces

1 medium eggplant
125 g (4¹/₂ ounces) mozzarella cheese
¹/₂ cup (125 ml) olive oil
oil for deep frying

Batter

1 cup (250 ml) plain flour
¹/₂ teaspoon (2 ml) dried yeast
1 cup (250 ml) and 1 tablespoon (20 ml) lukewarm water
1 teaspoon (5 ml) salt
¹/₄ teaspoon (1 ml) black pepper
¹/₂ teaspoon (2 ml) dried basil
¹/₄ teaspoon (1 ml) yellow asafoetida powder
salt for sprinkling

1. To make the batter: Sift the flour and yeast into a bowl, make a well in the centre, and add lukewarm water. Add salt, pepper, basil, and asafoetida, mix well, and allow to stand for ¹/₂ hour.

2. Slice the eggplant into 0.5 cm (¹/₄-inch) rings. Cut the mozzarella cheese into half as many rings as there are eggplant rings. Heat ¹/₄ cup (60 ml) olive oil in a frying pan and fry the eggplant rings until golden but still firm. Remove and drain carefully on paper towels.

3. Heat the oil for deep frying to 180°C/355°F. Place one piece of mozzarella cheese between 2 slices of eggplants, lift with the tongs, and dip into the batter. Repeat and deep-fry a few pieces at a time until they are golden brown. Remove and drain on paper towels. Repeat until all the eggplant rings are fried. Season the eggplant rings with the extra salt and serve hot.

Above: Eggplant Parmigiana

Vegetable Fritters (*Pakoras*)

Pakoras are popular spiced, batter-dipped, deep-fried, vegetables that make perfect snacks or hors d'oeuvres. *Ghee* is the preferred medium for frying *pakoras*, although you can use nut or vegetable oil. Serve hot *pakoras* with you favourite chutney or dip.

Try batter-frying various types of vegetables. Cauliflower *pakoras* are probably the most popular, but equally delicious are potato rings, zucchini chunks, spinach leaves, pumpkin slices, eggplant rings, baby tomatoes, sweet potatoes, red or green pepper slices, asparagus tips, and artichoke hearts.

Cook *pakoras* slowly to ensure that the batter and the vegetables cook simultaneously. You needn't precook the vegetables.

PREPARATION TIME: 10 minutes
BATTER SITTING
 TIME: 10-15 minutes
COOKING TIME: 30 minutes
YIELD: 2 dozen large or 3 dozen
 medium pakoras

2/3 cup (165 ml) chickpea flour
2/3 cup (165 ml) plain flour
2/3 cup (165 ml) self-raising flour
2 1/2 teaspoons (12 ml) salt
2 teaspoons (10 ml) yellow
 asafoetida powder
1 1/2 teaspoons (7 ml) turmeric
2 teaspoons (10 ml) cayenne pepper
1 1/2 teaspoons (7 ml) ground
 coriander
2 teaspoons (10 ml) green chilies,
 seeded and finely chopped
about 2 1/2 cups (625 ml) cold water,
 or enough to make a
 smooth batter
bite-sized vegetable pieces of
 your choice
ghee or oil for deep-frying

1. Combine the flours, salt, powdered spices, and green chilies in a bowl. Mix well with a wire whisk.
2. Slowly add cold water while whisking the batter until it achieves the consistency of medium-light cream. When you dip the vegetable in the batter, it should be completely coated but neither thick and heavy nor runny and thin. Have extra flour and water on hand to adjust the consistency as required. Let the batter sit for 10 to 15 minutes.

3. Heat fresh *ghee* or oil, to the depth of 6.5-7.5 cm (2 1/2-3 inches), in a wok or deep-frying vessel until the temperature reaches about 180°C/ 355°F. Dip 5 or 6 pieces of vegetable in the batter and, one at a time, carefully slip them into the hot oil.

4. The temperature will fall, but try to maintain it between 173°C-180°C (345°F-355°F) throughout the frying. Fry until the *pakoras* are golden brown, turning to cook them evenly on all sides. Remove with a slotted spoon and drain on paper towels. Continue cooking until all the *pakoras* are done. Serve immediately or keep warm, uncovered, in a preheated cool oven for up to 1/2 hour.

Above: Cauliflower Pakoras *served with* Tomato Relish (p. 127)

Tofu "Steaks"

Tofu "steaks" will vary in size according to the shape of the block of *tofu*. Generally, a 450 g (1-pound) block of *tofu* will make 4 good-sized *tofu* "steaks". Serve accompanied by *Boiled Rice*, vegetable dishes, and salad.

PREPARATION AND COOKING TIME: 10 minutes
MARINATING TIME: 2 hours
BAKING TIME: 20 minutes
YIELD: enough for 4 persons

2 tablespoons (40 ml) vegetable oil

¼ teaspoon (1 ml) yellow asafoetida powder

450 g (1 pound) firm tofu, sliced into 4 rectangles

4 tablespoons (80 ml) Japanese tamari (if unavailable, substitute with high quality soy sauce)

½ cup (125 ml) apple juice

½ cup (125 ml) dry white grape juice

1 tablespoon (20 ml) ginger juice (shredded ginger squeezed through a cloth)

1 tablespoon (20 ml) lemon juice

1 tablespoon (20 ml) raw sugar

1. Heat the vegetable oil over moderately low heat in a frying pan large enough to fit all 4 "steaks" at a time. Sauté the asafoetida in the hot oil and add the *tofu*. Sauté the *tofu* until golden brown on both sides, turning when required. Remove from the heat. Transfer the *tofu*, along with any remaining oil, into an ovenproof dish, laying the *tofu* "steaks" out flat.

2. Combine the *tamari*, apple juice, grape juice, ginger juice, lemon juice, and raw sugar in a bowl, stirring well to dissolve the sugar. Pour this mixture over the warm *tofu* "steaks". Leave to marinate for 2 hours.

3. Place the ovenproof dish in a preheated 200°C/390°F oven and bake for 20 minutes, uncovered. Serve hot.

Mashed Potato Puffs (Alu Vadas)

These are a favourite savoury item from Gujarat state on India's west coast. They're a good example of simple, tasty vegetarian "finger food". Most of the time spent to prepare these puffs lies in mashing and spicing the potatoes. The frying time is very quick because, even though they're cooked in a 'pakora-like' batter, the filling is already precooked, the wafer-thin crust cooking in only minutes. Serve *Alu Vadas* with *Coconut Chutney* for a tasty treat.

PREPARATION AND FRYING TIME: ½ hour
YIELD: enough for 6 persons (18 balls)

Potato Filling

2½ cups (625 ml) mashed potatoes, cooled

2 hot green chilies, seeded and chopped

½ teaspoon (2 ml) minced fresh ginger

1 teaspoon (5 ml) brown sugar

2 teaspoons (10 ml) fresh lemon juice

½ teaspoon (2 ml) salt

1 tablespoon (20 ml) minced raisins

1 tablespoon (20 ml) minced fresh coconut or desiccated coconut

1 tablespoon (20 ml) chopped fresh coriander leaves

Batter

¼ cup (60 ml) chickpea flour

¼ cup (60 ml) plain flour

¼ cup (60 ml) self-raising flour

¼ teaspoon (1 ml) ground ajowan seeds

1 teaspoon (5 ml) yellow asafoetida powder

½ teaspoon (2 ml) turmeric

1 teaspoon (5 ml) salt

about 1 cup (250 ml) cold water

ghee or oil for deep-frying

1. Mix the mashed potatoes with the other potato filling ingredients and roll into 18 balls.

2. Combine the 3 flours, spices, and salt in a mixing bowl. Adding water, whisk the batter to make a smooth, slightly thick pouring-consistency batter.

3. Heat *ghee* or oil, to the depth of 6.5-7.5 cm (2½-3 inches), in a wok or deep-frying pan over moderately high heat until it reaches 180°C/355°F. Dip 5 or 6 balls in the batter and carefully slip them into the hot oil. Deep-fry, turning gently after they float to the surface, for 3 to 4 minutes or until the puffs turn golden brown and crisp. Remove and drain them on paper towels. Serve immediately.

Sweet Potato Pie

This popular savoury pie features the delicious orange-fleshed kumeras, native New Zealand sweet potatoes. This recipe is from the lunch menu at Gopal's Restaurant in Auckland.

PREPARATION TIME: ½ hour
PASTRY RESTING TIME: ½ hour
TOTAL BAKING TIME: 25 to 35 minutes
YIELD: one 20 cm (8-inch) pie

Pie crust

1 cup (250 ml) unbleached plain flour

1 cup (250 ml) wholemeal flour

1 teaspoon (5 ml) salt

½ cup (125 ml) butter

up to ¾ cup (185 ml) iced water

Filling

3 cups (750 ml) kumeras, peeled, steamed, and mashed

¼ cup (60 ml) each of the following vegetables (all lightly steamed and drained): cauliflower pieces, french beans cut into 2.5 cm (1-inch) lengths, corn, chopped spinach, carrot cubes, and broccoli flowerets

¼ cup (60 ml) butter

1 tablespoon (20 ml) grated ginger, lightly sautéed

1½ teaspoons (7 ml) salt

½ teaspoon (2 ml) freshly ground black pepper

3 teaspoons (15 ml) soy sauce

½ teaspoon (2 ml) yellow asafoetida powder

2 tablespoons (40 ml) brown sugar

1. To prepare the crust: sift the 2 flours and salt into a large bowl. Rub in the butter until the mixture resembles a coarse meal. Add enough chilled water to hold the dough together. Knead briefly, working quickly to avoid over-handling. Cover the pastry in plastic wrap and refrigerate for ½ hour.

2. Pinch off two-thirds of the pastry and roll it into a smooth ball; then, with a rolling pin, roll it into a circle that comfortably fits inside and up the sides of one 20 cm (8-inch) buttered pie tin. Prick with a fork and bake in a preheated oven at 200°C/390°F for 10 to 12 minutes or until light golden brown.

3. Thoroughly combine all the ingredients for the filling. Spoon the filling into the pie base. Roll the remaining pastry to the required size, place it on top of the pie, and crimp the edges of the top over the pie base. Prick with a fork and place in the oven. Bake at 190°C/375°F for 15 to 20 minutes or until golden brown.

Variation: Place 1 cup (250 ml) grated cheese on top of the pie halfway through the baking.

Cauliflower and Pea Samosas

These triangular deep-fried stuffed savoury pastries are becoming world famous. The Gopal's Restaurants world-wide all feature *samosas* on their menu. Potato-and-peas, mixed-vegetables, or cauliflower-and-potato fillings can be substituted for cauliflower and peas. Fresh curd cheese can also be successfully added to *samosa* filling.

When you bite into a warm *samosa*, you'll notice it's wonderfully tender, thin pastry crust, golden brown from deep-frying in *ghee*, and the harmony of flavours of the vegetable filling.

Serve *samosas* with *Date and Tamarind Sauce*, *Peach Chutney*, or *Mint Chutney*. *Samosas* should be served warm or at room temperature and make a great travelling snack-food.

PREPARATION TIME: about 1 hour
FRYING TIME: 20 to 30 minutes
YIELD: 20 samosas

Filling

2 tablespoons (40 ml) ghee or oil

1 tablespoon (20 ml) cumin seeds

2 teaspoons (10 ml) minced fresh ginger

2 or 3 hot green chilies, seeded and minced

¾ teaspoon (3 ml) yellow asafoetida powder

1 small cauliflower (about 14 ounces, or 400 g), cored, trimmed, diced, and steamed until tender

1⅓ cups (335 ml) green peas, steamed

½ teaspoon (2 ml) turmeric

¼ teaspoon (1 ml) cinnamon powder

1½ teaspoons (7 ml) salt

1 tablespoon (20 ml) minced fresh coriander leaves or parsley

½ teaspoon (2 ml) lemon juice

ghee or oil for deep frying

Pastry

1¾ cups (435 ml) unbleached plain flour

¾ teaspoon (3 ml) salt

4 tablespoons (80 ml) melted butter or ghee

between ½ and ¾ cup (125 ml-185 ml) warm water

To make the filling

1. Heat 2 tablespoons (40 ml) of *ghee* or oil in a large frying pan over moderate heat. Sauté the cumin seeds in the hot oil until they turn golden brown. Add the ginger and chilies and stir-fry for 1 minute. Add the asafoetida and stir momentarily; then add the cauliflower and peas. Add the turmeric, cinnamon, and salt.

2. Reduce the heat to low, stir all the ingredients, and partially cover. Cook, stirring occasionally, for about 5 minutes or until the vegetables are tender and quite dry. Add the fresh coriander leaves and lemon juice. Remove from the heat and coarsely mash the vegetables. Allow the mixture to cool to room temperature. Divide the filling into 20 even portions.

To make the pastry

1. Mix the flour and salt in a large mixing bowl. Add the melted butter or *ghee* and rub it between your fingertips until it resembles a coarse meal.

At right: Preparing Cauliflower and Pea Samosas. The finished product is shown at left.

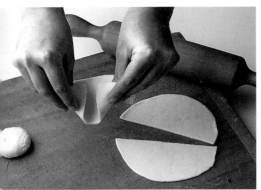

Fig. 1

Fig. 2

Fig. 3

Fig. 4

2. Make a depression in the centre of the mixture, add most of the water, and quickly mix and gather it into a ball. If the dough is too dry to cohere, add warm water to make a medium-soft pastry dough.

3. Knead the dough on a smooth surface for 8 to 10 minutes or until smooth and elastic. Cover with a cloth until the filling is cool.

To assemble the *samosas*

1. Roll the dough into a rope about 25 cm (10-inches) long and cut the rope into 10 equal-sized pieces. Cover with a moist cloth.

2. Take one piece of dough and press it into a smooth patty. Lightly oil a smooth working surface. With a rolling pin, flatten the patty into a round, thin disk about 16.5 cm (6½-inches) across. Cut the disk in half with a sharp knife.

3. Dip your finger into a bowl of water and moisten the straight edge of one semi-circle of pastry. Pick up the semi-circle and fold it in half, forming a cone. Gently but firmly press the moistened edges together, slightly overlapping them to ensure the seal. (Fig. 1)

4. Carefully spoon one portion of the vegetable stuffing into the pastry cone, leaving a 0.5-cm (¼-inch) border on top (Fig. 2). Dip your finger into the bowl of water and moisten the inside edge of the cone. Firmly press the moistened edges together, thoroughly sealing the filling inside the triangular pastry casing (Fig. 3). The top edge can be left plain, crimped with a fork or plaited with your fingers (Fig. 4). Place the *samosa* on a tray and finish rolling, filling, and shaping the remaining *samosas*.

5. Place *ghee* or oil to a level of 6.5-7.5 cm (2½-3 inches) in a wok or deep-frying pan over moderate heat. When the temperature reaches 145°C/290°F, slowly fry 8 to 10 *samosas* at a time for about 10 minutes or until they're flaky and pale golden brown. Remove with a slotted spoon and drain on paper towels. Serve warm or at room temperature.

Vegetarian Spring Rolls

Serve *Spring Rolls* hot with sweet chili sauce for a delicious snack as part of a multi-course banquet.

PREPARATION AND COOKING TIME: 20 minutes

FRYING TIME: 30 minutes

YIELD: about 30 spring rolls

2 tablespoons (40 ml) Chinese sesame oil

¼ teaspoon (1 ml) yellow asafoetida powder

1 tablespoon (20 ml) minced fresh ginger

4 or 5 medium carrots cut matchstick size (about 2 cups, 500 ml)

1 small cabbage or Chinese cabbage, cut into fine strips (about 6 cups, 1.5 litres)

2 cups (500 ml) mung bean shoots

100 g (3½ ounces) firm tofu, crumbled

1 tablespoon (20 ml) Chinese chili oil

2 tablespoons (40 ml) soy sauce

1 tablespoon (20 ml) brown sugar

1 teaspoon (5 ml) salt

½ teaspoon (2 ml) freshly ground black pepper

pinch of Chinese 5-spice

2 teaspoons (10 ml) cornflour

1 packet of 30 frozen, eggless spring roll wrappers (small size)

oil for deep-frying

1. To prepare the filling: heat the sesame oil in a wok over moderate-to-high heat until the oil is almost smoking. Sauté the asafoetida momentarily in the hot oil. Add the minced ginger and sauté for ½ minute; then add the carrots and, increasing the heat, sauté for 2 or 3 minutes. Add the cabbage and fry partially covered, stirring often. When the cabbage becomes soft, add the bean shoots, crumbled *tofu*, chili oil, soy sauce, sugar, salt, pepper, and

Chinese 5-spice. Stir-fry for another minute. Mix half the cornflour with cold water to form a paste and stir it into the mixture. Remove the filling from the heat, transfer to a tray, and allow it to cool.

2. Heat the oil in a wok over moderate heat until it reaches 185°C/365°F.

3. To prepare the rolls: unwrap the pastry and separate the sheets. Place 2 tablespoons (40 ml) of the filling in the corner of each sheet. Roll the sheet over the filling, tuck in the sides and continue rolling, sealing with a paste made from the remaining cornflour and a little cold water.

4. Place a few sealed rolls at a time in the oil. Deep-fry them, turning once, for about 45 seconds each side or until they are reddish brown. Drain them. Continue frying until all the rolls are cooked and serve them hot with an accompanying sauce.

Below: Sweet-and-Sour Walnuts served with Thai Rice (p.9)

Sweet-and-Sour Walnuts

This exotic dish from Shanghai features crispy walnuts in a delicious sweet-and-sour sauce. Serve with hot rice as an accompaniment to a main meal.

PREPARATION TIME: 25 minutes
BATTER RISING TIME: 45 minutes
COOKING TIME: 35 minutes
YIELD: enough for 6 to 8 persons

150 g (5 ounces) shelled walnut-halves

3 cups (750 ml) water

4 cups (1-litre) corn oil for deep-frying

Sauce

3 tablespoons (60 ml) corn oil

¾ teaspoon (3 ml) yellow asafoetida powder

2 stalks celery, finely chopped

2 cups (500 ml) ripe pineapple pieces

2 small green peppers, finely chopped

2 small green chilies, finely chopped

2 teaspoons (10 ml) salt

1 tablespoon (20 ml) brown sugar

4 tablespoons (80 ml) fresh lemon juice

4 tablespoons (80 ml) tomato purée

4 tablespoons (80 ml) sweet soy sauce

Batter

1 cup (250 ml) plain flour

1 tablespoon (20 ml) cornflour

2 teaspoons (10 ml) baking powder

¾ cup (185 ml) water

1 tablespoon (20 ml) corn oil

Thickening Paste

2 teaspoons (10 ml) cornflour

2 tablespoon (40 ml) water

2 teaspoons (10 ml) Chinese sesame oil

1. Bring water to the boil. Add walnuts, remove from heat and allow to soak for 30 minutes. Drain, pat dry, and place on a baking sheet. Toast in a preheated oven (120°C/250°F) for 20 minutes or until the walnuts are crisp.

2. Sift the plain flour, cornflour, and baking powder into a bowl. Add the water and set aside for ½ hour. Blend with the 1 tablespoon (20 ml) corn oil and leave for another 15 minutes.

3. Heat 4 cups (1 litre) corn oil in a wok to 180°C/355°F, and, dipping the walnuts in the batter, deep-fry until golden; then drain.

4. To make the sauce: heat 3 tablespoons (60 ml) corn oil in a wok over moderate heat. Sauté the asafoetida in the hot oil. Add the celery, pineapple, pepper, and chilies and cook for 7 to 10 minutes or until the celery and peppers become soft. Add the salt, brown sugar, lemon juice, tomato purée, and sweet soy sauce and heat until boiling. Combine the ingredients for the thickening paste and add to the sauce. Stir well and remove from the heat. Add the walnuts to the sauce, mix well, and serve hot.

Spicy Tofu Rolls

This tasty savoury is made from beancurd sheets, or "tofu skin", a dried *tofu* product, and stuffed with vegetables, such as choko. Choko is a green pear-shaped gourd that is sometimes called *chayote*. If choko is not available, substitute peeled, seeded, and shredded cucumber.

When purchasing the *tofu* skin, select the soft variety made especially for wrapping. All the Chinese ingredients are available at Asian grocers.

PREPARATION TIME: 30 minutes
COOKING TIME: 20 minutes
YIELD: 12 rolls

Filling

2 tablespoons (40 ml) corn oil

1 tablespoon (20 ml) shredded fresh ginger

1½ cups (375 ml) choko or cucumber, peeled and finely shredded

1½ cups (375 ml) carrots, peeled and shredded

1½ cups (375 ml) shredded Chinese bok choy leaves

1 tablespoon (20 ml) minced preserved turnip (choyboh)

½ teaspoon (2 ml) salt

1 teaspoon (5 ml) fresh lemon juice

3 tablespoons (60 ml) Chinese Vegetable Stock (or water)

½ teaspoon (2 ml) brown sugar

¼ teaspoon (1 ml) black pepper

1 cup (250 ml) mung bean shoots

1 large packet soft beancurd sheet

corn oil for shallow-frying

For thickening paste

½ teaspoon (2 ml) cornflour

2 teaspoons (10 ml) water

½ teaspoon (2 ml) Chinese sesame oil

Sauce

2 tablespoons (40 ml) brown sugar

2 tablespoons (40 ml) light soy sauce

2 tablespoons (40 ml) Chinese Vegetable Stock (or water)

1 teaspoon (5 ml) Chinese sesame paste

1 teaspoon (5 ml) sesame oil

2 teaspoons (10 ml) fresh lemon juice

1 teaspoon (5 ml) chili oil

tiny pinch Chinese 5-spice powder

2 teaspoons (10 ml) fresh red chili chopped for garnish

2 tablespoons (40 ml) chopped fresh parsley for garnish

1. Heat 2 tablespoons (40 ml) corn oil in a wok. Stir-fry the ginger, choko, and carrots in the hot oil over moderate heat for about 2 minutes. Add the shredded *bok choy* leaves and the preserved turnip, cover the vegetables, and cook until tender.

2. Combine thickening-paste ingredients. Remove lid and increase the heat; then add the salt, lemon juice, 3 tablespoons (60 ml) stock or water, brown sugar, black pepper, and the thickening paste. Add the bean shoots and stir. Spread the preparation on a plate to cool. Divide into 12 portions.

3. Unwrap the beancurd sheet and cut it into 30 cm (12-inch) squares. Dip a sheet momentarily into a bowl of cold water. Place it on a flat surface and pat dry. Place a portion of filling near the corner of the sheet and roll it over, tucking in the edges as you go until you make a tight roll. Repeat for all 12 rolls.

4. Place the corn oil in a shallow pan and, a batch at a time, shallow-fry the rolls over moderate heat (180°C/355°F) until they are golden brown on both sides. Remove and drain.

5. Mix all the ingredients for the sauce in a small pan (except the chilies and parsley). Cook over low heat until the mixture is smooth. Remove from the heat.

6. Pour the sauce over the rolls, garnish with parsley and chili, and serve immediately.

Potato and Pea Croquettes

These pan-fried delights are easy to make and are great served hot with sour cream or *Date and Tamarind Sauce*.

PREPARATION AND COOKING TIME: 30 to 40 minutes
YIELD: 1 dozen croquettes

3 medium potatoes, peeled and cut into 2.5 cm (1-inch) cubes

1 cup (250 ml) green peas

1 teaspoon (5 ml) salt

1 teaspoon (5 ml) freshly ground black pepper

¼ teaspoon (1 ml) yellow asafoetida powder

1 cup (250 ml) breadcrumbs

¼ cup (60 ml) minced fresh coriander leaves or parsley

¼ cup (60 ml) ghee or oil for pan frying

1. Boil the potato cubes in a saucepan of lightly salted water until very tender. Drain, mash, and set aside.

2. Steam the peas until tender. Drain and set aside.

3. Combine the salt, pepper, asafoetida, breadcrumbs, fresh herbs, and mashed potatoes in a bowl. Add the peas and mix well. Divide the mixture into 1 dozen even-sized balls. Flatten each ball into a 7.5 cm (3-inch) patty with the palms of your hand.

4. Heat a non-stick frying pan over moderate heat. Add half the *ghee* or oil and fry 6 of the patties on both sides until golden and crusted (about 3 or 4 minutes on each side). Remove and drain on paper towels.

5. Add the remaining *ghee* or oil to the pan and pan-fry the remaining croquettes. Serve hot.

Curd Pakoras

Home-made curd cheese is easy to make and is irresistible when batter-fried—crispy on the outside and smooth and creamy on the inside.

Serve hot *Curd Pakoras* with a wedge of lemon or lime and a spoonful of *Tartare Sauce*.

The curd cheese, or *panir*, should be home-made, pressed under a heavy weight, cut up while still hot and slightly moist, cooked in batter immediately, and served hot.

CURD MAKING TIME: about 15 minutes
PREPARATION TIME: 10 minutes
COOKING TIME: 20 minutes
YIELD: enough for 6 to 8 persons

8 cups (2-litres) milk
2-3 tablespoons (40-60 ml) fresh lemon juice
1/3 cup (85 ml) chickpea flour
1/3 cup (85 ml) plain flour
1/3 cup (85 ml) self-raising flour
2 teaspoons (10 ml) salt
1 teaspoon (5 ml) yellow asafoetida powder
1/4 teaspoon (1 ml) turmeric
1 1/2 teaspoons (7 ml) green chilies, minced
1 cup (250 ml) cold water, or as required
ghee or oil for deep-frying

1. Boil the milk in a heavy saucepan over moderate heat. Remove from the heat and add the lemon juice, a little at a time. When the curd has separated from the whey, place the pan of curds and whey aside.

2. Combine the flours, salt, spices, and chilies in a bowl and add cold water to form a thick batter. Leave for 10 minutes.

3. Drain the curd cheese and press it for 10 minutes under a heavy weight. Remove the weight and cut the cheese into 1.5 cm (3/4-inch) cubes or 3.75 cm (1 1/2-inch) long strips while the curd is still hot.

4. Pour 6.5-7.5 cm (2 1/2-3 inches) *ghee* or oil into a wok or deep-frying pan and heat to 180°C/355°F. Dip 6 or 7 pieces of curd cheese in the batter and carefully drop them into the hot oil one at a time. The temperature will fall but should be maintained at the frying temperature by adjusting the heat. Cook the *pakoras*, turning occasionally, until they are golden brown all over (about 4 to 5 minutes). Remove with a slotted spoon and drain on paper towels. Cook all the *pakoras* in the same manner and serve hot.

Crispy Flat-Rice and Cashews (Gujarati *Chidwa*)

Chidwa is a deep fried snack famous throughout India. This recipe from Gujarat combines nuts, dried fruits, fried potato straws, crispy flat-rice, and spices. Ajowan seeds, with a flavour reminiscent of oregano, give *chidwa* its authentic flavour. They are available from any Indian grocer.

PREPARATION AND SOAKING TIME: 1 hour
FRYING TIME: 30 minutes
YIELD: enough for 10 persons

1 large baking potato, peeled, and coarsely shredded
1/2 teaspoon (2 ml) cayenne pepper
1/2 teaspoon (2 ml) turmeric
1 1/4 teaspoons (6 ml) salt
1 tablespoon (20 ml) sugar
2 teaspoons (10 ml) ajowan seeds
1-2 hot green chilies, seeded and cut into long, wafer-thin strips
1 tablespoon (20 ml) fennel seeds
vegetable oil for deep-frying
1 1/4 cups (310 ml) flat-rice (the thick variety, called poha)
1/2 cup (125 ml) raw cashews
1/2 cup (125 ml) raisins

1. Rinse the shredded potato in batches of cold water until the water remains clear. Soak the shredded potato in cold water for 1/2 hour. Drain and pat dry.

2. Combine the cayenne, turmeric, salt, sugar, ajowan, and green chilies in a small bowl. Set aside.

3. Dry-roast the fennel seeds in a small frying pan over moderate heat until the seeds darken a few shades. Set aside.

4. Heat 5 cm (2 inches) oil in a deep pan or wok over high heat. When the temperature reaches 190°C/375°F, add a handful of the shredded potato and deep-fry until golden brown, stirring occasionally with a slotted spoon. Remove and drain in a colander lined with paper towels. Repeat until all the potato is fried.

5. Allow the oil temperature to fall to about 180°C/355°F. Place a small handful of flat-rice in a metal strainer and carefully lower it into the hot oil. The oil will froth initially. After one minute, the flat-rice will be crisp. Do not allow it to darken. Remove the strainer, drain, and transfer the flat-rice onto paper towels. Repeat until all the flat-rice is fried.

6. Deep-fry the cashew nuts in the same manner as the flat-rice until golden brown.

7. Allow all the fried ingredients to cool to room temperature. Combine them in a bowl with the spices and raisins, mixing well. Store in an airtight container.

For a more colourful variety of *chidwa* try the following: divide the shredded potatoes into 3 and soak in 3 separate small bowls of cold water, to which has been added 1 teaspoon (5 ml) each of edible red, blue, and green food dye. Soak the shredded potatoes, drain them, pat dry, and proceed as per the recipe.

Asparagus and Tomato Quiche

A quiche is an open faced tart with a savoury filling and is the perfect luncheon or supper dish accompanied by a green salad and French bread. It also makes a good first course for dinner. Quiche lends itself to advance preparation; the crust or base of the quiche should be cooked beforehand. A cold quiche is great for picnic fare or makes a quick, satisfying snack.

CRUST BAKING TIME: 15 minutes
FILLING PREPARATION
*   TIME: 10 minutes*
BAKING TIME: 30 minutes
YIELD: one 20 cm (8-inch) quiche

Pastry

½ cup (125 ml) melted butter

1½ cups (375 ml) wholemeal flour

3 tablespoons (60 ml) water, or as required

¼ cup (60 ml) grated parmesan cheese

Quiche filling

2 tablespoons (40 ml) sour cream

2 tablespoons (40 ml) softened cream cheese

2 tablespoons (40 ml) tomato paste

2 tablespoons (40 ml) cornflour

1 teaspoon (5 ml) salt

¼ teaspoon (1 ml) ground white pepper

1½ cups (375 ml) grated cheddar cheese

½ teaspoon (2 ml) dried thyme

½ teaspoon (2 ml) dried basil

½ teaspoon (2 ml) dried oregano

½ teaspoon (2 ml) yellow asafoetida powder

3½ cups (875 ml) fresh asparagus, diced and steamed

2 medium tomatoes, sliced into rings

1. Combine the butter and flour, rubbing well until it reaches a coarse meal consistency. Add the water and parmesan cheese to the mixture and mix to form a firm pastry. Press the mixture into a buttered 20 cm (8-inch) quiche or flan tin, being careful that the crust mixture is evenly distributed throughout the tin.

2. Bake the quiche crust in a hot oven (200°C/390°F) until light golden brown. Allow to cool.

3. Combine the sour cream, softened cream cheese, tomato paste, cornflour, salt, pepper, 1 cup (250 ml) cheese, herbs, and spices and mix well. Add the asparagus. Spoon the mixture into the cooled quiche crust, smooth out, press the slices of tomato on top, sprinkle with the remaining cheese, and bake in a preheated oven set on 190°C/375°F for about 20 minutes or until the filling is set and the top is golden.

Allow to cool before serving.

Pictured: Asparagus and Tomato Quiche

Spinach Filo Triangles (*Spanakopita*)

Spinach Filo Triangles feature the salty white Greek sheep's cheese called *feta* and wafer-thin continental filo pastry (both available at delicatessens and large stores). If you are not partial to the rather strong taste of *feta*, substitute ricotta cheese or home-made curd cheese (*panir*) or a combination of both. Include the optional cheddar cheese if you're using a substitute for *feta*. I have omitted salt from the recipe because *feta* cheese and spinach are both naturally salty. Add 1 teaspoon (5 ml) salt if you are not using *feta*. These crisp, savoury, baked pastries are great for party catering.

¼ teaspoon (1 ml) nutmeg

2 tablespoons (40 ml) plain flour

¾ cup (185 ml) milk

250 g (9 ounces) chopped feta cheese (or ricotta or curd cheese plus 1½ cups (375 ml) tasty cheddar cheese, grated)

375 g (13 ounces) filo pastry

2 tablespoons (40 ml) breadcrumbs (optional)

1 cup (250 ml) melted butter (for brushing on the pastry layers)

1. Place the spinach in a large, heavy saucepan over moderately high heat with 3 tablespoons (60 ml) of butter, salt, and pepper. Bring the

from the heat. Combine the spinach, cheese, and sauce. Place the mixture in a bowl and allow to cool. If the mixture is too moist, add the optional breadcrumbs.

3. Cut all the pastry sheets into long, 9 cm (4-inch) wide strips (Fig. 1). Using a pastry brush, brush 2 strips with melted butter (Fig. 2). Layer one buttered strip on top of another.

4. Place 1 heaped tablespoon of filling on the end of each double pastry strip and fold over to form a triangle, covering the filling (Fig. 3 & 4). Lifting the triangle up and over to form a second triangle, continue folding until you reach the end of the

Fig. 1

Fig. 2

Fig. 3

Fig. 4

Fig. 5

Fig. 6

PREPARATION TIME: 1-1½ hours

BAKING TIME: 15 to 20 minutes

YIELD: about 24 triangles

2 large bunches spinach, washed and coarsely chopped

5 tablespoons (100 ml) butter

1 teaspoon (5 ml) ground black pepper

1 teaspoon (5 ml) yellow asafoetida powder

spinach to a boil, reduce the heat, and cook uncovered until the spinach is tender and the liquid has evaporated.

2. Melt another 2 tablespoons (40 ml) butter in a separate pan, add asafoetida, and sauté for a few moments. Add the nutmeg and flour and sauté for about 1 minute. Add the milk and stir carefully until the sauce boils and thickens. Remove

pastry strip (Fig. 5). Adhere the last edge of the pastry with butter.

5. Fill all the triangles in this manner, brush the tops with butter (Fig. 6), and bake on unbuttered baking sheets in a preheated oven (180°C/ 355°F) for 20 to 30 minutes or until golden brown.

Ricotta Cheese-filled Pastries (*Calzone*)

Calzone are popular half-moon shaped stuffed savoury-or-sweet pastries from Italy. This is my version of the savoury variety eaten in the southern region of Campania, Basilicata, and Puglia. Serve *calzone* as part of a traditional Italian vegetarian meal or as an entrée or snack, either hot or cold.

PREPARATION TIME: 50 minutes
DOUGH RISING TIME: 1 hour 30 minutes
FRYING TIME: 20 minutes
YIELD: about 18 calzone

Pastry

3 teaspoons (15 ml) fresh yeast
1/2 cup (125 ml) warm water
1 teaspoon (5 ml) sugar
4 cups (1-litre) plain flour
1 teaspoon (5 ml) salt
3 tablespoons (60 ml) olive oil

Filling

1 tablespoon (20 ml) olive oil
1/4 teaspoon (1 ml) yellow asafoetida powder
2 tablespoons (40 ml) red or green peppers, finely diced
1/2 cup (125 ml) black olives, chopped

1 teaspoon (5 ml) salt
1/4 teaspoon (1 ml) black pepper
2 cups (500 ml) ricotta cheese (or cottage cheese or fresh curd, crumbled)
1/2 cup (125 ml) grated parmesan cheese
1/3 cup (85 ml) grated cheddar cheese,
1/2 cup (125 ml) spinach leaves, chopped and lightly-blanched
1/3 cup (85 ml) chopped fresh parsley
oil or ghee for deep frying

1. Dissolve the yeast in the warm water, add the sugar, mix well, and leave covered in a warm place for 10 minutes or until the mixture froths.

2. Sift the flour and salt into a large mixing bowl. Add the yeast, oil, and enough lukewarm water to make a smooth dough. Knead well for 5 minutes. Rub oil inside the bowl and over the dough. Place the dough in the bowl, cover, and let rise in a warm place for 1 hour or until doubled in size.

3. To prepare the pastry filling: heat the olive oil in a small frying pan over moderate heat. Sauté the asafoetida in the hot oil for a few seconds; then add the diced peppers and sauté for one minute. Add the chopped black olives, salt, and pepper and stir to mix; then remove from the heat and allow to cool.

4. Combine the ricotta cheese, parmesan cheese, cheddar cheese, cooled olives and pepper mixture, spinach, and parsley in a large bowl. Mix well and set aside.

5. After the dough has risen the first time, punch it down with your fist, remove it from the bowl onto a floured benchtop, and knead again for one minute. Roll the dough out with your hands into a long tube and cut into 18 portions. Roll each portion into a smooth ball and, with a rolling pin, roll out each ball into a 13 cm (5-inch) disk.

6. Divide the filling into 18 portions. Place a portion in the centre of each disk. Fold over and seal around the edge either with a fork or by pressure from your fingertips to make small semicircular pastries. Place all the pastries on a oiled tray and leave them covered with a cloth in a warm place for 30 minutes.

7. Heat the *ghee* or oil for deep-frying in a wok or large pan over moderate heat (180°C/355°F) and fry 6 pastries, turning when required, until they are golden brown. Remove and drain. Repeat until all the pastries are fried. Serve calzone either hot, warm, or cold.

Grated Cauliflower Balls in Tomato Sauce (*Gobi Kofta*)

Kofta are Indian-style vegetable balls of many varieties that are served with gravies and sauces. The most suitable vegetables for making *Kofta* are potato, cabbage, cauliflower, spinach, and white radish. These traditional cauliflower *Koftas* are served with tomato sauce. Try them with other sauces and serve them either as part of a main meal or as an accompanying savoury. *Kofta* balls are great served over hot rice or in your favourite spaghetti sauce over pasta.

PREPARATION AND COOKING TIME: 1 hour
YIELD: about 2 dozen kofta balls.

Tomato sauce

8 medium tomatoes, quartered
1/4 cup (60 ml) minced fresh coriander leaves
1 teaspoon (5 ml) minced fresh ginger

1 teaspoon (5 ml) hot green chilies, minced
1 tablespoon (20 ml) ground coriander
1 teaspoon (5 ml) ground cumin
1/4 cup (60 ml) olive oil
1 teaspoon (5 ml) black mustard seeds
1 tablespoon (20 ml) brown sugar
1 teaspoon (5 ml) salt

For cauliflower balls

3 cups (750 ml) cauliflower, finely minced (a food processor does an excellent job)

1 teaspoon (5 ml) minced fresh ginger

1 teaspoon (5 ml) hot green chilies, minced

3 tablespoons (60 ml) chopped fresh coriander leaves

1 teaspoon (5 ml) turmeric

1 tablespoon (20 ml) ground coriander

1 tablespoon (20 ml) dry-roasted cumin seeds, coarsely crushed

1 cup (250 ml) chickpea flour

1 teaspoon (5 ml) baking powder

3/4 teaspoon (3 ml) salt

ghee or oil for deep-frying

1. To prepare the sauce: boil the tomatoes in 1 cup (250 ml) water in a 2-litre/quart saucepan. Simmer, partially covered, for 15 minutes.

Remove the pan from the heat and cool for 10 minutes; then pour the sauce through a sieve until all of the tomato purée is separated from the seeds and skins. Set aside the purée while preparing the spices for the sauce.

2. Place the fresh coriander, minced ginger, chilies, ground coriander, cumin, and 1/2 cup (125 ml) water in a small bowl. Whisk until smooth.

3. Heat the olive oil in a 3-litre/quart saucepan over moderate heat. Sauté the mustard seeds in the hot oil until they crackle. Add the spice paste and bring to the boil. Simmer for 2 minutes, stirring occasionally. Add the tomato purée, brown sugar, and salt. Bring to the boil and simmer the sauce over a low heat while you prepare the kofta balls. When the sauce thickens, remove it from the heat.

4. To prepare the kofta balls: combine the grated cauliflower, ginger, chilies, fresh coriander, turmeric, ground coriander, and cumin in a mixing bowl and knead until well-mixed. In a smaller bowl, mix the chickpea flour, baking powder, and salt.

5. Heat the ghee in a wok or deep pan over moderate heat until it reaches 180°C/355°F. Combine the cauliflower and spices with the flour and salt. Roll the mixture into walnut-sized balls.

6. Slip 6 to 8 balls simultaneously into the hot oil, and after they rise to the surface reduce the heat to low and fry the kofta for 8 to 10 minutes or until they turn reddish gold. Remove and drain. When the oil reaches 180°C/355°F, fry the second batch of kofta. Remove and drain. Repeat until all koftas are fried. Before serving, place the koftas in a warmed, shallow serving dish and cover with the tomato sauce.

Potato and Cottage Cheese Rolls with Cranberry Sauce

This is my adaptation of a rich and unusual savoury dish from Lithuania. Large baking potatoes are mashed, mixed with fresh cottage cheese, rolled with rich pastry, baked, and served hot with a spoonful of sour cream and cranberry sauce. Present this stunning dish for a special dinner party.

PREPARATION TIME: 30 minutes
BAKING TIME: 30 minutes
YIELD: 8 rolls

2 to 3 medium baking potatoes, boiled and peeled to make 2 cups (500 ml) mashed potatoes

1 cup (250 ml) full-cream cottage cheese

1 1/2 teaspoons (7 ml) salt

1/8 teaspoon (0.5 ml) black pepper

2 cups (500 ml) plain flour

1 teaspoon (5 ml) baking powder

70 g (2 1/2 ounces) butter, cut into little pieces

2 cups (500 ml) sour cream

1 tablespoon (20 ml) butter, reserved

1 1/2 cups (375 ml) cranberry sauce

1. Mix the mashed potatoes with the cottage cheese, 1 teaspoon (5 ml) salt, and black pepper. Set aside.

2. Combine the flour, remaining salt, and baking powder and sieve into another large bowl.

3. Rub the butter into the flour mixture with your fingertips until it resembles a coarse meal. Add half the sour cream to this flour mixture and work into a soft but not sticky dough (you may need to add more flour). Knead the dough on a lightly floured board for a few minutes.

4. Gather the dough into a smooth ball and, with a rolling pin, roll it on the floured board into a 20 cm x 30 cm (8-inch x 12-inch) rectangle.

5. Spread the potato and cottage cheese mixture in a smooth even layer over the pastry. Roll the pastry to form a 30 cm (12-inch) long roll. Cut it into 8 sections.

6. Place the 8 swirls of pastry on a buttered baking tray. Melt the reserved butter and brush it over the pastries. Place the tray in the centre of a preheated 200°C/390°F oven and bake for about 1/2 hour or until the pastry rolls are golden brown.

7. Remove the rolls from the oven and place on individual serving plates topped with liberal spoonfuls of sour cream and cranberry sauce. Serve hot.

Potato Pancake (*Rosti*)

Almost a national dish in Switzerland, *Rosti* makes an elegant accompaniment to almost any main dish. Serve it hot and fresh with a small bowl of sour cream.

**PREPARATION AND COOKING
 TIME: 30 minutes**

YIELD: enough for 4 to 6

**1 kg (about 2 pounds) small
 potatoes, peeled and steamed
 until barely cooked (not soft)**

2 tablespoons (40 ml) butter

2 tablespoons (40 ml) olive oil

1 teaspoon (5 ml) salt

**½ teaspoon (2 ml) coarsely ground
 black pepper**

1. Grate the potatoes coarsely and set them aside.

2. Heat the butter with the oil in a large, heavy frying pan over moderate heat. When the butter melts and the foam subsides, place the grated potatoes in the pan and spread them out into a large pancake, taking care not to press it down too much. Season the potatoes with the salt and pepper.

3. Cover the pan and reduce the heat, cooking for 8 to 10 minutes or until the underside of the potato pancake begins to brown. Shake the pan occasionally to make sure the mixture doesn't stick.

4. Gently turn the potato pancake. Fry another 5 or 6 minutes or until the other side turns golden brown. Remove the pan from the heat and slide the potato pancake out of the pan onto a warmed serving dish. Slice and serve immediately.

Below: Potato and Cottage Cheese Rolls with Cranberry Sauce

PASTA AND GRAIN DISHES

Here's a wholesome collection of vegetarian pasta, noodle, and grain dishes from Greece, Japan, Italy, Morocco, India, and Malaysia.

Pictured: Spaghetti alla Napoletana

Vegetarian Lasagna

Tender pasta sandwiched between layers of tasty béchamel sauce, cheese, spinach, and herbed tomato sauce, topped with more cheese and baked until firm—whenever we serve *Vegetarian Lasagna* at Gopal's Restaurant our clientèle become practically ecstatic. "Could you possibly give us the recipe?" they ask. So here it is. This recipe calls for good quality imported Italian instant lasagna noodles. I like to use "Verde Ondine" instant lasagna. Otherwise, if you choose to use the non-instant variety, precook it according to the directions on the packet.

PREPARATION AND COOKING TIME: 1½ hours
BAKING TIME: 45 minutes
YIELD: 1 tray of lasagna, 30 cm x 20 cm x 8 cm (12 inches x 8 inches x 3 inches)

This lasagna has five distinct ingredients: pasta, tomato sauce, béchamel sauce, spinach, and cheese.

Pasta
about fifteen 17 cm x 17 cm (7-inch x 7-inch) sheets of instant lasagna (400 g, or about 14 ounces)

Tomato Sauce
½ cup (125 ml) olive oil

½ teaspoon (2 ml) yellow asafoetida powder

1 cup (250 ml) chopped fresh basil

1 teaspoon (5 ml) dried oregano

1 teaspoon (5 ml) dried marjoram

2 bay leaves

1 teaspoon (5 ml) freshly ground black pepper

1 medium eggplant, diced into 0.5 cm (¼-inch) cubes

3 medium peppers diced into 1.25 cm (½-inch) squares

24 medium tomatoes, blanched, peeled, and chopped, or six 250 g (9-ounce) tins Italian tomatoes, cut into 2.5 cm (1-inch) cubes (keep the juice)

½ cup (125 ml) black olives, chopped

2 tablespoons (40 ml) tomato paste

1 teaspoon (5 ml) salt

1 teaspoon (5 ml) brown sugar

2 tablespoons (40 ml) chopped fresh parsley

Béchamel Sauce
½ cup (125 ml) melted butter

¼ teaspoon (1 ml) ground nutmeg

½ teaspoon freshly ground black pepper

½ cup (125 ml) sifted plain flour

4 cups (1 litre) warm milk

Spinach
1 large bunch of spinach leaves, separated, stalks removed, washed, blanched in boiling water, and drained

Cheese
375 g (13 ounces) grated cheddar cheese

250 g (9 ounces) grated mozzarella cheese

60 g (2 ounces) grated parmesan cheese

1 tablespoon (20 ml) grated parmesan cheese, reserved for garnish.

To cook the tomato sauce

1. Heat the olive oil over moderate heat in a large, heavy-based saucepan. When hot, add the asafoetida. Sauté momentarily; then add the fresh basil, oregano, marjoram, bay leaves, and black pepper and sauté for another few seconds.

Add the eggplant cubes and stir-fry for 2 minutes. Add the peppers and, stirring occasionally, cook them along with the eggplant pieces until both are softened (about 3 or 4 minutes).

3. Add the tomatoes and olives and stir well. Bring to the boil, reduce the heat slightly, and cook uncovered, stirring often, for about ½ hour or until it reduces and thickens. Add tomato paste, salt, sugar, and parsley, mix well, and remove from the heat.

To cook the Béchamel Sauce

1. Place the melted butter in a heavy saucepan over low heat and stir in the nutmeg, black pepper, and flour and sauté until the mixture darkens slightly (about ½ minute). Remove from the heat.

2. Gradually pour in the warm milk, stirring with a whisk until the sauce is smooth. Return to moderate heat and stir until it boils. Reduce the heat and simmer, stirring constantly until the sauce thickens to a thick-custard consistency (about 5 minutes).

To assemble the lasagna

1. Combine all 3 cheeses (except the reserved parmesan) in a bowl. Divide the tomato sauce and béchamel sauce into 3. Divide the cheese and spinach into 2. Divide the pasta into 5.

2. Spread one-third of the tomato sauce in the bottom of the baking tray. Place one-fifth of the pasta sheets on top. Spread on one-third of the béchamel sauce then another one-fifth of the pasta. Spread one-half of the spinach leaves; then sprinkle half the grated cheese on top.

3. Repeat this process twice more and you should end up with the béchamel sauce on top. Sprinkle with parmesan cheese. Place the lasagna in the top of a pre-heated 200°C/390°F oven and cook for 30-45 minutes or until the top is slightly golden and the pasta "gives" when you stick a knife in it. It's best to let the lasagna set for at least another hour before serving, as this "plumps" the pasta. Cut into squares and serve.

Above right: Vegetarian Lasagna

Potato Dumplings with Tomato Sauce (*Gnocchi*)

Although not a true pasta, home-made *gnocchi* can replace pasta in a meal. These tasty and substantial dumplings originate in the style of the Molise region of Central Italy and are thus known as *Gnocchi alla Molisana*.

PREPARATION TIME: 10 minutes
COOKING TIME: 40 minutes
YIELD: enough for 6 persons

Sauce

3 tablespoons (60 ml) olive oil

1/4 teaspoon (1 ml) yellow asafoetida powder

3 1/2 cups (875 ml) tomatoes, blanched, peeled, and puréed

1 teaspoon (5 ml) salt

1/4 teaspoon (1 ml) freshly ground black pepper

2 tablespoons (40 ml) chopped fresh basil

grated parmesan cheese

2 tablespoons (40 ml) chopped fresh parsley

Dumplings

500 g (17 1/2 ounces) old potatoes

1 1/2 cups (375 ml) self-raising flour

1/2 teaspoon (2 ml) salt

1/4 teaspoon (1 ml) nutmeg

1 tablespoon (20 ml) milk

1. Heat the olive oil in a heavy 4-litre/quart saucepan over moderate heat until hot but not smoking. Sauté the asafoetida in the hot oil. Add the tomatoes, salt, pepper, and basil; stirring occasionally, simmer the sauce for about 30 minutes or until reduced somewhat. Remove from the heat, cover, and keep warm.

2. Meanwhile, peel and quarter the potatoes and boil them in a saucepan of slightly salted water until very tender. Drain well and push the potatoes through a fine sieve into a bowl. Add the sifted flour, salt, nutmeg, and milk. Mix well. Turn the mixture out onto a lightly floured surface. Knead for 2 minutes.

3. Take one-quarter of the mixture and form it into a roll on a floured surface. The roll should be 2.5 cm (1 inch) in diameter. Repeat with the remaining dough. Cut the rolls into 1.25 cm (1/2-inch) *gnocchi* lengths.

4. With two fingers, press each *gnocchi* against a cheese grater (medium holes) to roughen the surface on one side, at the same time making a dent in the other side where the fingers press. This gives the traditional *gnocchi* shape. Repeat with the remaining *gnocchi*.

5. Place one-quarter of the *gnocchi* into a large saucepan of boiling salted water over full heat. The *gnocchi* will go straight to the bottom of the pan and then start to float to the top. When the last dumpling rises to the top, boil for 1 minute; then remove them from the pan with a slotted spoon. Repeat with the remaining *gnocchi* in batches. Add the *gnocchi* to the prepared tomato sauce and simmer uncovered for 5 minutes over low heat. Place the *gnocchi* in a serving bowl and spoon over half the sauce. Serve the remaining sauce and grated parmesan cheese separately. Garnish with chopped parsley.

Baked Rigatoni with Vegetables (*Rigatoni al Forno*)

This is a vegetarian version of the famous Calabrian "*Rigatoni al Forno*".

PREPARATION AND COOKING TIME: 45 minutes

YIELD: enough for 4 to 6 persons

¼ cup (60 ml) olive oil

½ teaspoon (2 ml) yellow asafoetida powder

¼ cup (60 ml) red peppers, diced

3 cups (750 ml) tomato purée

1 cup (250 ml) tiny broccoli flowerets

1 cup (250 ml) tiny cauliflower flowerets

¼ cup (60 ml) cooked green peas

2 teaspoons (10 ml) salt

¼ teaspoon (1 ml) freshly ground black pepper

2 tablespoons (40 ml) chopped fresh basil

½ teaspoon (2 ml) grated nutmeg

1 cup (250 ml) heavy sour cream

¼ cup (60 ml) grated parmesan cheese

⅔ cup (165 ml) ricotta or cottage cheese

½ cup (125 ml) breadcrumbs

300 g (10 ounces) rigatoni *pasta*

1 cup (250 ml) grated mozzarella cheese

1 tablespoon (20 ml) fresh chopped parsley

1. Heat the olive oil in a heavy 4-litre/quart saucepan over moderately high heat. Sauté the asafoetida and diced red peppers for two minutes. Add the tomato purée, broccoli, cauliflower, green peas, salt, pepper, basil, and nutmeg. Simmer covered for 15-20 minutes or until all the vegetables are soft. Add the sour cream, parmesan cheese, ricotta cheese, and breadcrumbs. Remove from the heat and cover.

2. Cook the pasta in boiling salted water until cooked but still firm (*al dente*). Drain thoroughly.

3. Combine the pasta and the vegetable sauce. Empty the mixture into a large casserole dish, smooth over, sprinkle with the mozzarella cheese, and bake in a preheated oven (200°C/390°F) for 10 minutes. Serve hot, garnished with fresh chopped parsley.

Couscous with Vegetable Sauce

Couscous is the most common and well-known of all north African Arab dishes. *Couscous* is a grain product made from semolina, and it is also the name of the famous dish of which *couscous* is the main ingredient. Imported *couscous* can be obtained in some specialty supermarkets, although it can sometimes be a little costly. I have found it is much more economical to purchase a kilo or two from a well-stocked Middle Eastern grocer who has *couscous* in bulk, usually in huge sacks.

Traditionally, *couscous* is cooked in a *couscousier*—a special pot where the grains are steamed on top, the steam being generated from the sauce simultaneously cooking underneath. But if you don't have a *couscousier*, you will find this recipe from Morocco quick and easy. The *couscous* is cooked the "quick" method.

Couscous is always served in a mound with the sauce poured on top, the extra juice from the vegetables sometimes being served separately in little bowls on the side. Serve *couscous* as a filling main course with a spoonful of North African *Hot Pepper Sauce (Harissa)* added to the bowl of extra juice.

PREPARATION AND COOKING TIME: 1 hour
YIELD: enough for 8 to 10 persons

Sauce

3 tablespoons (60 ml) butter

½ teaspoon (2 ml) yellow asafoetida powder

6 small zucchinis, cut into 2.5 cm (1-inch) sections

2 medium green peppers, seeded, cored, and cut into thick strips

2 cups (500 ml) pumpkin, cubed

1 large potato, peeled and coarsely chopped

2 small turnips, cut in half and sliced lengthwise

at least 4 cups (1 litre) water

2 cups (500 ml) chickpeas, cooked and drained

8 medium tomatoes, diced

1½ teaspoons (7 ml) ground coriander

1½ teaspoons (7 ml) ground cumin

2 teaspoons (10 ml) turmeric

½ teaspoon (2 ml) cayenne pepper

2 small hot green chilies, chopped

1½ teaspoons (7 ml) salt

½ teaspoon (2 ml) freshly ground black pepper

Couscous

2 cups (500 ml) water

1 tablespoon (20 ml) oil

1 teaspoon (5 ml) salt

500 g (17½ ounces) couscous

2 tablespoons (40 ml) butter

Pictured: Couscous *with Vegetable Sauce with Hot Pepper Sauce (p. 131)*

To make the sauce

1. Melt the 3 tablespoons (60 ml) of butter over moderate heat in a heavy saucepan or in the bottom of a *couscousier*. Add the asafoetida, zucchinis, peppers, pumpkin, potato, and turnips and sauté for 10 minutes. Add half the water and bring to a boil. Reduce the heat and simmer for 30 minutes.

2. Add the chickpeas, tomatoes, ground coriander, cumin, turmeric, cayenne, chilies, salt, pepper, and the rest of the water, (adding more if needed). Stir well and reduce the heat to a simmer. Cook for another 15 minutes. Towards the end of the cooking time for the sauce, prepare the *couscous*.

To prepare the *couscous*

1. Pour 2 cups (500 ml) water into a large saucepan. Add 1 tablespoon (20 ml) oil and 1 teaspoon (5 ml) salt and bring to the boil. Remove from the heat.

2. Stirring constantly, add the *couscous*. Allow the grains to swell for 2 minutes. Add 2-3 tablespoons (40-60 ml) butter and heat the grains over low heat for 3 minutes whilst stirring with a fork.

To assemble the dish

Pile the *couscous* on a large pre-warmed serving dish. Drain some of the liquid from the vegetables (reserving it in little bowls to serve as an accompaniment), pour the vegetable sauce over the *couscous*, and serve immediately.

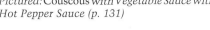

Spaghetti alla Napoletana

The famous city of Naples in Campania, Italy, produces the majority of commercially made pasta. Here is my version of the simple but famous Napolese spaghetti. Serve with a generous sprinkle of your favourite cheese.

PREPARATION AND COOKING TIME: 40 minutes

YIELD: enough for 4 persons

½ cup (125 ml) olive oil

½ teaspoon (2 ml) yellow asafoetida powder

1.2 kg (3 pounds) ripe tomatoes, blanched, peeled, and chopped; or three 400 g (14-ounce) tins Italian peeled tomatoes, chopped (save liquid)

2 tablespoons (40 ml) chopped fresh basil leaves

1 teaspoon (5 ml) salt

¼ teaspoon (1 ml) freshly ground black pepper

400 g (14 ounces) spaghetti

cheese for serving

1. Heat the olive oil in a heavy pan over moderate heat until hot but not smoking. Sauté the asafoetida in the hot oil. Add the tomatoes, basil, salt, and pepper and cook gently for 30 minutes. Meanwhile, cook the spaghetti in plenty of boiling salted water until cooked but still a little firm (al dente). Drain thoroughly and pile into a warmed serving dish. Pour the sauce over the top, sprinkle with cheese and serve immediately.

Pasta Pesto

Genoa, Northern Italy, is the home of the famous *"Pasta Pesto alla Genovese"*—pasta with a pungent sauce called *"pesto"*, made primarily of fresh basil leaves, parmesan cheese, and toasted pine nuts. Traditionally, ribbon-shaped pasta such as *trenette* or *linguine* are used.

PREPARATION AND COOKING TIME: 20 minutes

YIELD: enough for 6 persons

1½ cups (375 ml) chopped fresh basil leaves

1 teaspoon (5 ml) salt

½ cup (125 ml) olive oil (reserve 1 tablespoon, 20 ml)

3 tablespoons (60 ml) pinenuts lightly toasted and chopped

¾ teaspoon (3 ml) yellow asafoetida powder

125 g (4 ounces) grated parmesan cheese

575 g (1¼ pounds) pasta trenette or pasta linguine

1. Crush the basil with the salt and half the olive oil in a large pestle and mortar, or in a food processor. Add the rest of the oil and the pine nuts and three-quarters of the cheese. Blend until smooth. Add a little water if too thick.

2. Place one tablespoon (20 ml) olive oil in a small pan and place over moderate heat. Sauté the asafoetida powder in the hot oil. Add this mixture to the mortar or food processor.

3. Cook the pasta in plenty of salted boiling water until cooked but still a little firm (al dente). Drain thoroughly. Pile the pasta on a warmed serving dish, pour the sauce on top, and sprinkle on the remaining parmesan cheese. Serve immediately.

Pictured: Pasta Pesto

Stuffed Vine Leaves (*Dolmades*)

There are many versions of this stuffed appetizer, found in Armenia, Turkey, Greece, and the Middle East. A *dolma* is actually any dish prepared by stuffing a vine, fig, cabbage, or other edible leaf with a savoury filling. Here is a Greek version of vine leaves stuffed with rice, pine nuts, and currants and flavoured with dill and oregano. They can be served cold as an appetizer with salad, bread, and dips or heated in the oven with tomato sauce.

PREPARATION TIME: 45 minutes
COOKING TIME: 1-1½ hours
YIELD: 30 or 40 dolmades

2 cups (500 ml) boiling water
2 tablespoons (40 ml) olive oil
⅓ cup (85 ml) pine nuts
¾ teaspoon (3 ml) yellow asafoetida powder
1 cup (250 ml) long-grain rice
⅓ cup (85 ml) currants
1½ teaspoons (7 ml) dried oregano
1 teaspoon (5 ml) dried dill
1 teaspoon (5 ml) salt
¼ teaspoon (1 ml) freshly ground black pepper
1 tablespoon (20 ml) tomato paste
two 250 g (9-ounce) packets of vine leaves
juice of 2 lemons

1. Boil the water in a small pan over moderate heat.

2. Heat the olive oil in a non-stick 2-litre/quart pot over moderate heat. Stir-fry the pine nuts in the hot oil until they turn golden. Sauté the asafoetida; then add the rice and stir-fry for 2 minutes. Add the boiling water, the currants, oregano, dill, salt, and pepper. Boil, stir, reduce the heat to low, and simmer the rice covered without stirring for 20 minutes. Stir in the tomato paste. Empty the rice into a bowl and allow to cool.

3. Place the vine leaves in a bowl and scald them with boiling water. Leave them to soak for 10 minutes; then drain and rinse under cold water.

4. Open up each leaf, placing between 1 teaspoon and 1 tablespoon of the filling (depending on the size of the leaf), rolled into a short tubular shape, into the centre of each leaf. Roll up the leaf, tucking in the sides as you go (see illustrations).

5. Place some damaged or unused leaves on the bottom of a large, heavy pot and layer the stuffed leaves on top. If you have more than one layer, place some leaves in between.

6. Place an inverted plate or saucer on top of the stuffed leaves, add enough hot water just to cover them, add the lemon juice, and cover the pot. Simmer for one hour over low heat. After they are cooked, allow them to cool in the pot and carefully remove them.

Fig. 1

Fig. 2

Fig. 3

Malaysian Hot Noodles with Tofu
(Mie Goreng)

The basis of this chili-hot noodle dish is dried Chinese-style wheat noodles. They can be obtained in any Asian grocery or most good supermarkets. The soft, moist varieties of noodle found in the refrigerated display of Asian grocer shops are unsuitable for strict vegetarians since, like most fresh pasta in Italian shops, they contain eggs.

The chili-hot taste of this well-known Malaysian Chinese dish comes from *sambal oelek*, an Indonesian condiment made from minced fresh red chilies and salt. Be sure to obtain plain *sambal oelek*, as other varieties are loaded with garlic and onions. Alternatively make your own. The recipe is on page 177. The dried *tofu* that I use comes in the form of thick sheets about 5 cm x 10 cm (2 inches x 4 inches) and is called "Dry Sliced Bean Curd". *Choy sum* is a delicate Chinese green vegetable available at Chinese grocers. Select young, thin-stalked *choy sum*, cut off 2.5 cm (1-inch) from the base and use the rest.

PREPARATION AND COOKING TIME: 20-30 minutes

YIELD: enough for 10 to 12 persons

375 g (13 ounces) "Dry Sliced Bean Curd"

250 g (9 ounces) Chinese dried wheat noodles

oil for deep frying

400 g (14 ounces) firm tofu cut into 1.25 cm (½-inch) cubes

3 tablespoons (60 ml) Chinese sesame oil

3 tablespoons (60 ml) minced fresh ginger

½ teaspoon (2 ml) yellow asafoetida powder

1 bunch choy sum, chopped into 2.5 cm (1-inch) sections (leaves and stalk)

3 tablespoons (60 ml) soy sauce

2 tablespoons (40 ml) plain sambal oelek (or more if you want hotter noodles)

3 tablespoons (60 ml) fresh lemon juice

2 cups (500 ml) mung bean shoots

1. Soak the dried *tofu* slices in hot water for 15 minutes. When softened, cut into 2.5 cm (1-inch) squares, drain, and pat dry.

2. Cook the wheat noodles in a 5-litre/quart saucepan of boiling water until they are still a little firm (*al dente*). Drain, rinse under cold water, and drain again.

3. Heat the oil in a wok or pan over high heat. Deep-fry the *tofu* cubes until they turn golden brown, remove, and drain. Repeat for all the *tofu*. Next, deep-fry the squares of dried *tofu* until golden and slightly blistered. Remove and drain. Put aside.

4. Heat the sesame oil in another wok over full heat. Sauté the minced ginger for 1 minute. Add the asafoetida and *choy sum* and stir-fry until the vegetables become soft.

5. Add the soy sauce, *sambal oelek*, lemon juice, fried dry *tofu*, fried fresh *tofu*, and bean shoots and stir well. Increase the heat and add the drained wheat noodles. Stir-fry for another 2 minutes or until the noodles are hot.
Serve immediately.

Japanese Rice-Balls (Onigiri)

These traditional stuffed rice-balls, or *onigiri*, are quick and easy to prepare. They are served, as with all Japanese dishes, with great attention to colour and presentation. They are, in fact, not balls, but rather flattened triangular shapes. You will require two special ingredients to make *onigiri*, both available from Japanese or Asian speciality grocers: Japanese pickled plums (*umeboshi*) and yellow pickled daikon radish (*takuwan*).

Serve *onigiri* as a snack, or as part of a special picnic lunch, accompanied by yellow pickled radish, on a plate decorated with fresh green leaves. Allow 2 balls per person.

PREPARATION TIME: 10 minutes

YIELD: 8 balls

1 teaspoon (5 ml) salt

5 cups (1.25 litres) unsalted short-grain white rice, cooked to sticky consistency, and cooled

8 Japanese pickled plums (umeboshi)

2 tablespoons (40 ml) dry-roasted sesame seeds

yellow pickled daikon radish (takuwan) as accompaniment

1. Mix the salt thoroughly with the sticky rice. Roll into 8 even-sized balls and flatten each ball into a wheel shape with a flattened perimeter.

2. Make a slight indent in the side of each wheel with the thumb. Press one *umeboshi* into each hollow, allowing the plum to be visible on one face. Form the wheel of rice into a triangle with two flattened paralled faces. The plum should be visible on one of the faces. Press toasted sesame seeds around the plum on the flat face where the plum is visible and stand the savouries up on one of their three sides. Serve with yellow daikon radish pickles, allowing 2 or 3 small pieces of pickle per person. *Onigiri* with pickled plum will last 2-3 days without refrigeration.

Vegetable and Semolina Pudding (*Upma*)

Upma is a traditional grain dish much loved all over India. It consists of roasted semolina and sautéed spices, with added vegetables and nuts combined with water to form a moist, savoury pudding. Though *upma*'s texture resembles Italian *polenta* or North African *couscous*, its flavour is unique. Served with fresh lemon juice and a little yogurt, it makes a delicious breakfast.

**PREPARATION AND COOKING
TIME: about 30 minutes**

YIELD: enough for 6 to 8 persons

*1½ cups (375 ml) coarse-grain
semolina*

¼ cup (60 ml) ghee or oil

*1½ teaspoons (7 ml) black
mustard seeds*

2 teaspoons (10 ml) split **urad dal**

1½ teaspoons (7 ml) cumin seeds

*2 hot green chilies, seeded
and minced*

*2 cups (500 ml) cabbage,
finely shredded*

1 red pepper, seeded and diced

1 cup (250 ml) diced zucchini

*1 cup (250 ml) peeled
potatoes, cubed*

½ teaspoon (2 ml) turmeric

3 cups (750 ml) hot water

*1 cup (250 ml) green peas, cooked if
fresh, thawed if frozen*

1½ teaspoons (7 ml) salt

1 cup (250 ml) roasted cashew pieces

*2 tablespoons (40 ml) chopped
fresh coriander leaves*

*2 tablespoons (40 ml) fresh
lemon juice*

1. Stir-fry the semolina in a large, heavy frying pan over moderate heat for 6-8 minutes or until the grains darken a few shades. Transfer to a bowl and set aside.

2. Heat the *ghee* or oil in a heavy 4- or 5-litre/quart saucepan over moderately high heat. Sauté the black mustard seeds in the hot oil until they crackle. Add the *urad dal* and cumin seeds and sauté them until they darken; add the chilies and, stirring, add the cabbage, peppers, zucchini, potatoes, and turmeric. Stir-fry for 2 or 3 minutes. Reduce the heat to moderate and continue to cook for another 4 or 5 minutes or until the vegetables are limp and partly cooked.

3. Carefully add the hot water and bring to the boil. Add the cooked fresh peas or thawed frozen peas. Add the semolina, stirring continuously. Add the salt, reduce the heat to very low, and half-cover with a lid, stirring often until the *upma* becomes a light, fluffy pudding (about 10 minutes). If the *upma* appears too dry, add a little warm water.

4. Remove the *upma* from the heat, stir in the cashew nuts and fresh coriander leaves, and serve hot with a sprinkle of lemon juice.

Below: Malaysian Hot Noodles with Tofu

BEAN AND LEGUME DISHES

Beans and legumes are not only rich in essential iron, vitamin B, and proteins, but they're also delicious! Here are some of the many interesting ways to use them.

Pictured: *Lima-Bean and Cheese Croquettes*

Israeli Chickpea Croquettes (*Falafel*)

Falafel are spicy chickpea croquettes. The original Egyptian variety contained dried white broad beans and were called *ta'amia*. In Israel, chickpeas were substituted for the broad beans. *Falafel* are delicious served stuffed inside split *Middle Eastern Round Bread* (*Pita*) dressed with *Tahini Sauce* or *Hummus* and accompanied by green salad.

CHICKPEA SOAKING
   TIME: overnight
PREPARATION TIME: 10 minutes
MIXTURE RESTING TIME: ½ hour
COOKING TIME: 20 minutes
YIELD: 14 to 16 falafel

1¼ cups (310 ml) chickpeas, soaked overnight and drained

½ teaspoon (2 ml) yellow asafoetida powder

¾ cup (185 ml) finely chopped parsley

1 teaspoon (5 ml) ground coriander

1 teaspoon (5 ml) ground cumin

¼ teaspoon (1 ml) cayenne pepper

1½ teaspoons (7 ml) salt

¼ teaspoon (1 ml) freshly ground black pepper

½ teaspoon (2 ml) baking powder

oil for deep-frying

1. Place the chickpeas in a food processor and mince finely. Scrape the minced chickpeas into a bowl. Fold in the herbs, spices, salt, and baking powder. Mix well, knead, and leave for 30 minutes.

2. Form the mixture into 14 to 16 *falafel* balls. If they're too sticky, roll the *falafel* in a little flour. Repeat until all the mixture is rolled.

3. Fill a heavy pan or wok with *ghee* or oil to a depth of 6.5-7.5 cm (2½-3-inches). Heat until moderately hot (180°C/355°F). Deep-fry 6 to 8 *falafels* at a time, turning when required, for 5 or 6 minutes, or until they're evenly golden brown.

4. Remove and drain on paper towels. Cook all the *falafel*. Serve hot, as recommended above.

Below: Israeli Chickpea Croquettes, served with Middle Eastern Round Breads (p.39) and Chickpea and Sesame Dip (p.128)

Buckwheat Puffs

Buckwheat is not really a type of wheat or any kind of grain at all! A member of the *polygonaceae* family, it is related to rhubarb, sorrel, and dock. It is a grain-like food, however, and is rich in protein (11.7 percent), as well as fibre, iron, phosphorus, and potassium. These grain-free puffs are made from buckwheat flour, ground from unroasted buckwheat groats. Serve them warm with plain sour cream or *Horseradish Cream* as a side dish or snack.

PREPARATION TIME: 10 minutes
BATTER RESTING
   TIME: 10 minutes
COOKING TIME: 20 minutes
YIELD: 24 Puffs

3 cups (750 ml) buckwheat flour

1 tablespoon (20 ml) brown sugar

2 teaspoons (10 ml) salt

2 teaspoons (10 ml) baking powder

4 tablespoons (80 ml) yogurt

3 tablespoons (60 ml) melted butter

about 1½ cups (375 ml) warm milk

ghee or oil for deep-frying

1 to 2 cups (250-500 ml) sour cream or Horseradish Cream

1. Combine the buckwheat flour, sugar, salt, and baking powder in a bowl.

2. Add the yogurt and melted butter, and then gradually add enough warm milk to form a thick, spoonable batter. Allow the mixture to set for 10 minutes.

3. Heat *ghee* or oil in a deep pan or wok over medium heat. When the *ghee* is moderately hot (180°C/355°F), carefully place about 6 heaping tablespoons of batter into the oil. Deep-fry the puffs until they are rich golden brown on both sides. Remove with a slotted spoon and drain on paper towels. Repeat for all the batter. Serve *Buckwheat Puffs* warm with a generous spoonful of sour cream or *Horseradish Cream*.

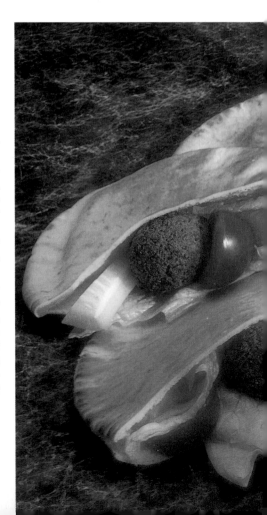

Lima-Bean and Cheese Croquettes

Serve these croquettes with a home-made sauce—such as *Tomato Relish* or *Date and Tamarind Sauce*—or with plain yogurt.

BEAN SOAKING TIME: overnight
PREPARATION TIME: about 25 minutes
FRYING TIME: 15 to 20 minutes
YIELD: 1 dozen large croquettes

Croquettes

1 cup (250 ml) lima beans, soaked overnight in 3 cups cold water

½ cup (125 ml) carrots, coarsely shredded

¾ cup (185 ml) cooked corn kernels

½ cup (125 ml) zucchini, coarsely shredded

2½ cups (625 ml) wholemeal breadcrumbs

1½ cups (375 ml) grated cheddar cheese

2 cups (500 ml) cold mashed potatoes

1 tablespoon (20 ml) ground dry-roasted sesame seeds

1½ teaspoons (7 ml) yellow asafoetida powder

2½ teaspoons (12 ml) salt

¼ teaspoon (1 ml) black pepper

¼ teaspoon (1 ml) nutmeg

1 tablespoon (20 ml) fresh lemon juice

2 tablespoons (40 ml) chopped fresh parsley

1 tablespoon (20 ml) chopped fresh coriander leaves

ghee or oil for deep-frying

Batter

1 cup (250 ml) plain flour

1½ cups (375 ml) water

½ teaspoon (5 ml) salt

1. Drain the lima beans. Boil them in unsalted water until soft. Drain them and mash them coarsely.

2. Combine all the croquette ingredients (except 1½ cups [375 ml] breadcrumbs) in a large bowl. Mix well. Form into 1 dozen croquettes about 6.25 cm x 2.5 cm x 2.5 cm (2½ inches x 1 inch x 1 inch).

3. Combine the flour and salt and add enough cold water to whisk into a smooth batter with the consistency of thin cream.

4. Heat the oil or *ghee* in a deep wok or pan. When the *ghee* is hot (185°C/365°F), dip a few croquettes in the batter, shake off the excess, roll them in breadcrumbs, and carefully lower them into the hot oil. Deep-fry until golden brown and crisp. Remove and drain on paper towels. Repeat until all the croquettes are fried. Serve hot.

Tomato 'Omelette'

Here's a delicious and unusual dish from Gujarat state in western India. It makes a wonderful breakfast or snack served with fried potato chips, sour cream, and chutney.

PREPARATION TIME: 10 minutes
COOKING TIME: a few minutes per omelette
YIELD: 10 to 12 omelettes

¾ cup (185 ml) tomatoes, peeled and finely chopped

1½ cups (375 ml) chickpea flour

2 hot green chilies, seeded and minced

1 small bunch fresh coriander leaves, minced

1 teaspoon (5 ml) dry-roasted sesame seeds

½ teaspoon (2 ml) turmeric

1 tablespoon (20 ml) sugar

1 teaspoon (5 ml) salt

1½ cups (375 ml) cold water

ghee or oil for griddle frying

1. Combine all the ingredients except the *ghee* or oil. If the batter is too thick, add a little more cold water to obtain a thin, pouring consistency.

2. Heat a heavy cast-iron griddle or non-stick frying pan over moderate heat until very hot. Reduce the heat and brush the griddle or frying-pan liberally with *ghee* or oil. Place 2 tablespoons (40 ml) batter on it and spread the batter as thin as you can. When the underside turns golden, put a little *ghee* or oil around the edges and turn the 'omelette' over. When golden brown on the other side, remove the 'omelette' from the pan. Fold and serve hot.

Spicy Beans with Corn Chips
(*Nachos*)

This simple combination of savoury beans, crisp corn chips, melted cheese, avocado dip, and sour cream can be served as an appetizer or as a snack.

BEAN SOAKING TIME: overnight
PREPARATION TIME: 40 minutes
COOKING TIME: 10 minutes
YIELD: enough for 4 persons

1 cup (250 ml) kidney or pinto beans soaked overnight to produce 2 cups soaked beans

2 tablespoons (40 ml) olive oil

½ teaspoon (2 ml) yellow asafoetida powder

2 teaspoons (10 ml) green chili, chopped

2 teaspoons (10 ml) ground cumin

1 tablespoon (20 ml) chopped fresh coriander leaves

2 tablespoons (40 ml) tomato paste

1 teaspoon (5 ml) salt

200 g (about 7 ounce) corn chips

1 cup (250 ml) grated cheddar cheese

2 cups (500 ml) **Guacamole**

½ cup (120 ml) sour cream

1 tablespoon (20 ml) chopped fresh parsley for garnish

1. Boil the beans until soft, then drain.

2. Heat the olive oil in a small saucepan and sauté the asafoetida. Add the chili, ground cumin, cooked beans, coriander leaves, tomato paste, and salt. Stirring often, cook on moderate heat for 2 to 3 minutes.

3. Arrange the corn chips on a 20 cm (8-inch) pie dish. Cover with the bean mixture and sprinkle the grated cheese on top. Place under a hot grill for 2 or 3 minutes, or until the cheese melts.

4. Top with *Guacamole*, sour cream and parsley. Serve immediately.

Pictured: Spicy Beans with Corn Chips

Dal Rissoles (*Baras*) Baked in Buttermilk

This recipe for *baras* baked in buttermilk has been a popular dish at the famous Hare Krishna Sunday Feasts throughout Australia for decades. I generally cook *baras* for at least 200 persons at a time, sometimes more. So I had to significantly reduce this recipe to a manageable size for home use. *Baras* easily lend themselves to bulk cooking, though, and they are always met with great enthusiasm. The little rissoles are wholesome and succulent and, when tasted, immediately dispel the notion that a vegetarian diet is dull and austere. (**Note**: The buttermilk used in this recipe is the cultured, reduced-fat variety. Yogurt may be substituted for the buttermilk.)

DAL SOAKING TIME: 5 or 6 hours
PREPARATION AND FRYING TIME: about 40 minutes
SECOND SOAKING TIME: about 10 to 15 minutes
BAKING TIME: about 1-1¼ hours
YIELD: about 60 small bara (allow 4 or 5 per person)

3 cups (750 ml) yellow split peas
1 tablespoon (20 ml) ground coriander
2 teaspoons (10 ml) ground cumin
2 teaspoons (10 ml) ginger powder
2 teaspoons (10 ml) garam masala
½ teaspoon (2 ml) cayenne pepper
1 teaspoon (5 ml) turmeric
2 teaspoons (10 ml) salt
1½ teaspoons (7 ml) baking powder
1½ teaspoons (7 ml) yellow asafoetida powder
ghee or oil for deep-frying
hot water for soaking baras
8 cups (2 litres) cultured buttermilk
10 to 12 medium tomatoes, each one sliced into about 5 rings
1 teaspoon (5 ml) sweet paprika

1. Soak the split peas for 5 or 6 hours in at least 12 cups (3 litres) of cold water.

2. Thoroughly drain the peas and, with the aid of a mincer, food processor, or grinder, mince them until they become a coarse paste. Add all the spices (except the paprika), the baking powder, and salt. Knead the mixture well.

3. Press out the paste on a flat, smooth surface until it is uniformly 1.25 cm (½-inch) thick. With a biscuit cutter or similar round object, cut out 3.75 cm (1½-inch) disks. With a spatula transfer the disks onto an oiled tray. Gather the remaining mixture and cut out some more disks, repeating until all the mixture has been used up.

4. Heat the *ghee* or oil until fairly hot (180°C/355°F). Carefully slip 10 or 12 disks into the hot *ghee* or oil, but do not touch them until they float to the surface. Then you can turn them over. Fry them for about 6 to 8 minutes or until both sides are dark golden brown. Remove and drain. Repeat until all the *baras* are fried and drained.

5. Place all the fried *baras* into a bowl of hot, lightly salted water and allow them to soak for 10 to 15 minutes or until they are soft and slightly spongy. Remove and thoroughly drain, squeezing gently to remove excess water.

6. In a deep 20 cm x 25 cm (8-inch x 10-inch) casserole dish, layer half the *baras*. Pour one-third of the buttermilk on top of the *baras*; then place one slice of tomato on top of each *bara*. Place another layer of *baras* on top of the tomatoes and cover with one-third of the buttermilk. Place another layer of tomatoes on top, cover with the rest of the buttermilk, and garnish with paprika. Place the dish in a pre-heated 200°C/390°F oven. Bake for about 1-1¼ hours or until the buttermilk forms a thick, slightly browned cheesy crust. Serve hot.

Gopal's Famous Vegie-Nut Burgers

Here's a wholesome combination of rice, lentils, and vegetables with spices and herbs in a patty that's first baked, then pan-fried. Serve *Vegie-Nut Burgers* on bread rolls with your favourite sauces, salads, and toppings.

PREPARATION AND COOKING TIME: 1 hour
YIELD: 16 burgers

1 cup (250 ml) cooked short-grain rice (it should be sticky)
1½ cups (375 ml) cooked brown lentils, thoroughly drained
½ cup (125 ml) carrots, coarsely shredded
1½ cups (375 ml) breadcrumbs
½ cup (125 ml) peanut butter
2 tablespoons (40 ml) soy sauce
1 teaspoon (5 ml) Chinese sesame oil
2 teaspoons (10 ml) dried basil
2 teaspoons (10 ml) dried oregano
1 teaspoon (5 ml) salt
1½ teaspoons (7 ml) yellow asafoetida powder
½ cup (125 ml) chopped fresh parsley
1 teaspoon (5 ml) sweet paprika

1. Combine all the ingredients in a large bowl and knead well.

2. Pinch off 16 portions of mixture, roll them into smooth balls, and with wet hands press out the balls into 8 cm (3-inch) patties.

3. Arrange the patties on lightly oiled baking sheets and place them in a preheated, moderately hot oven (200°C/390°F). Bake until the patties dry out somewhat and slightly darken.

4. The burgers can now be refrigerated or frozen until needed. Pan-fry them in butter or oil until they are hot; then use as required.

Mexican-Style Beans and Salad on Fried Tortilla (*Tacos*)

A *taco* is a Mexican corn pancake (*Tortilla*) that's crisped, folded, and stuffed with beans, salad, and cheese. For serving, you can either leave all the ingredients separate or fill the *tacos* ready to go—either way, they're great for party catering, with a minimum of fuss.

BEAN MARINATING TIME: 2 or 3 hours
PREPARATION AND ASSEMBLY TIME: 15 minutes
YIELD: 8 tacos (allow 2 per person)

Bean Marinade
½ teaspoon (2 ml) dry mustard
½ teaspoon (2 ml) ground cumin
1 tablespoon (20 ml) fresh lemon juice
2 tablespoons (40 ml) olive oil
¼ teaspoon (1 ml) cayenne pepper
¼ teaspoon (1 ml) salt

Salad dressing
1 tablespoon (20 ml) fresh lemon juice
3 tablespoons (60 ml) olive oil
¼ teaspoon (1 ml) yellow asafoetida powder
¼ teaspoon (1 ml) brown sugar
1 teaspoon (5 ml) salt

1½ cups (375 ml) cooked and drained red kidney beans
½ small lettuce torn into bite-sized pieces
½ green pepper, cored, seeded, and diced
2 tomatoes, chopped coarsely
1 ripe avocado, peeled, stoned, and cubed
1 teaspoon (5 ml) chopped fresh parsley
½ cup (125 ml) fresh alfalfa sprouts
8 taco shells
1 cup (250 ml) grated cheddar cheese

1. Combine the marinade ingredients, add the beans, and refrigerate to marinate for 2 or 3 hours.
2. Combine the dressing ingredients. Add the lettuce, green pepper, tomato, avocado, and parsley.
3. Crisp the *taco* shells (deep-fry or bake), fold them into wedge shapes, and stuff them with the beans, salad, and sprouts. Top with grated cheese and serve immediately.

Curried Chickpeas

This dish features chickpeas, with their faintly nut-like flavour and smooth texture. Chickpeas are rich in protein-nitrogen compounds. Cooked in this spicy sauce they're great served with *Puffed Fried Breads* (*Pooris*), with *Chapatis*, or with hot *Boiled Rice*.

DAL SOAKING TIME: overnight
PREPARATION TIME: 15 minutes
COOKING TIME: 1 hour
YIELD: enough for 4 to 6 servings

1¼ cups (310 ml) dried chickpeas
6 cups (1.5 litres) water
1 bay leaf
the seeds from 4 cardamom pods
6 whole cloves
5 black peppercorns
one 5 cm (2-inch) cinnamon stick, broken into bits
1 tablespoon (20 ml) cumin seeds
4 tablespoons (80 ml) ghee or oil
1 tablespoon (20 ml) fresh ginger, finely minced
1 teaspoon (5 ml) hot green chili, minced
½ teaspoon (2 ml) cayenne pepper
½ teaspoon (2 ml) yellow asafoetida powder
¾ teaspoon (3 ml) turmeric
2 teaspoons (10 ml) sweet paprika
1 tablespoon (20 ml) ground coriander
1 tablespoon (20 ml) fresh lemon juice
2 teaspoons (10 ml) salt
3 tablespoons (60 ml) chopped fresh coriander or parsley

1. Wash and drain the chickpeas; then soak well-covered in water overnight. Drain.
2. Place the chickpeas, water, and bay leaf in a heavy 3-litre/quart saucepan and bring to the boil over high heat. Reduce the heat to moderate and simmer the chickpeas for 1 hour or until they are butter-soft but not broken. Remove from the heat.
3. Drain, reserving the liquid. Remove the bay leaf.
4. Place ⅓ cup (85 ml) cooked and drained chickpeas in a blender or food processor with a little cooking liquid. Process to a smooth purée. Remove the chickpea purée and place it in a bowl. Set aside.
5. In a coffee grinder or blender or with a mortar and pestle, combine and crush to a powder the cardamom seeds, whole cloves, black peppercorns, cinnamon stick, and cumin seeds .
6. Heat the *ghee* or oil in a heavy 2-litre/quart saucepan over moderately high heat. When hot, stir in the fresh ginger and green chili and sauté for 1 minute. Remove the pan from the heat and add the cayenne, asafoetida, turmeric, paprika, and ground coriander. Add the ground spice powder, chickpeas, lemon juice, salt, the puréed chickpeas, and enough reserved chickpea cooking-water to make a gravy. Simmer for 6 to 8 minutes; then remove, garnish with minced fresh coriander, and serve hot.

Vegetarian Chili

This nourishing combination of beans and vegetables is given an extra protein boost with the addition of crumbled home-made curd cheese (*panir*). To make this a dairy-free dish, add frozen *tofu* that's been thawed and crumbled instead of the curd cheese. (Instructions for preparing *tofu* in this way are included in the recipe for *Vegetarian Stroganoff*.) Chili is delicious served with your choice of breads or rice.

PREPARATION AND COOKING TIME: 30 to 40 minutes

YIELD: enough for 6 to 8 persons

2 tablespoons (40 ml) olive oil

2 hot green chilies, seeded and minced

¼ teaspoon (1 ml) yellow asafoetida powder

½ cup (125 ml) diced green peppers

½ cup (125 ml) diced celery

½ cup (125 ml) cooked corn pieces

3 cups (750 ml) tomatoes, blanched, peeled and chopped

¾ cup (185 ml) tomato paste

3 cups (750 ml) cooked kidney beans (reserve the bean liquid separately)

1 cup (250 ml) crumbled curd cheese or frozen tofu that's been thawed and crumbled

1 teaspoon (5 ml) ground cumin

1½ teaspoons (7 ml) salt

¼ teaspoon (1 ml) freshly ground black pepper

1 teaspoon (5 ml) cayenne pepper, or to taste

1 tablespoon (20 ml) brown sugar

2 tablespoons (40 ml) chopped fresh parsley

1. Heat the oil in a heavy 3-litre/quart saucepan over moderate heat. When the oil is hot, add the minced green chili and sauté for 1 minute. Add the asafoetida powder and sauté momentarily. Add the diced peppers and celery. Sauté, stirring occasionally, for 5 minutes or until the vegetables soften.

2. Add the corn and the chopped tomato and cook, stirring occasionally, for another 10 minutes. Add all the remaining ingredients and simmer for 20 minutes, stirring occasionally. If the chili is too thick, add some reserved bean liquid. Serve hot.

Above: Mexican-Style Beans and Salad on Fried Tortilla

Chana Dal with Potatoes

Serve this thick *dal* with fancy rice, a simple vegetable, and bread.

DAL *SOAKING TIME: 5 hours*
PREPARATION TIME: 1 hour
YIELD: enough for 4 persons
1 cup (250 ml) chana dal
1½ cups (375 ml) water
one 2.5 cm (1-inch) cinnamon stick
4 tablespoons (80 ml) ghee or oil
2 medium potatoes, peeled and cut into 1.25 cm (½-inch) cubes
1½ teaspoons (7 ml) cumin seeds
¼ teaspoons (1 ml) yellow asafoetida powder
1½ teaspoons (7 ml) ground coriander
¼ teaspoon (1 ml) cayenne pepper

½ teaspoon (2 ml) turmeric
1 teaspoon (5 ml) salt
1 teaspoon (5 ml) fresh lemon juice
2 tablespoons (40 ml) coarsely chopped fresh coriander

1. Wash and drain the *dal* and place it in a bowl covered with hot water. Soak for 5 hours. Drain.

2. Boil the *dal*, water, cinnamon stick, and 1 tablespoon (20 ml) of *ghee* or oil over moderately high heat in a heavy 3-litre/quart saucepan with a tight-fitting lid. Reduce the heat to moderately low. Stir once and boil for 15 minutes.

3. Add the diced potatoes, stir once, replace the lid, and continue cooking until the *dal* is tender and plump and the potatoes are soft and tender.

4. Remove the *dal* from the heat and remove the cinnamon stick.

5. Pour the remaining *ghee* or oil into a large frying pan over moderate to moderately high heat. Sauté the cumin seeds in the hot oil until they turn brown. Add the asafoetida, ground coriander, cayenne, turmeric, and salt. Stir once; then add the *dal* and potatoes and stir well. Do not mash the *dal*. Add the lemon juice and fresh coriander. Mix well and remove from the heat, adding a little hot water if required. Serve hot.

Above: Tomato 'Omelette' (p.115)
Right: Dal Dumplings in Yogurt with Tamarind Sauce

Dal Dumplings in Yogurt with Tamarind Sauce (*Dahi Bada*)

I tasted *dahi bada* for the first time at the home of Chandra Shekhar Singh in Jaipur, Rajasthan. His wife had carefully soaked *dal*, ground it to a paste, added nuts, dried fruit and spices, fried little dumplings of the mixture, and then soaked them in water until spongy soft. She then carefully squeezed out the water, smothered them with yogurt and zesty tamarind sauce, and served them with a garnish of freshly ground spices and fresh coriander leaves. It was a sensory and culinary experience I've never forgotten.

DAL SOAKING TIME: 3 hours
PREPARATION AND COOKING TIME: 1 hour
CHILLING TIME: 2 hours
YIELD: 18 badas

For *badas*

1 cup (250 ml) split mung **dal**

⅓ cup (85 ml) split **urad dal**

1 tablespoon (20 ml) minced fresh ginger

1 tablespoon (20 ml) hot green chilies, minced

¼ teaspoon (1 ml) ground caraway seeds

1½ teaspoons (7 ml) salt

¼ teaspoon (1 ml) baking powder

2 tablespoons (40 ml) blanched almonds, minced

3 tablespoons (60 ml) raisins, soaked and minced

For yogurt sauce

1½ cups (375 ml) fresh plain yogurt

¾ cup (185 ml) sour cream

¼ teaspoon (1 ml) salt

For tamarind sauce

1 tablespoon (20 ml) tamarind concentrate

1 green chili, seeded and minced

¼ cup (60 ml) water

2 tablespoons (40 ml) brown sugar

½ teaspoon (2 ml) garam masala

½ teaspoon (2 ml) salt

Garnish

1 teaspoon (5 ml) dry-roasted cumin seeds, coarsely ground

1 teaspoon (5 ml) garam masala

½ teaspoon (2 ml) paprika

a few coriander leaves

1. Wash the *dals* and soak them in cold water for 3 hours. Drain.

2. Blend the drained *dals* in a food processor until the mixture is smooth and creamy. (You might have to add a little water).

3. Combine the *dals*, ginger, chilies, caraway, salt, and baking powder in a bowl. Add the almonds and minced raisins. Mix well. The mixture at this stage should be firm enough to scoop into portions. If not, add a little wholemeal flour. Divide the mixture into 18 *bada* portions.

4. Heat *ghee* or oil (which should be deep enough to cover the *badas*) in a wok or pan over moderate heat. When it reaches 175°C/345°F, carefully lift 6 *badas* into the *ghee* and fry them slowly for about 4 minutes on each side or until they are golden brown and puffed. Remove the *badas*

with a slotted spoon and drain in a colander. Continue frying all the *badas*.

5. Place a 2-litre/quart bowl of lightly salted water next to the stove. Remove the *badas* from the colander and drop them into the salted water. Soak the *badas* for 15 to 20 minutes or until they become spongy and soft.

6. When the *badas* have soaked enough, carefully remove them from the water and gently squeeze out the water by pressing them between your palms. Place them on a plate and refrigerate for at least 2 hours.

7. Combine the ingredients for the yogurt sauce in a bowl and whisk them until smooth. Combine all ingredients for the tamarind sauce and mix well. This can be done whilst the *badas* are refrigerating.

8. When you are ready to serve the *badas*, place 2 or 3 spoons of the yogurt sauce on individual serving plates, place 2 or 3 *badas* in the centre, place more yogurt sauce on top, and drizzle a spoon of sauce on top of that. Sprinkle on the ground cumin, the *garam masala*, and the paprika and garnish with the coriander leaves.

DIPS, SAUCES AND DRESSINGS

Here's a selection of meal enhancing dishes that display a variety of colour, texture, and flavour.

Pictured: Mexican Avocado Dip

Lebanese Eggplant Dip (*Babagannouj*)

This version of the famous Middle Eastern *mezze* (hors d'oeuvre) can be served as an appetizer with breads, salads, and a variety of other nourishing and substantial dishes. This delicious dip has a characteristic smoky flavour from roasting the eggplants until they blacken.

PREPARATION TIME: 10 minutes
OVEN ROASTING TIME: at least 1 hour
YIELD: enough for about 4 persons

2 large eggplants
1 tablespoon (20 ml) olive oil

½ cup (125 ml) tahini
juice of 2 large lemons
½ teaspoon (2 ml) salt
¼ teaspoon (1 ml) coarsely ground black pepper
½ teaspoon (2 ml) yellow asafoetida powder
1 tablespoon (20 ml) finely chopped fresh parsley
1 teaspoon (5 ml) paprika or cayenne pepper

1. Slit the eggplants with a sharp knife to allow the steam to escape whilst baking. Lightly oil the eggplants; then place them in a preheated oven (200°C/390°F). Bake them until the outside is charred and crisp.

2. Remove the eggplants from the oven, scoop out the pulp into a bowl (it should have a smoky aroma), and mash thoroughly. Mix with the *tahini*, lemon juice, salt, pepper, asafoetida, and parsley until it reaches a smooth consistency. If the mixture is too thick, add a little water. Spoon the dip into a suitable serving bowl, pour the olive oil into the centre, and garnish with paprika or cayenne. Serve immediately.

Indonesian Chili-and-Peanut Relish (*Sambal Pecal*)

Indonesian chili-based sauces or pickles are called *sambals*. This *sambal* functions as a dip with raw or cooked vegetables and can also be used as a salad dressing.

PREPARATION TIME: 5 minutes
COOKING TIME: 5 minutes
YIELD: enough for a dip for 4 or 5 or a salad dressing for 10 to 12

oil for deep-frying
¾ cup (185 ml) raw peanuts
3 tablespoons (60 ml) water
½ teaspoon (2 ml) tamarind concentrate
3 medium green chilies, seeded and chopped
1 teaspoon (5 ml) brown sugar
2 teaspoons (10 ml) light kecap manis (Indonesian sweet soy sauce)

¼ teaspoon (1 ml) salt
water
¼ teaspoon (1 ml) yellow asafoetida powder

1. Heat the oil in a wok or pan to 185°C/365°F and deep-fry the peanuts until golden brown. Remove and drain.

2. Mix the 3 tablespoons (60 ml) water with the tamarind concentrate to form tamarind juice.

3. In a blender or food processor, grind the peanuts to a fine sand-like consistency. Add the tamarind juice, chilies, sugar, soy sauce, salt, and 1 tablespoon (20 ml) water and blend or process until it reaches a stiff, grainy paste consistency. Add more water until it reaches a smooth paste consistency.

4. Heat 1 teaspoon (5 ml) oil in a small pan and momentarily fry the asafoetida until it becomes fragrant. Add this to the *sambal*. Blend or process the *sambal* a little more and then remove it from the blender or food processor. Serve warm or at room temperature.

Tartare Sauce

Here are two recipes for this famous sauce, using an eggless mayonnaise base. Both recipes call for capers which give *Tartare Sauce* its characteristic flavour. Non-vegetarians serve this sauce with seafood. However, I have discovered a wonderful karma-free use for *Tartare Sauce*—as an accompaniment to juicy *Curd Pakoras*. Serve this combination with a slice of lemon and amaze your dinner guests!

Tartare Sauce I

PREPARATION TIME : a few minutes
YIELD: almost 1 cup (250 ml)

¾ cup (185 ml) Eggless Mayonnaise II
1 tablespoon (20 ml) chopped green olives
1 tablespoon (20 ml) chopped gherkins
1 tablespoon (20 ml) chopped capers
½ teaspoon (2 ml) salt

1. Combine all the ingredients and refrigerate.

Tartare Sauce II

PREPARATION TIME: a few minutes
YIELD: almost 1 cup (250 ml)

⅔ cup (165 ml) Eggless Mayonnaise II
¼ cup (60 ml) chopped capers
1 tablespoon (20 ml) chopped gherkin
½ teaspoon (2 ml) salt
¼ teaspoon (1 ml) black pepper

1. Combine all the ingredients and refrigerate.

Left: Tartare Sauce served with Curd Pakoras (p. 96)

Date and Tamarind Sauce

Tamarind, the fruit pulp from the pods of the Asian tamarind tree, *Tamarindus indica*, is the most commonly used souring agent in Indian cuisine. When combined with dates, a delightful sweet-and-sour flavour results. This date and tamarind sauce is delicious served with *Potato and Pea Croquettes* or *Cauliflower and Pea Samosas*.

PREPARATION AND COOKING TIME: 20 minutes
SETTING TIME: 4 hours
YIELD: about 1 cup (250 ml)

3 tablespoons (60 ml) tamarind concentrate
2 green chilies, seeded and minced
1¼ cups (310 ml) boiling water
½ cup (125 ml) chopped dried dates
1 teaspoon (5 ml) minced ginger
2 tablespoons (40 ml) brown sugar
1 teaspoon (5 ml) garam masala
½ teaspoon (2 ml) chat masala
2 teaspoons (10 ml) salt

1. Blend the tamarind concentrate, chilies, water, dates, ginger, brown sugar, spices, and salt in a food processor or blender until smooth.
2. Place the sauce in a small saucepan and simmer it over moderate heat for 10 minutes, stirring occasionally.
3. Transfer the sauce to a bowl and set it aside for 4 hours to allow the sauce to thicken and the flavours to mingle. Serve at room temperature.

Greek Cucumber and Yogurt Dip
(*Tzatziki*)

Here's my version of the refreshing Greek cucumber-and-yogurt dip that is great served with crisp raw vegetables. The yogurt is hung for a few hours to drain off some of its whey; then it's folded with shredded cucumber and garnished with fresh herbs. Serve as a dip with chunks of vegetables such as blanched cauliflower and broccoli, squares of red or green peppers, celery wedges, baby tomatoes, carrot spears, or slices of fresh flat-bread.

PREPARATION TIME : 5 minutes
YOGURT HANGING TIME: 2 hours
YIELD: about 2 cups (500 ml)

2 cups (500 ml) plain yogurt
1 medium green cucumber
1 tablespoon (20 ml) fresh lemon juice
1 teaspoon (5 ml) salt
¼ teaspoon (1 ml) coarsely ground black pepper
2 teaspoons (10 ml) olive oil
¼ teaspoon (1 ml) yellow asafoetida powder
1 tablespoon (20 ml) chopped fresh parsley

1. Line a sieve with a double thickness of cheesecloth. Place it over a bowl, spoon the yogurt into it, and allow to drain for 2 hours, preferably in the refrigerator.
2. When the yogurt is drained, semipeel the cucumber, allowing some of the green under-skin to remain. Slit the cucumber in half, seed it, and grate it coarsely. Squeeze out the excess moisture.
3. Empty the drained yogurt into a bowl and add the cucumber, lemon juice, salt, and pepper.
4. Heat the olive oil in a small pan until slightly hot and momentarily sauté the asafoetida until it becomes fragrant. Add the oil and asafoetida to the bowl of yogurt and cucumber, add half the parsley, and combine well. Garnish with parsley and serve chilled.

Mexican Avocado Dip (*Guacamole*)

Here's my version of *Guacamole*, the famous dip or spread of Mexican origin that now enjoys great popularity around the world. In *Guacamole* the creaminess of the avocado combines wonderfully with the lemon and chili flavours. It is great served with *Nachos*, *Tacos*, or as a dip for corn chips.

I have found that the variety of avocado with the purple crinkly skin (known as the *Haas* variety in Australia) lends itself best to this dish.

PREPARATION TIME: 10 minutes
YIELD: enough for 4 or 6 persons

2 ripe medium avocados, peeled and stoned

3 or 4 inner leaves fresh crisp lettuce shredded very finely into long thin strips (chiffonade)

1 medium firm tomato, finely chopped

2 small green chilies, seeded and finely chopped

2 teaspoons (10 ml) fresh lemon or lime juice

¼ teaspoon (1 ml) coarsely ground black pepper

½ teaspoon (2 ml) salt

¼ teaspoon (1 ml) yellow asafoetida powder

1. Cut the avocado flesh into chunks and mash coarsely in a bowl.

2. Combine the avocado, lettuce, tomato, chilies, lemon or lime juice, pepper, salt, and asafoetida and transfer to a serving dish.

Note: If you would like to prepare *Guacomole* a few hours in advance, leave the avocado stone in the mixture. This will prevent browning. Remove the stone before serving.

Above clockwise from left: Greek Cucumber and Yogurt Dip [p.125], Lebanese Eggplant Dip [p.124] and Chickpea Pâté [p.127]

Chickpea Pâté

Chickpeas are a great source of protein and iron as well as fibre, vitamins A and B6, riboflavin, thiamin, niacin, calcium, phosphorus, sodium, and potassium. One cup of chick peas has the usable protein equivalent of one 130 g (4¼-ounce) steak. When chickpeas are combined with dairy products, the usable protein increases.

This chickpea pâté is very tasty and goes well as a dip or spread on bread or crackers.

CHICKPEA COOKING TIME: 1 to 2 hours
PREPARATION TIME: 10 minutes
YIELD: about 3 cups (750 ml)

1 cup (250 ml) raw chickpeas, soaked overnight

1½ teaspoons (7 ml) salt

1 cup (250 ml) sour cream

½ cup (125 ml) finely chopped fresh parsley

1 teaspoon (5 ml) ground coriander

1 tablespoon (20 ml) fresh lemon juice

¼ teaspoon (1 ml) ground black pepper

1 tablespoon (20 ml) olive oil

¼ teaspoon (1 ml) yellow asafoetida powder

½ cup (125 ml) celery, finely minced

1. Drain the soaked chickpeas and place them in a large saucepan with lots of water. Boil for 1 to 2 hours or until they're soft.

2. Drain the cooked chickpeas and blend them in a food processor or blender until they become smooth and creamy.

3. Add salt, sour cream, parsley, ground coriander, lemon juice, and black pepper and continue processing for 2 minutes.

4. Heat the olive oil in a pan and sauté the asafoetida. Add the minced celery and sauté for 1 minute or until the celery becomes soft. Add the celery mixture to the food processor and process a little more. Place the pâté in a suitable bowl and refrigerate until firm. The pâté can be refrigerated for two days.

Tahini Sauce

Tahini is a paste made from the finely ground seeds of the sesame plant, *Sesamum indicum*. It is cream or cream-grey in colour and has the texture, though not the taste, of runny peanut butter. In the Levant, *tahini* is used as a basis for various salad dressings and to flavour the famous *hummus*, or chick pea purée, which I have also included in this book. Here is an ultra-simple but delicious *tahini* sauce which can be served with fresh Middle Eastern breads and any of the following *mezze* or Middle Eastern hors d'oeuvres: slices of cucumber, lemon wedges, fresh raw cauliflower pieces, chunks of carrot, celery, lettuce leaves, tomato pieces, olives, nuts, or chickpeas.

PREPARATION TIME: a few minutes
YIELD: enough for 6 to 8 persons

1 cup (250 ml) tahini

½ teaspoon (2 ml) ground cumin

½ cup (125 ml) fresh lemon juice

½ teaspoon (2 ml) yellow asafoetida powder

1 teaspoon (5 ml) salt

1 tablespoon (20 ml) finely chopped fresh parsley

1. Combine all the ingredients (reserving half the parsley) with the aid of a food processor or blender. The sauce should resemble mayonnaise in consistency. Add a little water if required.

2. Pour the sauce into a serving bowl and garnish it with the reserved parsley. Serve at room temperature.

Tomato Relish

Here's the tomato sauce I use as the basis for many dishes at Gopal's Restaurant. It's ideal served with all types of pasta dishes, including *lasagna* and *gnocchi*. I also use it as the basis for various casseroles and as a dipping sauce. It's great on *pakoras*, especially cauliflower, and it's quick and easy to prepare.

PREPARATION AND COOKING TIME: 20 minutes
YIELD: 2 cups (500 ml)

3 tablespoons (60 ml) olive oil

½ teaspoon (2 ml) yellow asafoetida powder

¼ teaspoon (1 ml) ground black pepper

2½ cups (625 ml) puréed tomatoes

1½ teaspoons (7 ml) minced fresh basil leaves, or ½ teaspoon (2 ml) dried basil leaves

¼ teaspoon (1 ml) clove powder

1 teaspoon (5 ml) salt

1 teaspoon (5 ml) brown sugar

2 tablespoons (40 ml) tomato paste

1 teaspoon (5 ml) fresh lemon juice

2 tablespoons (40 ml) minced fresh parsley

1. Heat the olive oil in a medium sized saucepan over moderate heat. When the oil is hot but not smoking, add the asafoetida and sauté momentarily. Add the black pepper, sauté for a moment, and then add the tomatoes. Add the basil, cloves, salt, and sugar. Bring to a boil; then reduce the heat to low and simmer for 15 minutes, stirring occasionally.

2. Fold in the tomato paste, lemon juice, and parsley, combine and cook for another 1 minute, and remove from the heat. Serve hot, or if you prefer, allow it to cool, put it in a well-sealed glass jar, and use it when required for pasta dishes. This sauce can be refrigerated for about a week.

Chickpea and Sesame Dip
(*Hummus*)

Hummus, a chickpea and sesame dip, is the most popular and best known of the Middle Eastern bread dips. The chickpeas should be soaked the night before you prepare the dip. Serve *hummus* with warmed *Middle Eastern Breads*.

CHICKPEA COOKING TIME: 1 to 2 hours
PREPARATION TIME: 10 minutes
YIELD: enough for 6 persons

1½ cups (375 ml) chickpeas, soaked overnight in cold water

juice of 2 large lemons

1½ teaspoons (7 ml) salt

½ teaspoon (2 ml) yellow asafoetida powder

⅔ cup (165 ml) tahini

2 tablespoons (40 ml) olive oil for garnish

¼ teaspoon (1 ml) paprika for garnish

1 teaspoon (5 ml) chopped fresh parsley for garnish

1. Drain the soaked chickpeas and place them in a saucepan with lots of water. Boil for 1 to 2 hours or until the chickpeas are soft.
2. Drain the cooked chickpeas, reserving the water. Place the cooked and drained chickpeas, the lemon juice, salt, asafoetida, and *tahini* in a food processor or blender. Process until smooth, adding a little reserved cooking water if required to reach a purée consistency.
3. Transfer into a serving bowl and garnish with olive oil, paprika, and parsley. Serve at room temperature.

Béchamel Sauce

In French cuisine, béchamel sauce is considered to be the mother of all sauces because it is the basic white sauce from which so many others are made. It can be used as a flowing sauce or as a base for cream soups. Fold with grated cheese to make *sauce mornay*; pour it onto vegetables and bake it with more grated cheese on top and you have *Vegetables au gratin*; add cream or sour cream and you have cream sauce or sour cream sauce; fold with parsley and lemon juice for parsley sauce; and mix with powdered mustard seeds for mustard sauce.

Béchamel sauce is based on a *roux*, which is a combination of melted butter and flour to which warm milk is added. This recipe makes a thin béchamel sauce. For a sauce thick enough to coat vegetables, such as in *Vegetables Au Gratin*, the quantities of butter and flour are doubled.

PREPARATION AND COOKING TIME: 10 minutes
YIELD: about 2½ cups (625 ml)

2 tablespoons (40 ml) butter

2 tablespoons (40 ml) plain flour

2½ cups (625 ml) very warm milk

½ teaspoon (2 ml) salt

¼ teaspoon (1 ml) white pepper

pinch of nutmeg (optional)

1. Melt the butter in a medium-sized saucepan over moderate heat. Remove the pan from the heat. With a wooden spoon, add the flour to make a smooth paste. Gradually add the milk, stirring constantly.
2. Return the pan to the heat and bring the sauce to the boil, still stirring. Reduce the heat to low and simmer, stirring constantly for 2 or 3 minutes or until the sauce is smooth and thickened. Season with salt, pepper, and nutmeg. Serve immediately.

Italian Salad Dressing

Use this Italian-style herbed dressing on crisp green salads. This recipe makes a large quantity of dressing. It can be bottled and used as required.

PREPARATION TIME: a few minutes
YIELD: 2½ cups (625 ml)

1 cup (250 ml) olive oil

1 cup (250 ml) safflower oil

1½ cups (375 ml) fresh lemon juice

1 teaspoon (5 ml) each of the following: dried oregano, dried basil, freshly milled black pepper, dried sage, dried dill. (If fresh herbs are available use 1 tablespoon (20 ml) of each.)

2 teaspoons (10 ml) salt

2 teaspoons (10 ml) paprika

3 tablespoons (60 ml) honey (optional)

Process all the ingredients in a food processor or blender until thick and smooth. Pour the dressing into a bottle or jar which can be sealed. Refrigerate.

Right: Orange Fluff

Orange Fluff

Here's a gourmet salad dressing with a difference! *Orange Fluff* can be served with savoury or sweet salads with equally stunning results. Add the optional salt and serve with savoury salads, or add the optional honey when serving with fresh fruit salad.

PREPARATION TIME: 5 minutes
YIELD: a little over one cup (250 ml)

1 cup (250 ml) heavy sour cream

2 tablespoons (40 ml) orange juice concentrate

¼ teaspoon (1 ml) finely grated orange rind

½ teaspoon (2 ml) finely chopped fresh mint

1 teaspoon (5 ml) mild honey (optional)

¼ teaspoon (1 ml) salt (optional)

1. Combine all ingredients in a medium-sized bowl. Whip until smooth. Chill and serve cold.

Horseradish and Beetroot Relish
(*Khrain*)

This is a nose-tingling relish due to the presence of freshly grated horseradish. It is also a good example of central European Jewish cuisine. Serve *Khrain* with breads, soups, and savouries.

PREPARATION TIME: a few minutes
YIELD: just over 1½ cups (375 ml)

1 cup (250 ml) horseradish, peeled and grated

½ cup (125 ml) raw beetroot, peeled and grated

2 teaspoons (10 ml) brown sugar

1 tablespoon (20 ml) fresh lemon juice

Combine the ingredients in a bowl and mix well. Serve immediately.

Horseradish Cream

This delightfully simple accompaniment can be used as a relish, dip, or sauce and features the pungent horseradish (*Armoracia rusticana*). The root of the plant is grated and mixed with sour cream in this centuries-old European condiment. The pungent flavour of horseradish is due to the volatile essential oils it contains. If horseradish is cooked, however, most of its pungency disappears. If using fresh horseradish, do not allow the grated horseradish to sit around after grating—it quickly loses its pungency. Fresh horseradish can be obtained from good greengrocer shops. If fresh horseradish is unavailable, substitute with good quality dried horseradish powder. Serve with *Potato Pakoras* or *Buckwheat Puffs*.

PREPARATION TIME: a few minutes
YIELD: 1 cup (250 ml)

¾ cup (185 ml) sour cream

1 teaspoon (5 ml) fresh lemon juice

2 tablespoons (40 ml) freshly grated horseradish or dried horseradish powder

½ teaspoon (2 ml) salt

¼ teaspoon (1 ml) freshly ground black pepper

¼ teaspoon (1 ml) sugar

1. Place the sour cream in a bowl and beat until smooth. Add the lemon juice, horseradish, salt, pepper, and sugar and fold lightly. Chill, or serve at room temperature.

Eggless Mayonnaise

Here are three different recipes for eggless mayonnaise. The first recipe uses condensed milk as the base and is a sweet mayonnaise. The second recipe calls for evaporated milk, and the third is a dairy-free variety featuring puréed *tofu*.

Mayonnaise I

PREPARATION TIME: *a few minutes*
SETTING TIME: 10 minutes
YIELD: about 1½ cups (375 ml)

1 cup (250 ml) sweetened condensed milk

4 tablespoons (80 ml) olive oil

½ teaspoon (2 ml) salt

1 teaspoon (5 ml) mustard powder

4 tablespoons (80 ml) fresh lemon juice

¼ teaspoon (1 ml) black pepper

1. Combine all the ingredients except the lemon juice in a bowl. Gradually add the lemon juice whilst stirring with a whisk until the dressing thickens. Allow the mayonnaise to set for a further 10 minutes in the refrigerator.

Mayonnaise II

PREPARATION TIME: *a few minutes*
SETTING TIME: 10 minutes
YIELD: about 2¼ cups (560 ml)

1 cup (250 ml) evaporated milk (unsweetened)

1 cup (250 ml) safflower oil

½ teaspoon (2 ml) salt

1 teaspoon (5 ml) honey (optional)

4 tablespoons (80 ml) fresh lemon juice

1 teaspoon (5 ml) mustard powder

1. Place the evaporated milk in a blender. While the blender is on, gradually add the oil until the mixture slightly thickens. Add the salt, optional honey, lemon juice, and mustard powder. Continue blending until the mixture thickens further. Allow the mayonnaise to set for a further 10 minutes in the refrigerator.

Mayonnaise III

PREPARATION TIME: *a few minutes*
SETTING TIME: 10 minutes
YIELD: almost 2½ cups (625 ml)

2 cups (500 ml) mashed firm tofu

½ cup (125 ml) olive oil

4 tablespoons (80 ml) fresh lemon juice

1 teaspoon (5 ml) mustard powder

2 teaspoons (10 ml) honey (optional)

1 teaspoon (5 ml) salt

water (if required)

1. Combine all ingredients (except the lemon juice and water) in a blender. Blend until smooth and creamy. Gradually add the lemon juice. If the mayonnaise is too thick, add a little water. Refrigerate.

Hot-Pepper Sauce (*Harissa*)

This famous pungent sauce from North Africa is made from fresh hot red chilies and is a must for hot sauce *aficionados*. It is used as a condiment or as a dip to accompany *couscous*.

Serve with *Moroccan Couscous with Vegetable Sauce* or with *Middle Eastern Round Breads (Pita)* and a selection of Middle Eastern *mezze* (entrées).

PREPARATION TIME: 10 minutes
YIELD: 1½ cups (375 ml)

225 g (8 ounces) fresh hot red chilies, seeded

½ teaspoon (2 ml) yellow asafoetida powder

1 teaspoon (5 ml) ground caraway seeds

1 teaspoon (5 ml) salt

1½ teaspoons (7 ml) freshly ground black pepper

1½ teaspoons (7 ml) ground cumin

1 teaspoon (5 ml) ground coriander

olive oil

1. Place the chilies in a blender or food processor. Process until coarsely ground.

2. Add the remaining ingredients (except the olive oil) and process until almost smooth. Store the sauce in a small jar and top with a thin layer of olive oil. Refrigerate until required.

Walnut Sauce

This Italian purée-like sauce is called *"salsa di noci"*. It's great served with vegetarian rissoles or burgers, especially good with hot pasta, and can be prepared in minutes.

PREPARATION TIME: 10 minutes
YIELD: enough for 4 persons

½ cup (125 ml) walnut pieces

2 tablespoons (40 ml) finely chopped fresh marjoram or parsley

3 tablespoons (60 ml) cold water

½ cup (125 ml) heavy cream

1 tablespoon (20 ml) extra virgin olive oil

½ teaspoon (2 ml) salt

¼ teaspoon (1 ml) black pepper

1. Grind the walnuts to a paste in a food processor. Add the fresh herbs and water. Grind further. Transfer the nut-and-herb paste to a bowl. Fold in the cream, blending thoroughly. The paste should be fairly soft and pale green.

2. Gradually add the olive oil, salt, and pepper and refrigerate the sauce until ready to serve.

Left: Buckwheat Puffs (p.114) served with Eggless Mayonnaise

Satay Sauce

Satay sauce is delicious served with a variety of fried savouries. This recipe yields a fairly hot sauce. Adjust chilies as desired.

PREPARATION TIME: a few minutes
COOKING TIME: 15 minutes
YIELD: just under 2 cups (500 ml)

1 tablespoon (20 ml) olive oil

1 teaspoon (5 ml) minced fresh ginger

1 tablespoon (20 ml) hot green chilies, minced

¼ teaspoon (1 ml) yellow asafoetida powder

1½ cups (375 ml) tomato purée.

1½ teaspoons (7 ml) ground cumin

3 tablespoons (60 ml) peanut butter

4 tablespoons (80 ml) coconut milk

1½ teaspoons (7 ml) brown sugar

1 teaspoon (5 ml) salt

1 tablespoon (20 ml) minced parsley

1 tablespoon (20 ml) lemon juice

1. Heat the olive oil in a heavy pan until almost smoking. Sauté the ginger and chilies until they start to brown; then add the asafoetida. Sauté for just a few seconds; then add the tomato purée. Stirring often, bring the purée to a boil. Reduce the heat to low and simmer for 5 minutes.

2. Add the ground cumin and peanut butter, stirring the sauce until the peanut butter melts. Blend the coconut milk, sugar, salt, parsley, and lemon juice with the peanut butter and remove the sauce from the heat. Whisk until smooth. This sauce is best served hot.

French Salad Dressing

This simple French salad dressing can be used with *French Steamed Vegetable Salad* or crisp salads of your choice.

PREPARATION TIME: a few minutes
YIELD: 1½ cups (375 ml)

⅔ cup (165 ml) fresh lemon juice

½ teaspoon (2 ml) dry mustard

1 cup (250 ml) extra virgin olive oil

1 teaspoon (5 ml) salt

1 teaspoon (5 ml) freshly ground black pepper

1. Place all the ingredients in a food processor or blender and process at high speed for a short time. Bottle and refrigerate.

Cantonese Black Bean Sauce

Black beans are soya beans that have been fermented with malt, salt, and flour. *Black Bean Sauce* can accompany fried savoury items or can be used as a base in vegetable dishes.

PREPARATION TIME: 5 minutes
COOKING TIME: 10 minutes
YIELD: 1 cup (250 ml)

½ teaspoon (2 ml) chili oil
1½ teaspoons (7 ml) peanut oil
¼ teaspoon (1 ml) yellow asafoetida powder

¼ cup (60 ml) Chinese dried black beans
½ cup (125 ml) water
2 tablespoons (40 ml) soy sauce
1 teaspoon (5 ml) brown sugar
1 tablespoon (20 ml) corn flour mixed with 1 tablespoon (20 ml) water, as a thickening paste

1. Heat the chili oil and peanut oil together in a pan or wok. Momentarily sauté the asafoetida; then add the dried black beans and increase the heat to full. Sauté the beans, breaking them up a little, for 1 or 2 minutes. Add the water and place a lid on the pan or wok. Allow the beans to simmer and soften for another 2 minutes.

2. After the beans become soft, add the soy sauce and sugar and, stirring slowly, add the thickening paste. When the sauce thickens, remove the pan from the heat.

Serve this sauce immediately or let it cool and store it in the refrigerator to use as a sauce base for stir-fried vegetable dishes.

Mustard Sauce

This combination of dry mustard and sour cream can be served as a dip with raw salad vegetables or as an accompaniment to *Vegetables Fritters (Pakoras)*.

PREPARATION TIME: 15 minutes
YIELD: about 2 cups (500 ml)

6 teaspoons (30 ml) prepared mustard powder
2 tablespoons (40 ml) cold water
2 cups (500 ml) sour cream

½ teaspoon (2 ml) salt
¼ teaspoon (1 ml) freshly ground black pepper
¼ teaspoon (1 ml) yellow asafoetida powder
1 tablespoon (20 ml) minced fresh parsley

1. Combine the mustard and the cold water in a small bowl and set aside for 15 minutes.

2. Combine the sour cream, mustard paste, and all the other ingredients. Mix well and serve chilled, or at room temperature.

Syrian Yogurt-Cheese (*Labneh*)

In Middle Eastern cuisine, the ever-popular hors d'oeuvre is called *mezze*. Sometimes this abundant variety of mainly vegetarian entrées becomes the whole meal. Other famous *mezze* included in this book are *Hummus, Lebanese Eggplant Dip (Babbaganouj), Falafel,* and *Tabbouleh. Labneh,* a delightfully simple yogurt dip made from yogurt cheese, serves as a wonderful dip for fresh *Middle Eastern Round Bread (Pita)*.

YOGURT DRAINING TIME: 12 to 16 hours
PREPARATION TIME: a few minutes
YIELD: 2 cups (500 ml) (for 6 to 8 persons)

4 cups (1 litre) plain yogurt
½ teaspoon (2 ml) salt
1 tablespoon (20 ml) chopped fresh mint or 1 teaspoon (5 ml) dried mint for garnish
2 tablespoons (40 ml) extra virgin olive oil

1. Fold a large piece of damp cheesecloth in half and place it over a bowl. Pour the yogurt into the cloth, tie the corners of the cloth together with string, and suspend it over the top of the bowl overnight. Yogurt can also be hung in the refrigerator.

2. Next day, transfer the yogurt cheese from the cloth to a clean bowl, add the salt, and chill for some time (if necessary). Serve the dip garnished with chopped fresh mint and drizzle olive oil on top of the dip. Serve chilled.

Right: Vegetarian Spring rolls (p.93) served with Sweet-and-Sour Sesame Sauce

Sweet-and-Sour Sesame Sauce

This traditional sesame sauce, with a rich strong taste, enhances many Chinese savoury dishes. Use it as a dip for *Vegetarian Spring Rolls*, *Vegetable Fritters (Pakoras)*, or savouries of your choice.

PREPARATION TIME: *a few minutes*
COOKING TIME: *5 minutes*
YIELD: *about 1 cup (250 ml)*

4 tablespoons (80 ml) brown sugar

4 tablespoons (80 ml) salty soy sauce

4 tablespoons (80 ml) water

2 teaspoons (10 ml) Chinese sesame paste

2 teaspoons (10 ml) Chinese sesame oil

2 tablespoons (40 ml) fresh lemon juice

1 teaspoon (5 ml) Chinese chili oil

tiny pinch Chinese 5-spice

½ teaspoon (2 ml) fresh green chilies, seeded and minced

2 teaspoons (10 ml) minced fresh coriander leaves

1. Combine all the ingredients (except the fresh coriander leaves) in a small pan. Heat the sauce ingredients over low heat until a smooth sauce forms. Bring the sauce to a near boil, remove from the heat, add the fresh herb, and serve at room temperature.

SWEETS AND DESSERTS

"A meal is not complete without a sweet." With that in mind, why not plan your next meal with something from the following section?

Pictured: Baked Cheesecake

Carob and Hazelnut Fudge (*Burfi*)

As distinct from *Coconut Cream Fudge* which calls for the traditional method of cooking milk to a fudge by the process of slow reduction, here's a quick alternative using powdered milk. Flavoured with roasted hazelnuts and carob powder, it's a popular confectionery to make for special bulk catering.

PREPARATION TIME: 20 minutes
YIELD: 24 pieces

1 cup (250 ml) milk

¾ cup (185 ml) white sugar

3 tablespoons (60 ml) unsalted butter, softened

2 tablespoons (40 ml) carob powder

1¾ cups (435 ml) full-cream powdered milk (or as needed)

½ cup (85 ml) chopped, toasted hazelnuts

1. Combine the milk and sugar in a heavy-based 3-litre/quart nonstick saucepan and place over moderately low heat. Stir until the sugar dissolves; then raise the heat slightly and gently boil for 10 minutes. Remove the pan from the heat. Put aside for 5 minutes.

2. Combine the butter with the carob powder and mix into a paste. Add this paste to the milk syrup and, stirring constantly with a wire whisk, add the milk powder. When the mixture is smooth, place the pan over moderate heat and stir with a wooden spoon for about 4 minutes or until the mixture is reduced to a thick paste that draws away from the sides of the pan. Fold in the nuts.

3. Press the paste onto a buttered biscuit sheet and spread, pat, and mold the mixture into a square cake about 2 cm (³⁄₄ inch) thick. Refrigerate and, when cool, cut the fudge into 24 pieces. Keep the *burfi* refrigerated in an airtight container.

Carrot Cake

This moist carrot cake has a spicy, rich flavour and is iced with a vanilla cream-cheese frosting.

PREPARATION TIME: 15 minutes
BAKING TIME: 1 hour
YIELD: one 20 cm (8-inch) cake

3 teaspoons (15 ml) fresh lemon juice

1¼ cup (310 ml) milk

²⁄₃ cup (165 ml) corn oil

2 teaspoons (10 ml) finely grated orange rind

¾ cup (185 ml) soft brown sugar

3 teaspoons (15 ml) pure vanilla extract

1½ cups (375 ml) wholemeal pastry flour

1½ cups (375 ml) unbleached plain flour

1½ teaspoons (7 ml) baking powder

1½ teaspoons (7 ml) ground cinnamon

½ teaspoon (2 ml) ground cloves

½ teaspoon (2 ml) salt

1½ cups (375 ml) carrots, coarsely grated (packed)

½ cup (125 ml) chopped walnuts

Frosting

250 g (9 ounces) cream cheese, softened

¼ cup (60 ml) butter, softened

¼ cup (60 ml) icing sugar

1 teaspoon (5 ml) pure vanilla essence

1. Preheat the oven to 180°C/355°F.
2. Add the lemon juice to the milk and sour it.
3. Cream the oil, orange rind, and sugar and add the soured milk and vanilla.
4. Sift the flours together with the baking powder, spices, and salt. Add the liquid ingredients and beat until the mixture is smooth; then add the grated carrots and the nuts.
5. Butter a deep 20 cm (8-inch) cake tin. Pour in the batter and bake at 180°C/355°F for one hour or until a toothpick inserted into the centre of the cake comes out clean.
6. Allow the cake to cool in the tin until it pulls away from the sides of the pan; then, holding a cake rack over the pan, reverse the pan and allow the cake to fall out onto the rack.
7. Allow the cake to cool; then carefully lift it from the rack and place it on a serving plate.
8. Cream the frosting ingredients together with a beater and frost the cake.

Use within 2 days.

Pictured: Mango Ice Cream

Baked Cheesecake

Baked cheesecakes are rich and opulent and are a treat served with whipped cream and fresh sliced fruits.

PREPARATION TIME: 20 minutes
BAKING TIME: at least 1¼ hours
REFRIGERATION AND SETTING TIME: 24 hours
YIELD: one 20 cm (8-inch) cheesecake

Crust

¼ cup (60 ml) softened butter

¼ cup (60 ml) sugar

1 teaspoon (5 ml) pure vanilla essence

1 cup (250 ml) unbleached plain flour

1 teaspoon (5 ml) baking powder

Filling

500 g (17½ ounces) ricotta cheese

500 g (17½ ounces) softened cream cheese

⅓ cup (85 ml) fresh lemon juice

1½ cups (375 ml) sugar

2 tablespoons (40 ml) arrowroot powder, or 1 tablespoon (20 ml) cornflour

1⅓ cups (335 ml) fresh cream

1½ teaspoons (7 ml) pure vanilla essence

1. To prepare the crust: cream the butter and sugar and add the vanilla. Sift the flour and the baking powder. Combine the flour mixture with the creamed butter and sugar mixture. Pat it into the bottom of a buttered 25 cm (10-inch) cheesecake pan.

2. To prepare the filling: place all the ingredients in a large bowl and mix thoroughly with a beater until light and fluffy. Do not over-mix. Spoon the mixture into the pan on top of the uncooked crust.

3. Place in the middle of a pre-heated 180°C/355°F oven and bake for 1¼ hours or until lightly golden brown on top. The cake is done when the entire surface is golden brown.

4. Remove the cheesecake from the oven; allow it to cool. Refrigerate it for at least 20 to 24 hours before serving. Decorate it with cream and fruits if desired.

Mango Ice Cream

This delicious ice cream recipe uses a condensed milk and cream combination. It is best to make this ice cream when mangoes are in the peak of season, soft, ripe, and fragrant.

PREPARATION TIME: 15 minutes
FREEZING TIME: 10 to 12 hours
YIELD: enough for 6 persons

1½ cups (375 ml) heavy cream

1 cup (250 ml) cold milk

1 cup (250 ml) sweetened condensed milk

1½ cups (375 ml) fresh mango pulp

1. Pour the cream into a bowl and beat it until semi-whipped.

2. Beat the milk and condensed milk together in another bowl until well combined.

3. Pour the milk and condensed milk mixture into the semi-whipped cream and fold in the mango pulp. Mix well.

4. Pour into a metal freezer tray and freeze for about 10 to 12 hours or until solid. About an hour before serving, place the ice cream in the refrigerator to soften slightly.

Walnut and Raisin Semolina Halava

Semolina Halava is the most popular dessert served at any of the Gopal's Restaurants worldwide. This version of the famous hot, fluffy pudding—with juicy raisins, raw sugar, and walnut pieces—rates high in the "*halava*-top-ten". I have cooked *halava* for 4 or 5 persons and for 1500 persons; either way, following the same basic steps yields equally stunning results.

The secret of good *halava* is to roast the semolina very slowly for at least 20 minutes, with enough butter so as not to scorch the grains. Steam the finished *halava* over very low heat with a tight-fitting lid for 5 minutes to fully plump the semolina grains; then allow it to sit covered for another 5 minutes. Fluffy, plump-grained *halava* is best served hot, with a spoonful of cream or custard.

**PREPARATION AND COOKING
    TIME: about 30 minutes**
YIELD: enough for 6 to 8 persons

2½ cups (625 ml) water
1¼ cups (310 ml) raw sugar
½ cup (125 ml) raisins
140 g (5 ounces) unsalted butter
*1¼ cups (310 ml) coarse-grained
    semolina*
⅓ cup (85 ml) walnut pieces

1. Combine the water, sugar, and raisins in a 2-litre/quart saucepan. Place over moderate heat, stirring to dissolve the sugar. Bring to the boil, then reduce the heat to very low and cover with a tight-fitting lid.

2. Place the butter in a 2- or 3-litre/quart non-stick saucepan and over fairly low heat, stirring occasionally, melt the butter without scorching. Add the semolina. Slowly and rhythmically stir-fry the grains until they darken to a tan colour and become aromatic (about 20 minutes). (Add the walnut pieces about half-way through the roasting.) Stirring more carefully, raise the heat under the grains.

3. Raise the heat under the sugar water and bring the syrup to a rolling boil. Remove the saucepan of semolina and butter from the heat, slowly pouring the hot syrup into the semolina, stirring steadily. The grains may at first splutter, but will quickly cease as the liquid is absorbed.

4. Return the pan to the stove and stir steadily over low heat until the grains fully absorb the liquid, start to form into a pudding-like consistency, and pull away from the sides of the pan. Place a tight-fitting lid on the saucepan and cook over the lowest possible heat for 5 minutes. Turn off the heat, allow the *halava* to steam, covered, for an additional 5 minutes. Serve hot in dessert bowls as it is, or with the toppings suggested above.

---

*Above: Walnut and Raisin
Semolina Halava*

138

Apple and Blackberry Crumble

This version of the famous English dessert has delighted customers at Gopal's Restaurant in Melbourne for many years. Succulent stewed apples, folded with fresh blackberries, are baked with a buttery, crunchy topping and served with cream or hot custard.

PREPARATION AND COOKING TIME: 15 minutes

BAKING TIME: 20 minutes

YIELD: enough for 6 to 8 persons

6 medium green apples, peeled, cored, and thinly sliced

1½ cups (375 ml) fresh blackberries (or try raspberries, loganberries, or boysenberries)

1 tablespoon (20 ml) sugar

1 tablespoon (20 ml) fresh lemon juice

¾ cup (185 ml) raw oats

½ cup (125 ml) unbleached plain flour

½ cup (125 ml) wholemeal flour

½ cup (125 ml) raw sugar

½ cup (125 ml) brown sugar

½ cup (125 ml) melted butter

1. Place the sliced apples along with a sprinkle of water in a heavy 4-litre/quart saucepan. Cook covered over moderate heat until the apples soften. Fold in the fresh berries, one tablespoon (20 ml) sugar, and lemon juice. Remove from the heat.

2. In a bowl, combine the raw oats, unbleached plain flour, wholemeal flour, raw sugar, brown sugar, and melted butter, rubbing in the butter until a coarse meal-like consistency is achieved.

3. Spread the cooked apples and berries in the bottom of a 20 cm (8-inch) ovenproof baking dish. Without pressing down, spoon on all the topping.

4. Place the dish in the top one-third of a preheated 180°C/355°F oven and bake for 20 minutes or until the topping is golden brown. Serve hot.

Orange and Currant Simply Wonderfuls

Simply Wonderfuls are fudge-like sweets made from butter, sugar, and milk powder. They require no cooking—combine the ingredients, and the result is simply wonderful!

PREPARATION TIME: 20 minutes

YIELD: about 15 sweets

1¼ cups (310 ml) sifted icing sugar

190 g (7 ounces) unsalted butter

½ teaspoon (2 ml) finely grated orange rind

2 tablespoons (40 ml) currants

1½ cups (375 ml) sifted full cream milk powder

1. Cream the butter, sugar, and orange rind in a mixing bowl.

2. Fold in the currants and powdered milk and knead until a firm fondant-like dough is formed. Pinch off walnut-sized portions and roll into smooth even-sized balls. Chill and serve.

Pictured: Deep-Fried Milk Balls in Rose Syrup (p.140)

Deep-Fried Milk Balls in Rose Syrup (*Gulab Jamun*)

Whenever a special festival or feast day comes around, *Gulab Jamuns* are an ideal choice. When guests are confronted with them for the first time they invariably ask "What are they?" Guesses then range from preserved fruits to doughnuts. In fact, *Gulab Jamuns* are made from just milk powder and flour. They're fried slowly in *ghee* until golden brown and then soaked in rose-scented sugar syrup. Hence, the Hindi words *Gulab jamun* meaning "rose ball".

It is important to note that even though it only takes a few minutes to mix the dough, the *gulab jamuns* must be fried slowly. If you cook the *gulab jamuns* too quickly, they will be raw inside. They also must be constantly stirred.

PREPARATION AND COOKING TIME: about 45 minutes
YIELD: 20 gulab jamuns

4 cups (1 litre) water
3³/₄ cups (935 ml) sugar
5 teaspoons (25 ml) pure distilled rose water
ghee for deep-frying
6 teaspoons (30 ml) self-raising flour
2¹/₂ cups (625 ml) full-cream milk powder
³/₄ cup (185 ml) warm milk, or as required

1. Combine the water and sugar in a 3-litre/quart pan over moderate heat and stir constantly until the sugar has dissolved. Raise the heat and boil for 5 minutes. Remove the syrup from the heat. Add the rose water and set aside.
2. Pour the *ghee* to a depth of 6.7-7.5 cm (2¹/₂-3 inches) in a non-stick deep-frying vessel at least 25 cm (10 inches) in diameter. Place over very low heat.
3. To make the dough: sift the flour and milk powder into a small bowl. Pour the warm milk into a large bowl. Sprinkle the small bowl of milk powder and flour into the large bowl of warm milk while mixing with your other hand. Quickly mix and knead the combination into a moist, smooth, and pliable dough. Wash your hands, rub a film of warm *ghee* on them, and divide the dough into 20 portions. Roll those portions into 20 smooth balls. Place them onto an oiled tray or plate.
4. When the *ghee* temperature reaches 102°C/216°F, drop the balls in, one by one. The balls will initially sink to the bottom. Do not try to move them. You can, however, gently shake the deep-frying vessel from side to side occasionally until the balls start to rise to the surface. From this point on they must be gently and constantly stirred, rolling them over and over with the back of a slotted spoon, allowing them to brown evenly on all sides.
5. After 5 minutes, the temperature of the *ghee* will have increased to about 104°C/220°F and the balls will have started to expand. After 25 minutes, the *ghee* temperature should be about 110°C/230°F and the balls should be golden brown. Test one by dropping it into the warm syrup. If it doesn't collapse within a couple of minutes then remove all the balls (3 or 4 at a time) with the slotted spoon and place them in the syrup. Otherwise, cook the balls for another 5 minutes. When all the *gulab jamuns* have been placed in the syrup, turn off the heat under the *ghee* and allow the sweets to soak for at least 2 hours.

Gulab jamuns can be prepared a day in advance, allowing them to fully soak overnight. They can be served at room temperature or slightly warmed.

Coconut Cream Fudge

When sweetened milk is cooked down slowly until most of the water has evaporated, the resultant fudge is called *burfi*. This delicious version contains shredded fresh coconut, light cream, and optional *kewra* essence (available at all Indian grocers). Dried coconut can be substituted for fresh coconut.

PREPARATION AND COOKING TIME: 30 minutes
YIELD: 25 pieces

2 cups (500 ml) finely grated fresh coconut
1 cup (250 ml) milk
1 cup (250 ml) light cream
³/₄ cup (185 ml) caster sugar
3 drops kewra essence (optional)

1. Combine the coconut, milk, cream, and sugar in a heavy-based 5-litre/quart saucepan. Boil the mixture over high heat. Stirring constantly, cook the mixture vigorously until it is reduced to about one-half volume. Lower the heat to moderate and continue reducing while stirring rhythmically and steadily until the mixture forms a firm mass that pulls away from the sides of the pan. Add the *kewra* essence.
2. Scrape the coconut fudge onto a lightly buttered tray and press the mixture, with the aid of a spatula, into a 15 cm x 15 cm (6-inch x 6-inch) slab. When it is cool, cut into 25 squares. Store in an airtight container. It may be refrigerated for up to two weeks.

Creamy, Saffron Condensed Yogurt Dessert (*Shrikhand*)

This popular Gujarati sweet is simple to prepare. Yogurt is hung in a cloth to remove excess liquid. The solid residue, called yogurt cheese, or *dehin*, is sweetened, flavoured with saffron, pistacio nuts, cardamom, and rosewater, beaten until silky smooth, and served ice-cold in little cups.

As an alternative, replace the saffron, nuts, cardamom, and rosewater with ¼ cup (60 ml) fresh, vine-ripened chopped raspberries, strawberries, or blackberries.

Shrikhand is ideal for preparing in large quantities. Remember the simple sugar-to-yogurt ratio: good quality yogurt should yield 50% liquid (whey) when hung. Add sugar to the yogurt cheese in the ratio of one to four; in other words, the sugar content of *Shrikhand* is one-eighth part the original quantity of yogurt.

Reserve the liquid residue that drips out of the yogurt. It's a first-class curdling agent to make *Homemade Curd cheese (Panir)*. *Shrikhand* is delicious served with slices of fresh mango and puffed plain flour *pooris* sprinkled with sugar.

PREPARATION TIME: 15 minutes
YOGURT DRAINING
TIME: 12-16 hours
YIELD: enough for 8 to 12 persons

4 cups (1 litre) whole-milk yogurt

¼ teaspoon (1 ml) ground saffron threads

¼ teaspoon (1 ml) ground cardamom

1 tablespoon (20 ml) rosewater (or a few drops of rose essence)

2 tablespoons (40 ml) blanched raw slivered pistacio nuts

½ cup (125 ml) icing sugar

1. Place a triple thickness of cheesecloth in a colander. Spoon in the yogurt, gather-up the corners of the cloth, tie it into a bundle, and hang it either in the refrigerator or in a cool spot for 12 to 16 hours. Catch the drips in a bowl.

2. The residue yogurt cheese should have reduced to half the original quantity. Transfer it to a bowl, add the ground saffron, ground cardamom seeds, rose water, pistacio nuts, and sugar. Beat until light and fluffy.

Chinese Almond Cookies

These simple and tasty almond cookies are great served anytime.

PREPARATION AND COOKING
TIME: 30 minutes
YIELD: 1 dozen

½ cup (125 ml) softened butter

⅓ cup (85 ml) raw sugar

1 cup (250 ml) plain flour

3 tablespoons (60 ml) ground almonds

a few drops almond essence

1 dozen blanched almonds

1. Preheat the oven to 180°C/355°F.
2. Cream the butter and sugar together in a bowl. Add the flour, ground almonds, and almond essence and combine thoroughly.
3. Roll the mixture into 12 balls. Press each ball firmly in the palms of your hands to flatten. Press a blanched almond in the centre of each cookie.
4. Place the cookies on an ungreased biscuit sheet. Bake for 10 to 12 minutes or until golden around the edges. Allow to cool before serving.

Pictured: Creamy, Saffron Condensed Yogurt Dessert

Lemon Cream-Cheese Fudge
(*Nimbu Sandesh*)

Bengal is the home of Indian sweet manufacturing, and of all Bengali sweets, *sandesh* is the most famous. It is prepared from only two ingredients: homemade curd cheese and sugar. Use one-quarter part sugar to the volume of kneaded cheese curd. *Sandesh* is very simple to make, provided you prepare the curd cheese properly. You should also knead your cheese to the correct silky-smooth, neither-wet-nor-dry texture. *Sandesh* must be cooked in a scrupulously clean pan over very low heat. This sandesh derives its lemon flavour from the lemon oil contained in lemon rind, which is added during, and removed after, cooking.

**PREPARATION AND COOKING
   TIME: about 30 minutes**
YIELD: 16 to 20 pieces
**fresh homemade curd cheese from
   10 cups (2.5 litres) whole milk**
**at least ½ cup (125 ml) caster sugar
   or icing sugar**
**one 7.5 cm (3-inch) strip of
   lemon rind**

Pictured: Soft Cakes in Strawberry Yogurt

1. Knead and bray the curd cheese on a clean surface until it is silky smooth and creamy. Gather into one lump and calculate its volume with measuring cups. Measure one-quarter that volume of sugar. Combine the cheese, sugar, and lemon rind and again briefly knead and bray the cheese.

2. Place a heavy-bottomed pan on the lowest possible heat and, constantly stirring with a wooden spoon, cook the cheese for 10 to 15 minutes or until its surface becomes glossy and its texture slightly thickens.

3. Scrape the *sandesh* from the pan and remove the lemon rind. Press the *sandesh* onto a lightly buttered tray into a flat 1.25 cm (½-inch) thick cake. Cool to room temperature. Cut the cake into 2.5 cm (1-inch) squares. When completely cool, store in an airtight container in a single layer. The *sandesh* can be refrigerated for up to 4 days.

Lokshen Pudding

Lokshen pudding is a great favourite in the realm of Jewish cuisine. In this vegetarian version of my mother's recipe, vermicelli (*lokshen*) is baked with sultanas, butter, cream, and ground almonds. It's delicious and simple to make and is great served either hot or cold.

**PREPARATION AND BAKING
   TIME: about 50 minutes**
YIELD: enough for 4 persons

185 g (6 ounces) vermicelli noodles
1 cup (250 ml) heavy cream
2 teaspoons (10 ml) fresh lemon juice
¼ cup (60 ml) ground almonds
⅓ cup (85 ml) sugar
¼ teaspoon (1 ml) ground nutmeg
⅓ cup (85 ml) sultanas
**6 teaspoons (30 ml) melted butter
   (about 1 ounce or 30 g)**

1. Boil the vermicelli noodles in unsalted water until cooked but still a little firm (*al dente*). Rinse and drain.

2. Combine all the ingredients in a large bowl and mix well. Spoon the mixture into a buttered oven-proof baking dish and bake in a moderate oven (180°C/355°F) for about 45 minutes or until it becomes firm and golden-brown on top. Serve hot or cold.

Soft Cakes in Strawberry Yogurt
(*Malpoora*)

This luscious version of the well known Indian sweet *Malpoora* is not traditional but rather something that has been developed over 2 decades in the Sunday Feast kitchens of Hare Krishna Temples around the world. Spoonfuls of thick batter are deep-fried in *ghee* to produce doughnutlike soft cakes, which are suspended in sweetened, fruit flavoured yogurt. You can substitute any fresh ripe berry for the strawberries, or try banana, passionfruit, papaya, mango, or kiwifruit.

PREPARATION TIME: 15 minutes
BATTER RESTING
   TIME: 15 minutes
COOKING TIME: 20 minutes
YIELD: about 2 dozen

2¼ cups (560 ml) self-raising flour
1 cup (250 ml) icing sugar
1¼ cups (310 ml) cold water
ghee for deep-frying
5 cups (1.25 litres) plain yogurt, chilled
¾ cup (185 ml) caster sugar
1½ cups (375 ml) strawberries, washed and quartered

1. Sift together the flour and icing sugar in a bowl. Add the water gradually, while stirring with a wire whisk, until the mixture reaches a consistency somewhere between batter and dough. Spoon in one tablespoon (20 ml) of yogurt and whisk again. The finished batter should cling to a spoon. Allow to set for 15 minutes.

2. Meanwhile, heat the *ghee* to a depth of 6.5-7.5 cm (2½-3 inches) in a wok or deep-frying pan over moderately low heat (160°C/320°F).

3. Spoon out a tablespoon of batter from the bowl. With the aid of a second spoon, deftly slide the batter into the hot *ghee*. Quickly repeat the procedure for about 8 spoonfuls of batter. Allow the cakes to inflate in the *ghee*. Then turn them over with a slotted spoon and fry them, turning occasionally, for about 3 to 4 minutes, or until they are light golden brown all over. Remove and drain. Repeat until all the batter is used up.

4. Combine the yogurt and caster sugar in a large bowl. Crush a few berries through your fingers into the yogurt. Add the rest of the berries and combine well.

5. Carefully fold the fried cakes into the fruit yogurt and refrigerate, allowing the cakes to soak for about 30 minutes before serving. Serve the *malpoora* in individual dessert bowls with strawberry yogurt spooned on top.

Fruit Cake

This traditional fruit cake is ideal for weddings, birthdays, or any special occasion requiring a luscious, rich cake. It can be kept for several weeks after baking.

PREPARATION AND COOKING
   TIME: 2¼-2¾ hours
YIELD: one 20-cm (8-inch) round or square cake

1 tablespoon (20 ml) melted butter
1 cup (250 ml) self-raising flour
1 cup (250 ml) plain flour
450 g (1 pound) mixed dried fruit
1 cup (250 ml) sugar
225 g (8 ounces) butter
1 tablespoon (20 ml) golden syrup or dark corn syrup
1 cup (250 ml) water
1 teaspoon (5 ml) bicarbonate of soda
2 tablespoons (40 ml) yogurt
1 cup (250 ml) smoothly mashed pumpkin or potato

1. Line the base of a 20 cm (8-inch) cake tin with greaseproof paper. Dip a pastry brush in melted butter and brush the sides of the tin to give an even shine.

2. Sift both flours into a large bowl and set aside.

3. Combine the fruit, sugar, butter, syrup, and water in a heavy 4-litre/quart saucepan. Heat slowly over low heat, stirring constantly until the sugar dissolves. Raise the heat and allow the mixture to boil. Reduce the heat and simmer for 20 minutes. Remove the saucepan from the heat, mix in the bicarbonate of soda, and set aside to cool.

4. When the mixture has cooled to room temperature, fold in the yogurt and mashed potato or pumpkin. Beat the mixture until smooth.

5. Gently fold in the flour mixture with the fruit mixture, combining carefully.

6. Spoon the combined mixture into the prepared cake tin. Smooth out the mixture. Cover the tin with aluminium foil (or brown paper secured with an elastic band) and bake in a moderate oven (180°C/355°F) for 1½ to 2 hours. The cake can be uncovered for the last ½ hour of the cooking. To test whether the cake is done, insert a skewer through the centre of the cake. The cake is cooked if the skewer comes out clean. If the cake is done, remove it from the oven, allowing it to cool in the tin. (This will stop the cake from breaking.)

7. When the cake is cool, carefully remove it from the tin and peel off the greaseproof paper. Now the cake is ready for icing, if desired.

Vietnamese Sweet Mung Bean Cakes
(Dau Xanh Vung)

In Thai and Vietnamese cuisine, split mung beans are often used as a stuffing for sweet pastries. This recipe is no exception, featuring glutinous rice flour as the main ingredient for the pastry wrapping. Both split mung beans and glutinous rice flour are available from any Vietnamese or Chinese grocer.

PREPARATION AND COOKING TIME: 1 hour

YIELD: 12 cakes

½ cup (125 ml) yellow split mung beans

1¼ cups (310 ml) water

½ cup (125 ml) sugar (reserve one tablespoon, 20 ml)

2 cups (500 ml) glutinous rice flour

1 teaspoon (5 ml) baking powder

½ teaspoon (2 ml) salt

2 medium potatoes, boiled, peeled and mashed

½ cup (125 ml) boiling water

4 tablespoons (80 ml) sesame seeds

oil for deep frying

To make the filling

1. Thoroughly rinse the mung beans under cold running water. Boil the beans and water in a saucepan over full heat. Reduce the heat and simmer for about 25 minutes or until the beans are soft and tender. Raise the heat to evaporate the rest of the water and when the beans are dry, remove the saucepan from the heat. Mash the beans and add the ½ cup (125 ml) sugar. Return the saucepan to the heat and cook until the mixture thickens and leaves the sides of the pan. Transfer the bean mixture to a plate and allow it to cool.

To make the pastry wrapping

1. Combine the glutinous rice flour, baking powder, salt, the reserved sugar, and mashed potatoes, and mix well. Slowly add the boiling water. Knead the mixture into a smooth ball.

To prepare the cakes

1. Divide the pastry into 12 even-sized portions, roll into smooth balls, and cover with a cloth. Flatten each ball into a 7.5 cm (3-inch) disk. Place 1 teaspoon (5 ml) of the filling into the centre of each pastry disk and gather the wrapping together to enclose the filling, sealing well, shaping it into a ball.

2. Sprinkle the sesame seeds into a heavy frying pan which has been preheated until very hot. Stir-fry the seeds in the dry pan until they are dark golden brown. Place the sesame seeds on a plate and roll all the cakes in the seeds until completely coated, pressing so the seeds adhere well.

3. Heat the oil to 180°C/355°F and deep-fry the cakes one batch at a time for about 10 minutes or until golden brown.

4. Remove the cakes, drain them on absorbent paper, allow them to cool, and serve.

Easy Apple Pie

Pastry making is not difficult as long as you follow some basic guidelines: keep the ingredients cool; always use cold water and the coldest possible surface for rolling out; measure your ingredients carefully; take care with the amount of flour dredged onto the rolling surface; always roll the pastry in one direction—do not turn it over or overstretch it during rolling; the rolling should be light but firm. Don't handle the dough more than necessary—the less handling pastry receives, the better it is.

PASTRY PREPARATION
   TIME: 15 minutes
PASTRY CHILLING
   TIME: 30 minutes
FILLING PREPARATION
   TIME: 15 minutes
TOTAL BAKING TIME: 45 minutes
   (the top and bottom of the pie are cooked separately.
YIELD: one 20 cm (8-inch) pie

Left: Vietnamese Sweet Mung Bean Cakes
Above: Easy Apple Pie

Pastry

1 cup (250 ml) plain flour

1 cup (250 ml) self-raising flour

pinch salt

155 g (5½ ounces) cold unsalted butter

3 tablespoons (60 ml) caster sugar

scant ¼ cup (60 ml) cold plain yogurt

a little milk for glazing

sugar for sprinkling

Filling

6 to 8 medium green cooking apples, peeled, cored, and thinly sliced

2 tablespoons (40 ml) sugar

½ teaspoon (2 ml) cinnamon powder

1. Sift the flours and salt into a mixing bowl. Cut the cold butter into little pieces and add it to the flour. Rub the butter into the flour with your fingertips until there are no lumps and the mixture resembles breadcrumbs.

2. Sprinkle in the sugar; then add most of the yogurt. Mix quickly until it forms a ball. If the pastry feels a little dry, add a little more yogurt. Gently knead for 10 seconds.

3. Wrap the pastry in plastic wrap and chill for 30 minutes. Preheat the oven to 220°C/430°F.

4. Place the apples, cinnamon, and sugar with a sprinkle of water in a 2-litre/quart saucepan over moderate heat and cook until the apples are soft. Drain any liquid.

5. Roll out two-thirds of the pastry to line a 20 cm (8-inch) pie dish. Prick with a fork. Place in the oven, and cook for 20 minutes at 220°C/430°F.

6. Remove the pie shell from the oven and fill with the apple filling. Roll out the remaining pastry and cover the pie. Trim the edges and seal them with a fluted pattern with your fingertips or a fork.

7. Brush the top of the pie with milk, sprinkle with sugar, and bake at 220°C/430°F for 25 minutes or until golden brown. Allow the pie to cool before cutting.

Italian-style Lemon Doughnuts

A friend's grandmother from Tuscany, Italy, parted with this recipe for doughnuts (called *Bomboloni*). Serve them hot at afternoon tea for a delicious treat.

PREPARATION TIME: a few minutes

DOUGH RISING TIME: 2 hours

FRYING TIME: 5 minutes each batch

YIELD: 15 to 20 doughnuts

4 cups (1 litre) plain flour

¾ cup (185 ml) caster sugar

pinch of salt

75 g (2½ ounces) butter, softened and cut into pieces

3 teaspoons (15 ml) fresh yeast dissolved in 2 tablespoons (30 ml) warm water

finely grated rind of 1 lemon

ghee or oil for deep-frying

1. Sift the flour into a bowl and stir in ⅓ cup (85 ml) of sugar and the salt. Mix well. Make a well in the centre and add the butter, the yeast water, and the lemon rind. Mix well, adding enough lukewarm water to form a soft dough. Knead until smooth, shape into a ball, and cover with a damp cloth. Let it rise in a warm place for 1 hour or until the dough has doubled in bulk. Punch the dough down with your fist.

2. Roll out the dough into a long rope and cut into 15 or 20 even-sized portions. Roll each into a smooth ball. Place on a buttered baking sheet and let rise in a warm place for another hour. The balls should double in size.

3. Heat *ghee* or oil to 180°C/355°F in a wok or deep pan and very carefully lower 3 or 4 doughnuts at a time into the hot oil. Deep fry, maintaining a constant temperature, for about 5 minutes, turning often until the doughnuts are dark golden brown. Drain and dredge in the remaining sugar. Serve hot.

Pictured: Turkish Nut Pastries in Syrup

Turkish Nut Pastries in Syrup (*Baklava*)

Baklava is probably one of the best known of all Middle Eastern sweets. In this delightful version of Turkish origin, sheets of buttered wafer-thin filo pastry are layered with nuts and baked; then they're soaked in a lemony orange-blossom flavoured sugar-and-honey syrup.

PREPARATION TIME: 30 minutes
COOKING TIME: 45 minutes
BAKLAVA SOAKING TIME: overnight, or at least 2 hours
YIELD: about 18 large pieces

450 g (1 pound) filo pastry (about 30 sheets)

250 g (9 ounces) unsalted butter, melted

250 g (9 ounces) finely chopped walnuts (or almonds, pistacios, or a combination)

1 teaspoon (5 ml) cinnamon powder

1/4 cup (60 ml) sugar

Syrup

1 1/4 cups (310 ml) sugar

1 cup (250 ml) water

2 tablespoons (40 ml) lemon juice

1/4 cup (60 ml) honey

1 tablespoon (20 ml) orange-blossom water (available at Middle Eastern grocers)

1. Butter a 28-cm x 18-cm (11-inch x 7-inch) tin. If necessary, cut the pastry the size of the tin. Place one sheet of pastry on the bottom of the tin and butter it with a pastry brush. Repeat for 1/2 the pastry (about 15 sheets).

2. Combine the nuts, cinnamon, and sugar and sprinkle the mixture evenly over the top layer of buttered filo pastry. Continue layering the remaining pastry on top of the nut mixture, again brushing each layer of pastry with melted butter.

3. After the final layer of pastry is placed on top, brush it with butter. Carefully cut the tray of pastry into diagonal diamond shapes with a sharp knife, cutting directly to the base. Bake in a moderate oven (180°C/355°F) for about 45 minutes or until the top is crisp and golden.

4. While the pastry is baking, combine the sugar, water, and lemon juice in a pan, stir over low heat to dissolve the sugar, and then boil for 5 minutes. Remove from the heat, add the honey, stir to dissolve, and add the orange-blossom water. Chill the syrup. Pour the cold syrup over the hot *baklava*. Let set for at least 2 hours, or for best results leave overnight for the syrup to be fully absorbed.

Fruit Fritters with Orange Sauce

These are a popular item on the lunch menu at the Hare Krishna Restaurant in Hong Kong.

PREPARATION TIME: 15 minutes
BATTER RESTING: 15 minutes
COOKING TIME: about 25 minutes
YIELD: 2 to 3 dozen medium fritters

1 cup (250 ml) plain flour

1/2 cup (125 ml) cornflour

1 tablespoon (20 ml) sugar

1/2 teaspoon (2 ml) cinnamon powder

2 teaspoons (10 ml) baking powder

1 cup (250 ml) milk

4 tablespoons (80 ml) corn oil

2 to 3 dozen chunks of fruit, cut into approximately 2.5 cm (1-inch cubes) (try bananas, papaya, apples, or pineapple)

oil or ghee for deep-frying

sugar for sprinkling

Sauce

1 cup (250 ml) orange juice

2 tablespoons (40 ml) sugar

1 tablespoon (20 ml) soy sauce

1/4 teaspoon (1 ml) chili powder (optional)

1 teaspoon (1 ml) cinnamon powder

1 teaspoon (5 ml) grated orange rind

1 tablespoon (20 ml) cornflour

water

1. Combine the flours, sugar, cinnamon, and baking powder in a medium-sized bowl. Pour in the milk and whisk until smooth and creamy. Set aside for 15 minutes. Add the oil, whisking well. Add a little extra milk if the batter is too thick.

2. Heat the *ghee* or frying oil until moderately hot (180°C/355°F). Dip 5 or 6 chunks of fruit in the batter and deep-fry them, turning often, until the fritters are golden brown on both sides. Remove and drain. Repeat for all fritters.

3. Combine the orange juice, sugar, soy sauce, chili powder, cinnamon powder, and orange rind in a small pan and bring to the boil. Mix the cornflour with a little cold water to form a smooth, thin paste. Whisk the thickening paste into the sauce until the required consistency is reached. Remove from the heat.

4. Sprinkle sugar on top of all the fritters and serve with the hot orange sauce.

Peanut Butter Fudge

Homemade confectioneries are fun to prepare and make great gifts. The sugar syrup for this delicious fudge is boiled to the 'soft ball' stage and is then beaten to encourage crystallization of the sugar. This gives the fudge its characteristic texture and appearance.

Use a heavy-based saucepan that has a capacity for at least four times the volume of the ingredients. Measure the temperature with a cooking thermometer suitable for sweet-making (sometimes called a candy thermometer). Be sure to stand the thermometer in a glass of very hot water before plunging it into the boiling sugar syrup.

PREPARATION AND COOKING TIME: about ½ hour
YIELD: about 36 pieces

2½ cups (625 ml) sugar
¾ cup (185 ml) milk
2 tablespoons (40 ml) golden syrup or light corn syrup
½ cup (60 ml) peanut butter
a few drops of vanilla essence

1. Butter a pan approximately 20 cm (8 inches) square.
2. Heat the sugar, milk, and syrup gently in a heavy saucepan, stirring with a wooden spoon until the sugar has dissolved and the syrup melted.
3. Bring to the boil, cover, and boil for 2 to 3 minutes.
4. Uncover the pan and continue to boil until the temperature reaches 116°C/240°F.
5. Remove the pan from the heat and stand it in cold water until the temperature of the syrup falls to 43°C/110°F.
6. Add the peanut butter and vanilla and beat the mixture until it thickens and becomes paler.
7. Pour the fudge mixture into the pan and leave it undisturbed until it is just about set. At this stage, mark the fudge into squares and leave until it sets completely.
8. When set, cut or break the fudge into pieces, wrap it in waxed paper, and store in an airtight container in a cool place for up to 2 weeks.

Creamy Condensed-milk Rice Pudding (*Chaval Ksira*)

Ksira is a Sanskrit word for condensed milk. It is commonly known as *kheer* in North India, and regional variations are known as *payasa*, *payesh*, etc. When milk is slowly condensed with rice, the result is this creamy dessert known as *Chaval Ksira*, sometimes just referred to as "sweet-rice".

I always start off with a scant one-sixteenth part rice to milk. When the sweet-rice has been cooked and chilled, it should be a "just drinkable" consistency.

The following recipe is for a simple cardamom-flavoured sweet-rice. Try the varieties listed below as alternatives.

PREPARATION AND COOKING TIME: about 50 minutes
YIELD: 4 to 5 cups

a bit less than ½ cup (about 120 ml) short-grain rice
4 green cardamom pods
8 cups (2 litres) fresh whole milk
¾ - 1 cup (185 ml - 250 ml) sugar

1. Clean, wash, and drain the short-grain rice.
2. Tap the cardamom pods until they slightly open.
3. Pour the milk and cardamom pods into a heavy-based 5- or 6-litre/quart saucepan and, stirring constantly with a wooden spoon, bring the milk to the boil over moderately high heat. Reduce the heat, add the rice, and, stirring attentively, boil gently for 25 to 30 minutes.
4. Reduce the heat to moderately low and boil the milk for another 10 to 15 minutes, still stirring constantly with a smooth, sweeping action. When the sweet-rice becomes creamy and slightly thick, remove the pan from the heat. Extract the cardamom pods and discard. Stir in the sugar, mix well, and allow the sweet-rice to cool. Refrigerate for at least 3 hours. Serve chilled.

Note: If the sweet-rice thickens too much after it cools, add a little cold milk or light cream to thin it out.

Saffron Sweet-Rice: Omit the cardamom pods and add a pinch of high quality saffron threads to the milk halfway through the cooking.

Camphor Sweet-Rice: Omit the cardamom pods and add a tiny pinch of pure camphor crystals after the sweet-rice has been removed from the heat.

Bengali-Style Sweet-Rice: Omit the cardamom pods and add 1 small bay leaf and 2 tablespoons (40 ml) butter at the beginning of the cooking. Add ½ teaspoon (2 ml) ground cardamom seeds and ¼ cup (60 ml) currants halfway through the cooking.

Vanilla Sweet-Rice: Omit the cardamom pods and add one 5 cm (2-inch) length of dried vanilla bean at the beginning of the cooking. Remove the bean after the sweet-rice cools.

Berry Sweet-Rice: Omit the cardamom pods. Cook the rice and milk together. Add the sweetener. Refrigerate until ice cold. Fold in 1 cup (250 ml) fresh, washed berries (ripe strawberries or raspberries are ideal).

Walnut and Chickpea-Flour Fudgeballs (*Laddu*)

You can purchase chickpea flour at Indian grocery stores under different names such as *gram* flour, peas meal, or *besan*. It is made from roasted *chana dal*, and when toasted in butter and sweetened it forms the basis of this delightful and popular confectionery, *laddu*.

COOKING AND PREPARATION TIME: about 20 minutes

COOLING AND ROLLING TIME: about 40 minutes

YIELD: 2 dozen sweets

¾ cup (185 ml) unsalted butter

2 cups (500 ml) chickpea flour, sifted after measuring

2 tablespoons (40 ml) chopped walnuts

¼ teaspoon (1 ml) ground nutmeg

1 cup (250 ml) icing sugar, sifted after measuring

1. Melt the butter in a heavy-based frying pan or small saucepan over a low heat. Add the sifted chickpea flour, walnut pieces, and nutmeg. Cook, stirring constantly with a wooden spoon, for about 15 to 20 minutes or until the mixture becomes deep golden brown and loose in consistency.

2. Remove the pan from the heat and add the icing sugar until it is well combined.

3. Spoon the mixture into a dish and spread it out. When cool enough to handle, roll the mixture into balls. Alternatively, you can spread the hot mixture into an even slab in a lightly-buttered dish and slice into squares when cool. Refrigerate until the *laddu* becomes firm. Serve cool or at room temperature.

Above: Walnut and Chickpea-Flour Fudgeballs along with Orange and Currant Simply Wonderfuls (p.139)

Algerian Ramadan Dessert

This deliciously simple dessert made almost entirely from dried fruit is traditionally taken at dusk at the end of the Muslim fast during the period of *Ramadan*. All the fruits should be soaked overnight.

SOAKING TIME: overnight
PREPARATION TIME: 10 minutes
COOKING TIME: 1½ to 2 hours
YIELD: enough for 10 persons

All measurements are for
unsoaked fruit.

1 cup (250 ml) dried prunes

1 cup (250 ml) raisins

1 cup (250 ml) whole dried apricots

¼ cup (60 ml) sultanas

¼ cup (60 ml) candied orange peel

¼ cup (60 ml) currants

4 dried figs, chopped

5 cups (1.25 litres) water

1 cup (250 ml) sugar

1 cup (250 ml) chopped mixed nuts
(pinenuts, walnuts, and almonds)

light cream for topping
grated nutmeg for garnish

1. Place the prunes, raisins, dried apricots, sultanas, candied orange peel, currants, and chopped figs in a large bowl. Add cold water until the level rises 2.5 cm (1 inch) above the fruit. Soak overnight.

2. Next day, drain the fruit. Place the 5 cups (1.25 litres) of water and sugar in a heavy saucepan, cover, and gently boil for 15 to 20 minutes. Add all the fruits which have been soaked and drained; simmer covered, for 1½ to 2 hours over low heat. About halfway through the cooking, add the nuts and mix well.

3. Remove the mixture from the heat and allow to cool. Transfer into a bowl and refrigerate until cold. Serve in individual decorative glass dessert bowls with a topping of light cream and a garnish of grated nutmeg.

Celestial Bananas

Having its origins in the West Indies, this opulent sweet really shows the versatility of the humble banana.

Sautéed in butter and baked with cream cheese, it is a delightful year-round dessert.

PREPARATION AND COOKING
TIME: about 30 minutes

YIELD: enough for 4 to 6 persons

185 g (6½ ounces) soft spreadable
cream cheese

¼ cup (60 ml) brown sugar

¾ teaspoon (3 ml) cinnamon powder

4 tablespoons (80 ml) unsalted
butter

4 large or 8 small ripe bananas,
peeled and halved lengthways

3 tablespoons (60 ml) pouring-
consistency cream

1. Beat the cream cheese, sugar, and ½ teaspoon (2 ml) of the cinnamon together until well-blended. Set aside.

2. Heat the butter in a heavy frying pan and sauté the banana halves until they are lightly browned on both sides.

3. Lay half of the banana halves in a buttered shallow, fire-proof serving dish. Spread half the cream cheese mixture on the bananas and top with the remaining banana halves. Spread them with the rest of the cream cheese mixture. Pour the cream over them.

4. Bake in a preheated 180°C/355°F oven for about 15 minutes or until the cream cheese mixture is golden brown.

Sprinkle with the remaining ¼ teaspoon (1 ml) cinnamon and serve immediately.

Orange Cheesecake

This delicious cheesecake requires no cooking and features orange-flavoured cream cheese in a biscuit crumb base.

PREPARATION TIME: 20 minutes
CHILLING TIME: at least 12 hours
YIELD: one 20 cm (8-inch) cake

Crust

2 cups (500 ml) biscuit crumbs,
coarsely ground

¼ teaspoon (1 ml) ginger powder

⅓ cup (85 ml) melted butter

Filling

350 g (12 ounces) cream cheese

¾ cup (185 ml) sweetened
condensed milk

½ cup (125 ml) fresh lemon juice

2 teaspoons (10 ml) grated
orange rind

1. To prepare the crust: combine the biscuit crumbs, ginger, and butter. Press the crumb mixture into the base and 2.5 cm (1-inch) up the sides of a 20 cm (8-inch) spring-form pan. Chill the base for ½ hour.

2. To prepare the filling: beat the cream cheese until smooth and gradually add the condensed milk, lemon juice, and orange rind, beating thoroughly. Alternatively, the ingredients can be combined in a food processor.

3. Pour the mixture into the crust, smooth it out, and chill to set.

Decorate the cake with the whipped cream and orange segments, or as desired.

Above right: Carob Fudge Cake

Carob Fudge Cake

This two-tiered carob cake is light in texture without the use of any eggs. The cake's light texture is due to the sour milk. Filled and iced with *Carob Vienna Icing*, it is an irresistible dessert.

PREPARATION TIME: 15 minutes
BAKING TIME: 30 minutes
YIELD: 1 two-tiered 20 cm (8-inch) carob fudge cake

125 g (4 ounces) butter, room-temperature
1 cup (250 ml) caster sugar
1 teaspoon (5 ml) vanilla essence
1 cup (250 ml) carob powder
½ cup (125 ml) hot water
2 teaspoons (10 ml) imitation chocolate essence (optional)
2 teaspoons (10 ml) fresh lemon juice
1 cup (250 ml) milk
1¾ cups (435 ml) plain flour
1 teaspoon (5 ml) baking powder
1 teaspoon (5 ml) bicarbonate of soda
pinch salt
Carob Vienna Icing

1. Cream the butter, sugar, and vanilla until light and fluffy. Blend the carob powder in the hot water, add the imitation chocolate essence, and mix to a smooth paste. Gradually add the carob mixture to the butter and sugar mixture.
2. Add the lemon juice to the milk to sour it.
3. Sift the flour, baking powder, bicarbonate of soda, and salt and add it to the creamed mixture alternately with sour milk. Mix thoroughly.
4. Spoon the cake mixture into two buttered 20 cm (8-inch) cake tins and bake in a moderate oven (180°C/355°F) for 30 minutes or until the tops spring back when lightly pressed.
5. Allow the cakes to cool in their tins for 10 minutes. Turn out and allow to cool completely. Fill and ice with Carob Vienna Icing.

Carob Vienna Icing

125 g (4 ounces) butter
2½ cups (625 ml) icing sugar
4 tablespoons (80 ml) carob powder
2 tablespoons (40 ml) hot water
1 teaspoon (5 ml) imitation chocolate essence (optional)

1. Beat the butter until creamy. Sift the sugar. Blend the carob powder with the hot water and chocolate essence. Add the icing sugar to the butter alternately with the carob mixture until it reaches a spreading consistency.

Alternative: spread the centre with jam and whipped cream. Cover and ice as above.

DRINKS

What better way to express one's hospitality than offering a drink to guests? This selection of non-alcoholic beverages has something for everyone.

Pictured: Mango Yogurt Smoothie

Homemade Lime Squash

Fresh limes (*Citrus aurantifolia*) impart a wonderful tart flavour to this thirst-quenching drink. The essential oil contained in the lime is released by the process of infusion when the lime skins are steeped in hot water. This recipe yields concentrated syrup, ideal for party punch. Lemons may be substituted for limes.

PREPARATION AND COOKING TIME: 45 minutes

YIELD: concentrated syrup for about 30 to 40 cups of lime squash

5 cups (1.25 litres) freshly squeezed lime juice, strained (about 60 large limes)

½ cup (125 ml) water

1½ cups (375 ml) sugar

2 cups (500 ml) light corn syrup

1. Peel the outside rind from 8 of the limes in thin strips, avoiding the white part of the fruit. Place the rinds in a bowl.

2. Boil the water and pour it onto the reserved fruit peel. Cover and let it stand for 30 minutes. Pour the lime water through a sieve placed over a bowl and squeeze. Collect the juice and discard the rest.

3. Heat the lime-rind water in a saucepan over moderate heat. Add the sugar and light corn syrup until it completely dissolves. Remove from the heat.

4. Add the lime juice to the contents of the saucepan and allow the mixture to cool. Pour the syrup into a bottle or jar and refrigerate.

To serve, add approximately ¼ cup (60 ml) of concentrate to a tall glass, add cracked ice, and fill with cold water, mineral water, or soda.

Watermelon Sherbet

This refreshing preparation can be served as either a drink or a dessert. For the best results *Watermelon Sherbet* should be made with the juice from ripe red watermelon flesh at the peak of melon season.

PREPARATION TIME: 15 minutes
CHILLING TIME: a few hours
YIELD: enough for 6 persons

6 cups (1.5 litres) watermelon juice

1 cup (250 ml) sugar

6 teaspoons (30 ml) fresh lemon juice

2 cups (500 ml) reduced cream (light cream)

6 sprigs fresh mint

1. Combine the watermelon juice, sugar, and lemon juice and place in a steel bowl in the freezer. Freeze until slushy.

2. Remove from the freezer and scoop into individual glass dessert bowls. Pour cream over each serving and garnish with a sprig of fresh mint. Serve immediately.

Note: alternatively, you can freeze the watermelon juice overnight and blend it in a food processor next day, reducing it to a sorbet consistency.

Middle Eastern Lemonade

The special ingredient in this refreshing drink is orange-flower water (sometimes called orange-blossom water). This distilled essence of orange blossom can be purchased in most well-stocked specialty grocery stores. Most orange-flower water comes from the south of France and from the Levant.

PREPARATION TIME: 10 minutes
YIELD: enough for 6 persons

¾ cup (185 ml) lemon juice

¾ cup (185 ml) sugar

2 teaspoons (10 ml) orange-blossom water, or as required

2 tablespoons (40 ml) finely chopped fresh mint

8 cups (2 litres) water, soda, or mineral water

ice cubes

1. Blend the lemon juice, sugar, orange-blossom water, and mint. Combine with the water or soda and serve in individual chilled glasses over ice.

Lemon Barley Water

Barley water is famous as a tonic and great thirst quencher. It is very nutritious and soothing to the stomach and kidneys.

PREPARATION AND COOKING TIME: 15 minutes
SOAKING TIME: 1 hour
YIELD: about 12 glasses

1/4 cup (60 ml) pearl barley
6 3/4 cups (1.7 litres) water
8 lemons
3/4 cup (185 ml) sugar

1. Wash the barley in several changes of water. Drain it and place it into a saucepan with 4 1/2 cups (1.125 litres) of water. With a citrus peeler, peel very thin rinds off the lemons and add the rinds to the barley water. Bring to a boil; then simmer for 10 minutes.

2. Juice the lemons and place the juice into a large bowl. Add the sugar and the barley mixture, stir well, and add the remaining 2 1/4 cups (560 ml) of water; then let the mixture soak for 1 hour.

3. Strain the mixture into a large jug or suitable container and chill. To serve, pour into chilled glasses half filled with ice; garnish with a slice of lemon.

Orange and Almond Nectar

This protein-rich non-dairy drink combines the smoothness and delicate flavour of almond milk with the refreshment of orange juice. Serve anytime for a delicious surprise.

PREPARATION TIME: a few minutes
SOAKING TIME: overnight
YIELD: enough for 4 to 6 persons

1 cup (250 ml) whole blanched almonds
1 cup (250 ml) fresh orange juice
5 cups (1.25 litres) water
1/2 cup (125 ml) sugar

1. Soak the almonds in the water overnight in a sealed container.

2. Pour the water and almonds through a strainer and collect the liquid in a bowl. Place the almonds and a little soaking water into a blender or food processor, cover, and blend until smooth (about 3 to 4 minutes).

3. Line a sieve with three thicknesses of cheesecloth. Pour the nut milk through the sieve; then extract as much liquid as possible by squeezing. (The residual pulp can be kept for cutlets or salad dressing). Combine this with the water the nuts were soaked in.

4. Combine the almond milk, orange juice, and sugar in a bowl and mix well. Refrigerate and serve ice cold.

Pictured from left: Homemade Lime Squash, Watermelon Sherbet and Middle Eastern Lemonade

Anise Flavoured Fruit-and-Nut Shake (*Thandhai*)

This drink is well known throughout India, although the recipe varies slightly from place to place. *Thandhai* is a summer drink only, generally taken either in the morning or late afternoon. It cools the body and head.

PREPARATION TIME: 20 minutes
YIELD: one litre/quart

10 whole green cardamom pods
15 whole black peppercorns
5½ teaspoons (27 ml) fennel seeds
½ cup (125 ml) white poppy seeds
6 teaspoons (30 ml) broken raw cashew nuts
16 blanched raw almonds
16 raisins
2½ cups (625 ml) chilled water
1 teaspoon (5 ml) rosewater
5 tablespoons (100 ml) raw sugar
1½ cups (375 ml) fresh cold milk

1. Grind the cardamom pods, peppercorns, and fennel seeds to a fine powder in a coffee mill. Set aside in a large bowl.

2. Grind the poppy seeds in a coffee mill and add to the bowl.

3. Grind the cashew nuts, almonds, and raisins to a fine paste in a food processor or blender with the aid, if required, of a little water.

4. Add the bowl of ground spices and ½ cup (125 ml) of the water and blend for 3 or 4 minutes until the mixture is smooth and creamy. Add the remaining water and process for another 2 minutes.

5. Place a sieve in a bowl and line the sieve with two or three layers of cheesecloth. Pour the contents of the blender through the sieve, gathering the corners of the cheesecloth and squeezing all the liquid into the bowl (save the contents of the bag for cutlets or sauces). To this liquid, add the sugar, rosewater, and milk. Mix well and chill. Serve in chilled glasses.

Yogurt Smoothie (*Lassi*)

India's yogurt-based smoothie drinks, called *lassi*, are world famous. Rejuvenating one's strength and cooling the head and stomach, they're ideal for counteracting the heat of a midsummer's day.

Rose *Lassi*

In this version of *lassi*, popular throughout India, the smoothness of sweetened yogurt is offset with a splash of rosewater.

PREPARATION TIME: 10 minutes
YIELD: enough for 4 persons

2½ cups (625 ml) homemade or plain yogurt

½ cup (125 ml) caster sugar or equivalent sweetener

2 teaspoons (10 ml) rosewater

¾ cup (185 ml) iced water

1 cup (250 ml) ice cubes, cracked

a few fragrant rose petals for garnish (optional)

1. Blend the yogurt, sugar, rosewater, and iced water in a blender or food processor for 2 minutes. Add the ice and process for another 2 minutes. Pour into chilled glasses and garnish with rose petals.

Cumin *Lassi*

With the subtle flavour of dry-roasted cumin seeds and a hint of lemon or lime juice, this is, alongside sweet *lassi*, India's favourite summertime drink.

PREPARATION TIME: 10 minutes
YIELD: enough for 4 persons

3 cups (750 ml) plain yogurt

2 tablespoons (40 ml) lemon or lime juice

⅓ cup (85 ml) iced water

½ teaspoon (2 ml) salt

8 ice cubes

2 teaspoons (10 ml) coarsely ground dry-roasted cumin seeds

1. Blend the yogurt, citrus juice, iced water, and salt in a food processor or blender for 2 minutes. Add the ice cubes and most of the cumin and blend for another minute.
2. Pour the *lassi* into frosted glasses and garnish with the reserved cumin. Serve immediately.

Fruit *Lassis* are a popular Western innovation. Here are two great varieties.

Strawberry *Lassi*

Choose fresh, ripe, sweet strawberries for this recipe. Any ripe berries can be substituted for the strawberries.

PREPARATION AND CHILLING TIME: ½ hour
YIELD: enough for 6 persons

2 cups (500 ml) fresh strawberries

⅔ cup (165 ml) sugar or honey

3 cups (750 ml) plain yogurt

1½ cups (375 ml) iced water

1 cup (250 ml) crushed ice

1. Blend the strawberries and sweetener in a food processor or blender. Transfer the purée to a bowl. Freeze for 20 minutes.
2. Blend the yogurt, water, and ice in a blender and add the chilled strawberry pulp. Blend until frothy and serve in chilled glasses.

Mango *Lassi*

Mango is sometimes called "the king of fruits". There are dozens of varieties of mango. Select ripe, sweet fruits for this thick and rich mango nectar drink.

PREPARATION AND CHILLING TIME: 30 minutes
YIELD: enough for 6 to 8 persons

2 cups (500 ml) diced fresh mango pulp (about 4 or 5 small mangoes)

½ cup (125 ml) orange juice

¼ cup (60 ml) honey or vanilla sugar

3 cups (750 ml) plain yogurt

1 cup (250 ml) iced water

1 cup (250 ml) crushed ice

1. Blend the mango, orange juice, and sweetener in a food processor or blender. Transfer to a bowl and place in the freezer for 20 minutes.
2. Blend the yogurt, water, and ice in the blender and add the chilled mango pulp. Blend until frothy and serve in chilled glasses.

Pictured from left: Orange Ginger Cooler (p. 160), Anise Flavoured Fruit-and-Nut Shake and Strawberry Lassi

157

Peach Sorbet

Fresh, ripe peaches in season are puréed and chilled in this frozen peach dessert from Sicily. Serve *Peach Sorbet* as a dessert or between the entrée and first course of a full meal.

PREPARATION TIME: 20 minutes
FREEZING TIME: 4 hours
YIELD: enough for 4 persons

½ *cup (125 ml) sugar*
⅔ *cup (165 ml) water*
4 large white-fleshed peaches
juice of 1 lemon

1. Heat the water and sugar in a small saucepan over low heat until the sugar dissolves; then boil for 3 to 4 minutes. Set aside until quite cold.

2. Immerse the peaches in boiling water for 1 minute. Drain and remove the skins and stones.

3. Blend the peaches until smooth in a blender or food processor. Add the lemon juice and blend for 1 more minute. Empty the fruit into a bowl, add the cold syrup, pour into a shallow freezer tray, and freeze until half firm. Remove, transfer to a bowl, and whisk vigorously. Return to the tray and freeze again until firm.

4. About 40 minutes before serving, transfer the sorbet to the refrigerator, allowing it to soften. Scoop the sorbet into tall glasses and serve immediately.

Pictured: Pineapple Coconut Punch

Pineapple and Coconut Punch

This tropical refresher comes from Jamaica and calls for fresh pineapple juice. You can substitute fresh pineapples with bottled or canned unsweetened pineapple juice.

PREPARATION TIME: 10 minutes
YIELD: enough for 6 persons
2 cups (500 ml) canned coconut milk
4 cups (1 litre) unsweetened pineapple juice, chilled
2 tablespoons (40 ml) caster sugar
1 cup (250 ml) crushed ice
¼ *teaspoon (1 ml) coconut essence*

1. Blend the coconut milk, pineapple juice, sugar, and ice in a blender at high speed until the mixture is very smooth.

2. Strain the mixture through a fine sieve into a clean bowl. Add the coconut essence to the bowl of juice.

3. Pour the juice into a jug and refrigerate until thoroughly chilled. Serve in chilled glasses with or without ice.

Hot Saffron Milk with Pistachios

PREPARATION TIME: 15 minutes
YIELD: enough for 4 persons
12 saffron threads
4 cups (1 litre) milk
1 tablespoon (20 ml) powdered raw pistachio nuts
3 tablespoons (60 ml) sugar or honey

1. Grind the saffron threads to a powder with a mortar and pestle; alternatively, powder them in a coffee grinder.

2. Boil the milk, saffron, and most of the pistachio powder in a heavy-based saucepan over moderate heat. Stirring constantly, bring the milk to a full boil, allow it to froth twice; then remove from the heat. Dissolve the sweetener in the milk. Serve immediately, garnishing each serving with the remaining pistachio nut powder.

Lemon Mint and Whey Nectar

Whey is the liquid by-product in the basic cheese-making process. When this cheese, or "curd" (as it is commonly called), is prepared, almost 90% of the total volume of milk is transformed into whey. Whey can be substituted for water when preparing vegetables, soups, bread, and this refreshing minted lemon drink.

PREPARATION TIME: 15 minutes
YIELD: enough for 6 persons
1 small bunch of mint
½ cup (125 ml) sugar
½ cup (125 ml) boiling water
3 cups (750 ml) chilled water or soda water
1 cup (250 ml) whey, strained through a fine sieve to remove any sediment
½ cup (125 ml) fresh lemon juice
1 cup (250 ml) crushed ice

1. Crush 2 dozen mint leaves with one teaspoon (5 ml) sugar in a mortar and pestle or food processor. Pour on the boiling water. Allow the mixture to steep for 10 minutes. Strain through a fine cloth and collect the liquid.

2. Blend the mint liquid, the rest of the sugar, the water or soda water, the whey, and the lemon juice in a food processor or blender for 1 minute. Serve over ice in chilled glasses and garnish with mint leaves.

Spiced Hot Apple Juice Drink

Use freshly squeezed or bottled apple juice for this winter's-night beverage.

PREPARATION TIME: 25 minutes
YIELD: enough for 6 persons

6 cups (1.5 litres) apple juice
one 10 cm (4-inch) cinnamon stick
6 whole cloves
¼ teaspoon (1 ml) whole cardamom seeds
lemon slices
honey as sweetener, if required

1. Boil the apple juice and the spices in a large heavy-based pan over high heat. Cover the saucepan and reduce the heat to low, simmering for 20 minutes.

2. Just before serving, strain the spices from the juice. Serve hot with slices of lemon and honey (optional).

Pictured: Spiced Hot Apple Juice Drink

Orange Ginger Cooler

Orange juice combined with fresh ginger, cardamom, and fresh mint make this a thirst-quenching drink.

PREPARATION AND COOLING TIME: 1 hour
YIELD: about 8 cups (2 litres)

1/4 cup (60 ml) fresh mint leaves

1 teaspoon (5 ml) minced fresh ginger

1/8 teaspoon (0.5 ml) finely ground cardamom seeds

2 cups (500 ml) hot water

1/3 cup (85 ml) honey

3 cups crushed ice

1/3 cup (85 ml) fresh lemon juice

3 cups (750 ml) fresh orange juice

1. Grind the mint leaves, ginger, and cardamom to a paste with a mortar and pestle or mince them in a food processor. Steep the pulp in the hot water for 1/2 hour. Strain the mixture through a cloth or sieve, collect the juice, and discard the pulp.

2. Blend the mint and ginger juice and the honey in a large bowl. Add the ice, lemon juice, and orange juice. Serve in chilled glasses garnished with an orange ring and mint leaves.

Fruity Chamomile Tea

A refreshing, digestive beverage with a hint of spice.

PREPARATION AND COOKING TIME: 10 minutes
YIELD: enough for 2 persons

2 sachets chamomile tea

2 cups (500 ml) boiling hot water

2 cloves

juice from one small orange

juice from one small lemon

1 tablespoon (20 ml) mild-tasting honey

2 orange slices, as garnish

1. Infuse the chamomile tea sachets along with the cloves in the boiling hot water for 10 minutes.

2. Discard the sachets, add the orange and lemon juice to the tea and heat the mixture in a small pan until boiling. Remove from the heat, stir in the honey and discard the cloves.

Serve hot with the orange slice garnish.

Orange Buttermilk Smoothie

Buttermilk aids digestion by increasing the secretion of digestive enzymes, and it soothes the stomach. This cultured, low-fat dairy product is combined with freshly squeezed orange juice in this refreshing drink.

PREPARATION TIME: 5 minutes
YIELD: enough for 4 persons

2 cups (500 ml) low-fat, cultured buttermilk

2 cups (500 ml) freshly squeezed orange juice

2 tablespoons (40 ml) sugar or equivalent sweetener

2 cups (500 ml) crushed ice

1. Blend all the ingredients in a food processor or blender for 2 minutes. Pour into chilled glasses and serve immediately.

Pictured from left: Raspberry and Rhubarb Punch, Banana Milk Smoothie and Saffron and Lemon Sherbet

Raspberry and Rhubarb Punch

Raspberries, fresh rhubarb, and ginger combine wonderfully in this delicious party punch.

PREPARATION AND COOKING TIME: 30 minutes
YIELD: about 6 cups (1½ litres)

500 g (17½ ounces) fresh rhubarb stalks, chopped

3 cups (750 ml) water

¾ cup (185 ml) caster sugar

200 g (7 ounces) raspberries (reserve a few for garnish)

1 tablespoon (20 ml) fresh lemon juice

½ teaspoon (2 ml) minced fresh ginger

1 cup (250 ml) dry ginger ale

1½ cups (375 ml) lemonade

ice cubes

Banana Milk Smoothie

Frothy, ice-cold banana smoothie with a hint of nutmeg is an opulent and rich summertime drink. Bananas have a natural sweetness, as does milk, so there is no need to add much extra sweetener. Bananas also add significant body to this substantial beverage.

PREPARATION TIME: 10 minutes
YIELD: enough for 4 persons

3 medium-sized ripe bananas, peeled and sliced

2 cups (500 ml) cold milk

1 to 2 tablespoons (20 to 40 ml) mild honey

1 cup (250 ml) ice

pinch of nutmeg

1. Blend the bananas, milk, and honey in a blender or food processor for 2 minutes. Add the ice and process for another minute. Pour into chilled glasses, garnish with nutmeg, and serve.

chilled water (optional)

1. Place the rhubarb, water, and sugar in a medium-sized saucepan. Cover with a lid and simmer over low heat until the rhubarb softens. Transfer into a bowl and refrigerate.

2. Purée the rhubarb in a blender or food processor. Strain it, and discard the pulp. Purée the raspberries with the lemon juice and combine with the rhubarb juice.

3. Just before serving, stir in the fresh ginger, ginger ale, lemonade, and ice cubes. For a thinner punch, add chilled water.

Saffron and Lemon Sherbet

This is an unusual and refreshing drink. Incorporating the subtle flavour of saffron ("the king of spices"), the aromatic freshness of cardamom, and the tang of lemon juice, this is a real summer thirst-quencher.

PREPARATION TIME: 5 minutes
YIELD: enough for 6 persons

8 strands pure saffron thread

4 tablespoons (80 ml) fresh lemon juice

6 tablespoons (120 ml) sugar

¼ teaspoon (1 ml) powdered cardamom seeds

4½ cups (1.125 litres) iced water

¼ teaspoon (1 ml) salt

crushed ice

1. Grind the saffron threads with a mortar and pestle until pulverized. Alternatively, mix with a few drops of warm water and pulverize with a spoon.

2. Transfer the saffron powder or saffron water to a large bowl and add the lemon juice, sugar, powdered cardamom seeds, water, and salt. Mix thoroughly. Refrigerate. Serve over crushed ice in chilled glasses.

Suggested Menus

INDIAN-STYLE WINTER BREAKFAST
Rice and Mung Bean Stew
Puffed Fried Bread
Cauliflower and Pea *Samosas*
Mint Chutney
Freshly cut Fruits
Banana Milk Smoothie

INDIAN-STYLE SUMMER BREAKFAST
Scrambled Curd
Puffed Fried Bread
Tomato Chutney
Freshly cut Fruits
Homemade Lime Squash
or
Fruity Chamomile Tea

LIGHT INTERNATIONAL-STYLE LUNCH
Malaysian Hot Noodles with *Tofu*
Mediterranean Salad
Orange Ginger Cooler

LIGHT EAST MEETS WEST LUNCH I
Zucchini, Green Peppers, and Tomato
Griddle Baked Bread
Lokshen Pudding

LIGHT EAST MEETS WEST LUNCH II
Yellow Split-pea Soup with Pumpkin
Yellow Rice
Asparagus, Green Bean and Broccoli Salad

LIGHT SUMMER LUNCH
Hawaiian Brown Rice Salad
Green Beans
Middle Eastern Round Bread

MEDITERRANEAN LUNCH
Minestrone Soup
Vegetarian Lasagna
Asparagus, Green Bean and Broccoli Salad
Peach Sorbet

LIGHT MIDDLE-EASTERN LUNCH
Middle Eastern Round Bread
Israeli Chickpea Croquettes
Chickpea and Sesame Dip
Mediterranean Salad

SUMMER PATIO LUNCH OR PICNIC
Pasta Salad
Soft Breadrolls
Ricotta Cheese-filled Pastries
Tomato Relish
Asparagus and Tomato Quiche
Crispy Flat-Rice and Cashews
Mango Ice cream
Middle Eastern Lemonade

EUROPEAN WINTER DINNER
Vegetable Soup
Italian Eggplant and Tomato Appetizer
Wholemeal Bread
Vegetables au Gratin
Italian Market Salad
Easy Apple Pie
Spiced Hot Apple Juice Drink

ASIAN-STYLE DINNER
Thai Clear Soup with *Tofu*
Thai Rice
Cantonese Stir-Fried Vegetables
Sweet-and-Sour Walnuts
Chinese Almond Cookies

SPECIAL EAST MEETS WEST DINNER
Tomato Soup
Savoury Cantonese Fried Rice
Baked Stuffed Avocados
Yeasted, Puffed Fried-Bread
Italian Market Salad
Carob Fudge Cake
Lemon Barley Water

EUROPEAN DINNER PARTY
Cream of Pumpkin Soup
Spinach Filo Triangles
Eggplant Parmigiana
Mediterranean Salad
Apple and Blackberry Crumble
Lemon Barley Water

LIGHT INDIAN DINNER
Sautéed Rice with Poppy Seeds
Split-Mung Dal
Griddle-Baked Bread
North Indian Curried Cauliflower and Potatoes
Mixed Vegetable and Yogurt Salad
Creamy Condensed-milk Rice Pudding
Lemon Mint and Whey Nectar
or
Spiced Hot Apple Juice Drink

SPECIAL INDIAN DINNER PARTY
South Indian Sweet-and-Sour Tamarind Rice
Green Split-Pea Dal with Spinach and Coconut Milk
Puffed Fried-Bread
Green Beans
Tomato, Peas, and Home-made Curd
Pineapple Chutney
Cauliflower and Pea *Samosas*
Creamy, Saffron Condensed Yogurt Dessert
Lemon Mint and Whey Nectar

LIGHT INTERNATIONAL SUMMER BUFFET
Mexican Oatmeal Corn and Cheese Bread
Tomato Relish
Japanese Rice-Balls
Tacos
Baked Cheesecake
Pineapple and Coconut Punch

ITALIAN-STYLE BUFFET
Asparagus with Oil and Lemon Sauce
Tomato Rice with Herbs
Mozzarella and Tomato Pizza
Italian Market Salad
Sicilian Radicchio and Fennel Salad
Ricotta Cheese-filled Pastries
Eggplant Rings with Cheese
Peach Sorbet

INTERNATIONAL BUFFET
Chickpea Pâté with Vegetable Crudités
Italian Fried Corn-Bread
Gauranga Potatoes
Cauliflower *Pakoras* with Peach Chutney
French Braised Summer Vegetables
Yellow Rice
Mexican Oatmeal Corn and Cheese Bread
Peanut Butter Fudge
Mango Ice cream
Saffron and Lemon Sherbet

MIDDLE EASTERN BANQUET
Stuffed Vine Leaves
Middle Eastern Round Bread (*Pita*)
Couscous with Vegetable Sauce
Lebanese Bulgur-Wheat Salad
Lebanese Eggplant Dip
Chickpea and Sesame Dip
Syrian Yogurt-Cheese
Assorted Vegetable Crudités
Turkish Nut Pastries in Syrup
Middle Eastern Lemonade

ASIAN BUFFET-STYLE BANQUET
Mashed Potato Puffs
Grated Cauliflower Balls in Tomato Sauce
Baked Vegetable Rice
Curried Chickpeas
North Indian Potato Salad
Cantonese Stir-Fried Vegetables
North Indian Cabbage and Peanut Salad
Fig and Apple Relish
Fresh Coconut Chutney
Date and Tamarind Sauce
Crispy Dal Wafers
Fresh Fruits with Cream
Fruit Fritters with Orange Sauce
Homemade Lime Squash
or
Rose *Lassi*

INDIAN-STYLE FEAST
Bengali Royal Rice
Puffed Fried Bread
Cauliflower and Potato Supreme
Spinach, Tomato, Eggplant, and Chickpea Stew
Mixed Vegetable and Yogurt Salad
Pineapple Chutney
Curd *Pakoras*
Peanut and Coriander Chutney
Walnut and Raisin Semolina *Halava*
Deep-Fried Milk Balls in Rose Syrup
Orange Ginger Cooler

Glossary

AJOWAN SEEDS: Tiny, light-brown spice seeds closely related to caraway and cumin with a very strong, thyme and oregano flavour. Ajowan, *Carum ajowan* is used in many North Indian savoury dishes, especially in fried snacks.

Ajowan aids digestion and is used to relieve stomach problems. The seeds keep indefinitely and are available from Indian and Middle Eastern grocers.

ALFALFA SPROUTS: The nutritional content of the seeds of the perennial plant *Medicado sativa*, alfalfa, is increased dramatically when they are sprouted. Alfalfa sprouts contain 40% protein and are very high in vitamins A, B, and C, as well as B vitamins, and the vitamins K and U. Alfalfa sprouts also contain good amounts of sodium, potassium, sulphur, phosphorus, and magnesium. The high nutrition, as well as the mild, slightly sweet flavour of alfalfa sprouts make them a popular salad ingredient.

Ajowan

AMCHOOR: A tan coloured powder made from grinding small sun-dried green mangoes. Amchoor is used in North Indian dishes to give a slightly sour, pungent taste. It is a predominant flavour in the spice blend called *chat masala* and is available at all Indian grocery stores.

ANISE SEEDS: The highly aromatic seeds of the annual herb *Pimpinella anisum*. These greenish-grey, slightly crescent-shaped seeds have a very strong licorice-like flavour and odour, although they are not related to the perennial plant of the pea family whose sweet roots are the source of true licorice. Although anise is generally used as a flavouring for drinks, sweets, and creams, it is delicious sautéed in *ghee* or oil and cooked in vegetable dishes such as *Cabbage, Potato and Yogurt with Anise*. Anise seeds are available at supermarkets and specialty stores.

ANTIPASTO: A light starter or an appetizer served before an Italian meal. It can also be used as a light snack. Vegetables and salads (served raw or lightly cooked) make delicious antipasto, as do simple hot dishes, fried breads (*crostini*), or miniature pizzas.

ARHAR DAL: (see **TOOVAR DAL**)

ARROWROOT: A very fine white starch derived from the rootstock of the South American tropical plant *Maranta arundinacea*. Arrowroot is used much like cornflour in sauces, except that it

Asafoetida

is a non-grain flour and thickens at a lower temperature. It is also used as a binding agent. It is available at most supermarkets or grocers.

ASAFOETIDA: The aromatic resin from the root of the giant fennel, *Ferula asafoetida*. Asafoetida (also known as *hing*) is extracted from the stems of these giant perennial plants that grow wild in Central Asia. In the spring, when the plant is about to bloom, the stems and roots are cut. Milky resin exudes from the cut surface and is scraped off. More exudes as successive slices of root are removed over a period of 3 months. The gummy resin is sun-dried into a solid mass that is then sold in solid, wax-like pieces, or more conveniently, in powdered form. Due to the presence of sulphur compounds, asafoetida has a distinctive pungent flavour reminiscent of shallots or garlic. Used in minute quantities, it adds a delicious flavour to various savoury dishes. I always use the mild Vandevi brand of yellow asafetida powder and not the grey variety. All recipes for this book using asafoetida were tested using this yellow variety. If using other varieties, reduce the quantities to one half of the suggested amount. Asafoetida is available at Indian grocers.

ATTA FLOUR: Also known as *chapati* flour, this low-gluten flour is derived from a strain of soft wheat popular throughout India. The entire wheat kernel, including the bran, germ, and endosperm, is ground very finely making a nutritious flour. *Atta* flour is suitable for all Indian flatbreads, such as *pooris*, *chapatis*, and *parathas*. Doughs made with *atta* flour are velvety smooth, knead readily, and respond easily to shaping and rolling. *Atta* flour is available from Indian and Asian grocery stores.

BAMBOO SHOOTS: The tender, inner part of the young shoots of the bamboo tree. They are used as an ingredient in Chinese, Japanese, and South East Asian dishes. The best quality bamboo is the first growth of shoots that sprout early in the new year and is known as winter bamboo. Fresh bamboo shoots are more or less unavailable in the West. Substitute canned bamboo shoots, available at any Asian grocer.

BARLEY: Barley (*Hordeum vulgare*) is an annual cereal grass widely cultivated as a food grain. The most familiar form is called pearl barley, which has had the husk removed and has been steamed and polished. It is inexpensive and has a pleasant, nutty flavour. Barley is high in carbohydrate content, containing useful amounts of protein, calcium, and phosphorus, as well as small amounts of B vitamins. It is excellent in soups, stews, and side dishes, as well as the refreshing barley water. Pearl barley is available at any grocer or supermarket.

BASIL: The fragrant aromatic herb *Ocimum basilicum*, known also as sweet basil. It is a small, profusely branched, bushy plant, whose tender green leaves are used worldwide, especially in Italian cuisine, where it is used mostly in dishes containing tomatoes, and in salads and soups, on pizzas, and in pasta dishes. Freshly chopped basil should be used whenever possible, as dried basil makes a poor substitute. Fresh basil is available at good greengrocer shops.

BASMATI RICE: A superb, light-textured long-grain, aromatic rice from North India and Pakistan with a wonderful fragrance and flavour. Even served plain with a little *ghee* or butter, *basmati* rice is a treat. I have found Dehradun *basmati* to be most superior in flavour and texture. *Basmati* rice is easy to cook, and although more costly than other long-grain rices, it is well worth the extra expense. *Basmati* rice is available at Indian, Middle Eastern, and Asian grocers.

BAY LEAVES: The leaves of the sweet bay or laurel tree, *Laurus nobilis*, an evergreen member of the laurel family native to the Mediterranean region and Asia Minor. The highly aromatic leaves are thick, dark green, and glossy on the upper surface.

Bay leaves used in their fresh or dried form are quite pungent with a slightly bitter, spicy flavour. They are popular in French cuisine.

BEAN CURD: (see *TOFU*)

BESAN: (see **CHICKPEA FLOUR**)

BLACK BEANS: Soya beans fermented with malt and salt. They have a strong, salty flavour. Dry in texture, they keep for a long time in the refrigerator. They are popular in Chinese and Indonesian cooking, especially as the basis for black bean sauce. They're available at Chinese and South East Asian grocers.

BLACK CUMIN SEEDS: Often confused with *nigella* or *kalonji* seeds, which are tear-drop shaped. Black cumin seeds (*Cumin nigrum*) are blacker and thinner than cumin seeds. They are exclusively used in North Indian cuisine, especially in Kashmir. They're available at well-stocked Indian grocers.

BLACK PEPPER: (see **PEPPER**)

BLACK SALT: A reddish-grey variety of salt with a distinct "hard-boiled egg-yolk" flavour. Black salt, or *kala namak*, as it is known in Indian cuisine, is a major ingredient in the spice blend *chat masala*. I like to sprinkle black salt in *Scrambled Curd*. It is available at Indian grocers.

BOK CHOY: The common Cantonese name for Chinese cabbage. These small cabbages, used in Chinese cooking, have dark green leaves and wide white stalks joined near the base of the stem. They resemble a miniature Swiss chard (silverbeet). The smaller the individual cabbage, the more delicate the flavour. They're available at Chinese grocers.

BORLOTTI BEANS: One of the most popular varieties of "*legumi secchi*", legumes, in Italian cuisine. They are from the same family as red kidney beans and vary in colour considerably from pale pink to dark red. They are always speckled. Borlotti beans should, like all dried beans, be soaked in cold water overnight, rinsed well, and then boiled in fresh water until tender. They are delicious in soups such as *Minestrone*. If borlotti beans are unavailable, substitute red kidney beans.

BRAN: The tough outer pericarp layer of the wheat grain. It is removed together with the germ during milling to produce flour. It is a rich source of protein, B vitamins, phosphorus, and, of course, fibre.

BUCKWHEAT: Buckwheat is not a grain in the botanical sense, as it is related to dock and rhubarb, although some cookbooks classify it as such. Native to China, Nepal, and Siberia, it is rich in iron and contains 11% protein and almost the entire range of B-complex vitamins. Buckwheat is available in the form of the whole seeds, called groats; finely cracked groats, called grits; roasted whole groats, called *kasha*; and flour.

Buckwheat is popular in Russian and Jewish cooking. It is available at health food stores and specialty grocers.

BULGUR WHEAT: A grain product made by par-boiling and drying whole wheat kernels and crushing them into various sizes. Bulgur is popular in Middle Eastern cuisine, especially in the famous *tabbouleh* salad. It has a chewy texture and a pleasant nutty taste, and is rich in protein, calcium, phosphorus and iron. Bulgur wheat is available at health food shops and Middle Eastern grocers.

BUTTERMILK: Real buttermilk is the liquid residue after cream has been churned into butter. However, the buttermilk referred to here (and used in this book) is cultured buttermilk, which is low-fat milk cultured (in a similar way to yogurt) to produce a pleasant, mild-tasting dairy product the consistency of light cream.

Anise

Basil

165

Cultured buttermilk is delicious in drinks, soups, and vegetable dishes.

CAMPHOR: A pure white crystalline powder derived from steam distillation of the camphor tree, *Cinnamomum camphera*, which grows in China and India. It is used in tiny amounts to flavour Indian milk sweets and puddings. It is available at some Indian grocers and pharmacies.

CANNELINI BEANS: The long, white cannelini beans are probably used more than any other dried beans in Italian dishes. They resemble dried white haricot (navy) beans, although they are smaller. Soaked and boiled in water until soft, they feature in many vegetable dishes and soups.

CARAWAY: Caraway seeds are the fruits of the hardy biennial herb *Carum carvi*, a native of Europe, Asia, and North Africa. The brown seeds are curved and tapered at each end, and are sometimes mistaken for cumin seeds, although they taste quite different. Caraway seeds are warm, sweet, biting, and pleasantly acrid. They are a favourite flavouring for many kinds of rye bread and are also widely used in cheese, cakes, and biscuits.

CARDAMOM: The aromatic seeds of the fruit of the tropical plant *Elettaria cardamomum*, a member of the ginger family which grows in the moist tropical regions of South India and Sri Lanka. Cardamom is the world's third most costly spice, topped only by saffron and vanilla.

The odour and flavour of cardamom is quite pronounced—reminiscent of lemon rind and eucalyptus. Cardamom is popular in some Middle Eastern dishes. In Indian cuisine, cardamom is used in rice dishes, milk sweets, and *halava*. It is also chewed as a breath freshener and digestive aid after a meal.

Cardamom is available in the pod (green or bleached), as decorticated seeds (the outer shell having been removed), or powdered. I would suggest you shun the latter two forms and purchase whole pods, available at Indian and Middle Eastern grocery stores, for the freshest and most flavoursome cardamom seeds.

CAROB: The edible beans of the carob tree, a legume belonging to the locust family. The beans grown on this tall evergreen tree are dried, ground into powder, and used as one would use

Cardamom

Carob

cocoa. Carob powder is rich in protein and is delicious in confectionery. It also contains pectin, which is an excellent tonic for the stomach. Carob powder is available at health food stores and specialty shops.

CAPERS: The pickled flower buds of the wild Mediterranean bush *Capparis rupestris*. Capers have been used as a condiment for thousands of years, and today feature especially in French and Italian cuisine. They have a distinct sour, salty flavour and are featured in this book in *Tartare Sauce*.

CAYENNE PEPPER: The orange-red to deep-red powder derived from small, sun-dried, pungent red chili peppers (*Capsicum frutescens*). This bitingly hot condiment should be used with restraint, for a small amount will add considerable zest and flavour to dishes. It's used in a number of hot dishes, notably in Mexican and Indian cuisine. Cayenne is available from supermarkets or well-stocked grocers.

CHAMOMILE: Both Roman and German chamomile grow wild over much of Europe and temperate Asia. An aromatic herb with a delicate flavour and fruity aroma reminiscent of apples, it is made from the dried flower heads of Roman chamomile (*Anthemis nobilis*). Taken as a tea, it is good for relieving colic and flatulence and is a stomach tonic. It is available at any well-stocked supermarket or health food shop.

CHANA DAL: Husked, split whole dried brown chickpeas (a relative of the common chickpea). They are very popular in Indian cuisine, especially in *dal* dishes and savouries, being tasty, nutritious, and easy to digest. *Chana dal* is roasted and ground into chickpea flour (*besan*) and used throughout India for savouries and sweets. *Chana dal* is featured in this book in *Chana Dal with Potatoes*, and chickpea flour appears in *Assorted Vegetable Fritters (Pakoras)* and *Walnut and Chickpea Flour Fudgeballs (Laddu)*. *Chana dal* is available at Indian grocery stores.
See also: **CHICKPEA FLOUR**

CHAPATI FLOUR: (see *ATTA*)

CHAT MASALA: A traditional companion to freshly-cut fruit in Indian cuisine. This light-brown spice blend contains a number of ingredients, notably black salt, mango powder, and asafoetida. Sprinkled on fruit with a few drops of fresh lime juice, it makes a deliciously different dessert. Available from Indian grocery stores.

CHERVIL: A close relative of cow parsley, lacy-leaved garden chervil (*Anthriscus cerefolium*) is an annual plant mainly cultivated in France as a kitchen herb. Its flavour is delicate and less robust than parsley, with the distinctive aroma of anise.

It is used raw, fresh, chopped, or broken into tiny sprigs. It is generally not cooked, but sometimes it is added to a dish just before serving.

Chervil can be grown without difficulty in almost any garden or window box, or can be purchased at, or ordered from, well-stocked specialty greengrocers.

CHICKPEAS: Known as *garbanzos* in Spanish-speaking countries or *ceci* in Italy, chickpeas are the peas from the pods of the plant *Cicer arietinum*. They are popular in India in their immature green state, whereas they are commonly known outside of India in their dried state. These large, light-brown, wrinkled peas must be soaked before use, then boiled until soft. They are used extensively in many cuisines around the world, especially Indian, Mexican, and Middle Eastern. They are rich in protein—100 grams (3½ ounces) cooked chickpeas contain 20 g protein. Chickpeas provide nearly double the amont of iron and more vitamin C than most legumes. Chickpeas are available at Continental, Indian, and Middle Eastern grocers, and at well-stocked supermarkets.

CHICKPEA FLOUR: The finely milled pale-yellow flour from ground, roasted *chana dal*. It is popular in Indian cuisine for making batter, as a binding agent, and in confectionery. It is also known as *besan* flour, *gram* flour, and peas meal, and is available at Indian grocers.
See also: ***CHANA DAL***

CHILIES, dried: The dried pods of plants of the genus *Capsicum*, they are indigenous to Mexico, Central America, the West Indies, and much of South America. Dried chilies vary in size and heat, and can be obtained whole or crushed. In Indian cuisine, chilies are sautéed in *ghee* or oil with other spices and added to *dals*, chutneys, and sauces to impart heat. Obtain dried red chilies at Indian or Middle Eastern grocery stores, or at supermarkets.

CHILIES, green: The unripe green pods of various chili peppers are available in the markets of most hot countries. Choose firm, green specimens. Fresh green chilies have an advantage over dried chilies, as they impart a delicious flavour as well as heat. The seeds are the hottest part, and often a recipe calls for removing the seeds to tame the heat of the chili. Green chilies are indispensable in Indian, Mexican, Indonesian, and Italian dishes.

Fresh chilies are also nutritious, being rich in vitamins A and C. They also stimulate sluggish digestion. Fresh green chilies are available at most greengrocers and supermarkets.

CHILI OIL: A fiery hot oil used in Chinese cooking. To make your own chili oil, stir-fry 3 or 4 dried red chilies in a few tablespoons of oil over moderate heat for 3 minutes. Strain the oil and use as required. Alternatively, chili oil can be purchased at any Chinese or South East Asian grocer.

CHOKO: Used in Mexican, Chinese, and Indonesian cooking, this delicate, pale-green, pear-shaped vegetable, which is related to the gourd family, originally came from Mexico, where it is known as *chayote*. When buying chokos, look for young tender ones with pale, green, almost translucent skin. The spikes on the skin should be short and soft. Chokos add a subtle flavour and an apple-like texture to any dish.

Chickpeas

CHOY BOH: Preserved turnips, used in Chinese and Japanese cooking. Sold in small packets, they are not expensive and will keep for a long time in the refrigerator. Preserved turnips impart a pleasant, slightly salty flavour to vegetable dishes and savouries. They're available at Asian grocery stores.

CHOY SUM: Although this plant, also known as Rape (its seeds are the source of Rapeseed oil), is grown in various parts of the world, it is used extensively in Chinese and Japanese cuisine as a vegetable. It is delicately flavoured, with yellow flowers, succulent green stalks, and small bright-green leaves branching from a central stem. This attractive vegetable is available from Chinese grocers all year round.

CINNAMON: *Cinnamomum zeylanicum* is a moderate-sized, bushy evergreen tree of the laurel family whose dried inner bark is true cinnamon. Native to southern India and Sri Lanka, the thin bark sheaths are sun-dried and packed one inside the other to produce "sticks" or "quills".

Confusion sometimes exists in distinguishing cinnamon from cassia. In some countries, what is sold as cinnamon is in fact cassia (*Cinnamomum cassia*). Cassia is a taller tree with smaller flowers and fruits than true cinnamon. In general, cassia is prepared for the market in much the same way as cinnamon, and their flavours are similar, although cinnamon is less pungent and more delicate than cassia. Cassia powder is reddish-brown, while cinnamon powder is tan. Cinnamon or cassia sticks impart a sweet, aromatic flavour to fancy Indian rice dishes, vegetables, and *dals*. Ground to a powder, cinnamon is an important ingredient in the North Indian spice blend *garam masala*. Cinnamon also features extensively in Mid-

Cinnamon

Coriander

Cumin

dle Eastern and European cuisine. It is available at supermarkets and Indian and Middle Eastern grocers.

CITRIC ACID: Powdered citric acid crystals can be used as a souring agent in preparing dishes where moisture must be avoided. It is also effective in curdling milk when making *Home-made Curd Cheese* (*Panir*). These sugar-like white crystals are available at Indian grocery stores, supermarkets, and chemist shops.

CLOVES: The dried nail-shaped buds from the evergreen tree *Eugenia aromatica*. Clove trees are neat evergreens with aromatic pink buds. These buds, when hand picked and dried, turn reddish brown to become the cloves with which we are familiar.

Good cloves should have a strong, pungent, sweet aroma and flavour and should be well-formed, plump, and oily. Cloves have diverse uses in different cuisines of the world, being used for cakes, tarts and pastries, fancy rice dishes, soup stocks, sweet cooked fruits, and in various spice blends, including some North Indian *garam masalas*. Cloves are available at supermarkets and Indian grocery stores.

COCONUT: The coconut palm, *Cocos nucifera*, is grown on tropical coasts all over the world and is the source of many products. Most important are the nuts (technically called drupes in this case). When coconuts are picked green, one can extract their sweet juice as a beverage. The pulp inside is used in many South Indian savoury dishes. When coconuts ripen on the tree, the picked fruits yield moist, white "meat", which is excellent in varieties of vegetable dishes, savouries, rice dishes, sweets, chutneys, and beverages, especially in Indian and South-East Asian cuisine.

Dried coconut is dessicated and is familiar in Western cuisine as an ingredient in sweets and cakes. When a recipe calls for fresh coconut, dried dessicated coconut is a poor substitute. Fresh coconuts are easily available in tropical areas and can even be found for sale far from their place of origin. These will be suitable as long as they are still full of juice and have no cracks or signs of mould around their "eyes". Once cracked open, separated from their husk, and peeled, fresh coconut can be sliced, grated, shredded, stored in the refrigerator for several days, or frozen.

COCONUT CREAM: An unsweetened, fatty coconut product sold in blocks in Asian and Western supermarkets. Imparting a rich texture and coconut flavour, it is used in varieties of sweet and savoury Indonesian, Thai,

and occasionally Indian dishes.

COCONUT MILK: Known as *santan* in Indonesian cooking, this creamy white liquid with a fresh, coconut flavour is extracted from fresh coconut pulp and is used in varieties of South East Asian and Indonesian dishes. It is available in cans from supermarkets and Asian grocers.

COCONUT OIL: Extracted from coconut 'meat', this oil is solid white fat at room temperature but clear when heated. It is used extensively in South Indian cuisine.

CORNFLOUR: When I mention cornflour in this book, I am referring to what Americans call "cornstarch", and not to the flour milled from corn. Cornflour, sometimes referred to as wheat starch, is the dry white powdered starch remaining when the protein has been removed from wheat flour. It is used in many cuisines, especially Chinese, as a thickener for sauces. It is available from any grocer or supermarket.

CORN MEAL: (see **POLENTA**)

CORN OIL: Extracted from maize, or corn, it is a light oil and one of the most unsaturated of grain oils. It can be used as an alternative to olive oil as a salad dressing ingredient, and since it has a high smoking point, it is an excellent frying oil.

CORIANDER LEAVES, fresh: The fresh leaves of the hardy annual plant *Coriandrum sativum*. Fresh coriander is one of the most commonly used flavouring herbs in the world, certainly on par with parsley. It is found in markets throughout the Middle East, China, South East Asia, India, and South and Central America. Bunches of coriander can be recognised by their smell and their fan-like lower leaves and feathery upper ones.

Also known as *cilantro*, Chinese Parsley, and *har dhania*, fresh coriander is a zesty and delicious addition to many varieties of the world's cuisines. Its unique warm-bodied taste is found in Indian vegetable dishes, *dals*, savouries, and fresh chutneys (see *Peanut and Coriander Chutney*). It also makes a very beautiful garnish. Purchase fresh coriander from Oriental and Latin American grocers or well-stocked produce markets and greengrocers.

CORIANDER SEEDS: The seeds of the annual herb *Coriandrum sativum*. Coriander seeds are a favourite flavouring spice in Indian, Cypriot, and some Latin American (especially Peruvian) cuisines. They are almost round, brown to yellowish-red, with a warm, distinctive fragrance and a pleasant taste—mild and sweet yet slightly pungent, reminiscent of a combination of sage and lemon. Coriander is available whole or ground, although I recommend obtaining the whole seeds and grinding them yourself when you need the freshest coriander flavour. Known as *dhania* in Indian cuisine, coriander complements the flavour of many savoury dishes. They are available at Indian and Middle Eastern grocery stores.

COUSCOUS: A grain product made from semolina. It is also the name of the famous dish of which *couscous* is the main ingredient, being one of the most common and widely known North African Arab dishes. I have included a recipe for *Couscous with Vegetable Sauce* in this book.

CUMIN SEEDS: The seeds of the small annual herb of the parsley family *Cuminum cyminum*. Cumin seeds are oval and yellowish-brown, similar in appearance to the caraway seed but longer. They have a warm, strongly aromatic, and slightly bitter flavour and are used extensively in Indian, Middle Eastern, and Latin American cuisine (especially in Mexican dishes).

The flavour and aroma of cumin, like most spice seeds, emerge best after they have been dry-roasted or added to hot oil. In Indian cuisine cumin is popular in vegetable dishes, yogurt-based salads (*raitas*), *dals*, and savouries.

Cumin seeds can be obtained from any Indian or Middle Eastern grocer.

CURD CHEESE (*Panir*): The simplest type of unripened fresh cheese, produced by adding an acidic curdling agent to boiled raw milk. This versatile food ingredient is popular in all varieties of Indian cuisine, and it can also be used as a substitute for *tofu*, *feta*, or farmer's cheese. It is high in protein, has a soft consistency, and is sweeter and creamier than *tofu*. It can be cubed and deep-fried, and added to moist vegetable dishes and rice dishes, crumbled into salads, kneaded and rolled into smooth balls, and made into confectionery.

CURRY LEAVES: The thin, shiny, dark-green leaves of the South East Asian tree *Murraya koenigii*. Curry leaves are highly aromatic when fresh. Used especially in South Indian kitchens, they are generally sautéed in *ghee* with mustard seeds and asafoetida and added to *dals*, fresh coconut chutney, or vegetable dishes. They are an important ingredient in one variety of curry powder used in Tamil Nadu.

Dried leaves are inferior but sometimes all that is available. Obtain curry leaves from Indian grocery stores.

DAIKON RADISH: This large white radish is commonly grown in Japan. It is eaten cooked or raw, and is also grated and pickled. Pickled daikon radish is called *Takuwan* and is eaten as a condiment with savouries such as *Japanese Rice Balls* (*Onigiri*).

DAL: The name for any type of dried bean, lentil, or pea in India. It is also the name for thick gravy-like or thin soup-like dishes prepared from these beans, lentils, or peas.

Most raw *dal* in India is split. The following *dals* are used in this book: brown lentils, yellow and green split peas, whole mung beans, *arhar dal*, *chana dal*, green split peas, and *urad dal*.

DHANIA: (see **CORIANDER**)

DEHIN: When yogurt is drained of its whey content, the resultant thickened, rather solid cheesy residue is called yogurt cheese, or *dehin* in Indian cuisine. Yogurt cheese is featured in this book in the famous dessert called *Shrikhand*, and also in *Greek Cucumber and Yogurt Dip* (*Tzatziki*) and *Syrian Yogurt Cheese* (*Labneh*).

DILL: A medium-sized herb with small feathery leaves and yellow flowers. Dill (*Anethum graveolens*) is related to anise, caraway, coriander, cumin, fennel, and parsley. Dill seeds are oval, tan, and light in weight, with a clean odour faintly reminiscent of caraway—pungent and pleasantly aromatic. They are most frequently used as a condiment, either whole or ground, especially in pickling cucumbers, and in breads. In France, dill seeds are used extensively in pastries and sauces, while in India they are used in traditional medicines.

The feathery fresh herb known as 'dill weed' is excellent in potato salads. It can be obtained dried. Fresh dill is available at quality produce markets or greengrocers, and dried dill weed and dill seeds can be obtained from health food stores, specialty shops, or well-stocked supermarkets.

Dill

FENNEL: The tall, hardy, aromatic perennial of the parsley family native to southern Europe and the Mediterranean area. Fennel (*Foeniculum vulgare*) is distinguished by its finely divided feathery green foliage and its golden-yellow flowers. It is used both as a herb and for its aromatic seed. In Italian cuisine, the bulb of the Florence fennel, or *finocchio*, is used whole, sliced, or quartered as a vegetable, and either braised or baked *au gratin*. It is also chopped raw in salads. Wild fennel stems and the frondy leaves, with their slightly bitter anise flavour, are used in cooking, especially to flavour sauces.

Fennel seeds, although used to some extent in European cooking, are especially favoured in Indian cuisine.

Fennel

169

The oval, greenish or yellowish-brown seeds resemble tiny watermelons. They emit an agreeable, warm, sweet fragrance, similar to that of anise. Fennel seeds appear in Kashmiri and Punjabi dishes and are one of the five spices in the Bengali spice blend called *panch puran*. They are prominent in the famous beverage *Thandhai*, and in a variety of vegetable dishes, *dals*, and pastries. The most common use of fennel seeds in Indian cuisine is as an after-dinner digestive. They are dry-roasted and chewed, freshening the breath and stimulating digestion. Fresh fennel bulbs are available seasonally at good greengrocer shops. The seeds are available at Indian grocers.

Curry leaves

FENUGREEK: An erect annual herb of the bean family indigenous to western Asia and southeastern Europe. Fenugreek (*Trigonella foenum-graecum*) is cultivated for its seeds, which, although legumes, are used as a spice.

The seeds are small, hard, yellowish-brown, smooth, and oblong, with a little groove across one corner. Fenugreek has a warm, slightly bitter taste reminiscent of burnt sugar and maple.

The seeds are used in Greece and Egypt and especially India, where they are lightly dry-roasted or fried to extract their characteristic flavour. One should note however that over-roasting or-frying results in excessive bitter flavours.

The leaves of the fenugreek plant are also popular in Indian cuisine. Known as *methi*, they are used in vegetable dishes, breads, and savouries. Easily home-grown, fresh young fenugreek leaves are wonderful in salads dressed with oil and lemon.

Fenugreek seeds are available at Indian or Middle Eastern grocers. The fresh leaves (if you are shopping outside India) can occasionally be found in markets, or can be home-grown.

FETA: A crumbly, strong-tasting white cheese usually made from sheep's milk and ripened in brine. *Feta* cheese is especially well-known in Greek cuisine (see *Greek Salad* and *Spinach and Filo Triangles, [Spanakopita]*). *Feta* cheese is available at Greek shops and well-stocked supermarkets.

Fenugreek

FILO PASTRY: A very light and paper-thin pastry popular throughout the Middle East and in Greece. This delicate pastry is used for either sweet or savoury dishes. Filo pastry is featured in this book in *Spinach and Filo Triangles (Spanakopita)*, and in *Turkish Nut Pastries in Syrup (Baklava)*. Filo is difficult to prepare at home and is best purchased refrigerated from well-stocked supermarkets, delicatessens, and health food stores.

FIVE-SPICE: Two varieties of five-spice are prominent in the world of vegetarian cuisine: Chinese five-spice powder and Indian *panch puran*, a blend of five whole spices.

Chinese five-spice powder is a combination of five dried, ground spices, generally cinnamon, cloves, fennel, star anise, and Sichuan peppercorns, the pungent brown peppercorns native to the Sichuan province.

When used as a condiment for fried food, it is used in sparing quantities because it is very potent. Try making your own by grinding together 2 or 3 small sections of cinnamon stick, a dozen cloves, 2 teaspoons of fennel seeds, 2 teaspoons of Sichuan peppercorns, and 3 or 4 star anise. Keep the powder in a well-sealed jar in a cool, dry place. Obtain your ingredients at any Asian grocery store. You can also purchase Chinese five-spice ready-made.

Panch puran is most often associated with Bengali cuisine. It is a combination of equal quantities of fenugreek seeds, cumin seeds, fennel seeds, black mustard seeds, and *nigella (kalonji)* seeds. *Panch puran* is always fried in *ghee* or oil before use to release the dormant flavour in the seeds. Mix your own, or purchase it ready-mixed at Indian grocery stores.

FLAT RICE: Flat, pounded rice, also known as *poha*. Popular in Indian cuisine, it is sometimes deep-fried and added to fried potato straws, peanuts, and raisins and eaten as a tasty snack.

GALANGAL: There are two varieties of *galangal*—greater and lesser. Both are closely related, although the lesser is more important. Greater *galangal* (*Alpinia galanga*), native to Indonesia, is related to ginger. Its large, knobby, spicy roots taste rather like ginger and are used in Indonesian cooking.

Lesser *galangal* (*Alpinia officinarum*) is the rhizome of a plant native to China. Its roots have a pepper-ginger flavour and are used in many Indonesian and Malaysian dishes. In Indonesia it is also known as *laos*.

Laos or *galangal* can occasionally be obtained fresh from Chinese or Indonesian shops. Peel and slice it before use. If unavailable, substitute fresh ginger. *Laos* powder is also used, especially in Indonesian cooking. It is less hot and more bitter than fresh *laos*. Use very sparingly or substitute slices of fresh ginger.

GARAM MASALA: A blend of dry-roasted and ground spices well-used in Indian cuisine. The spices used for *garam masala* warm the body (*garam* means warm). Such spices include dried chilies, black pepper, cardamom, coriander, cinnamon, cloves, and cumin. Other spices, such as ajowan, mace, nutmeg, fennel, bay leaves, ginger, and white and green pepper, as well as other ingredients, such as sesame seeds, coconut, and saffron, are also used according to the region, since Indian cooking styles vary immensely according to the geographical location. Generally, *garam masala* is added towards the end of cooking. It is available at Indian grocery stores.

GHEE: The oil produced by clarifying butter over gentle heat until all the moisture is driven off and the milk-solids are fully separated from the clear butterfat. *Ghee* is an excellent choice for sautéeing and frying and is much favoured in Indian cooking, as well as some French, Saudi Arabian, and other Middle Eastern cuisines. The best *ghee* comes from Holland, Scandinavia, and Australia, although home-made *ghee* is easy to prepare and cheaper than purchasing ready-made *ghee*.

See page 2 for detailed information on making *ghee*. Alternatively, *ghee* can be purchased at Indian or Middle Eastern grocery stores, or some well-stocked supermarkets.

GINGER: The thick, white, tuberous underground stems, or rhizomes, of the plant *Zingiber officinale*, which thrives in the tropical areas of the world.

Fresh ginger root has a spicy-sweet aroma and a hot, clean taste and is used in many cuisines, especially throughout China, Japan, Thailand, and India. The young "green" ginger is especially appreciated for its fibre-free texture and mild flavour. Mature ginger root is more readily available at produce markets, Asian grocery stores and some supermarkets.

Fresh ginger should be peeled before use. It can be minced, sliced, puréed, shredded, or cut into fine julienne strips and used in vegetable dishes, *dals* and soups, savouries, fried dishes, chutneys, rices, sweets, and drinks.

Ginger powder is not a substitute for fresh ginger, having lost its volatile essential oil, and being sometimes stale or adulterated. Ginger powder is used mostly in European cooking in puddings, creams, beverages, biscuits, breads, and cakes. It is available at most grocery shops or supermarkets.

GLUTEN FLOUR: A flour made from the protein constituent of wheat flour. It creates an extra-spongy texture when added to breads, by virtue of the elastic network it forms in the dough when water is added.

GLUTINOUS RICE FLOUR: A pure-white, starch-like flour made from a special round-grain, matt-white rice, which is much stickier than ordinary rice when cooked. It is used in Chinese, Japanese, Vietnamese, and Korean cooking for batters (savoury and sweet) and pastries (see *Vietnamese Sweet Mung Bean Cakes*). Glutinous rice flour is available at any Asian grocery store.

HARICOT BEANS: A member of the *Phaseolus vulgaris* species, which includes not only haricot but kidney beans, great northern beans, and pinto beans. These dried white beans, also knows as navy beans, are popular in soups, stews, and casseroles. They are well-used in Italian cooking and are known as *fagiolo secco*. They are available at grocery stores and supermarkets.

HING: (See **ASAFOETIDA**)

HORSERADISH ROOT: The root of the hardy perennial plant *Armoracia rusticana*. When scraped or bruised, these stout, white, fleshy, cylindrical roots emit their characteristic highly pungent, penetrating odour, plus volatile oils which cause tears to flow. Horseradish roots are generally peeled and grated and made into sauces to accompany savoury dishes. When choosing horseradish select large roots. The inside core is woody and is not used. Shred or grate the outside of the root, but use straight away and do not cook it, or else the pungent flavour will fade.

Dehydrated powdered horseradish can be used as a substitute, but fresh is better. Fresh horseradish root is sometimes available at quality produce markets and greengrocer shops. The powdered horseradish is available at specialty shops and some supermarkets.

Horseradish

KALAMATA OLIVES: Large, ink-black olives with pointed ends and shiny skin, named after the seaside town of Southern Greece where they are grown. Popular in Greek cuisine, they are flavoursome and full-bodied.

KALA NAMAK: (see **BLACK SALT**)

Kalonji (nigella)

KALONJI SEEDS: Also known as *nigella* or black onion seed (no relation to the onion). Very often these small, jet-black, tear-drop-shaped seeds are confused with, or called, black cumin seeds, which in fact, they are not. *Kalonji* seeds (*Nigella sativa*) have a peppery taste and, when heated, have an herbal aroma. They are an important ingredient in the Bengali spice blend called *panch puran*. They are available at Indian grocery stores.

KARMA: This Sanskrit word means 'action' or, more specifically, any material action that brings a reaction binding us to the material world. According

171

Mint

to the law of *karma*, if we cause pain and suffering to other living beings, we must endure pain and suffering in return.

KECAP MANIS: A thick, sweet variety of soy sauce from Indonesia featured in Indonesian and Malaysian cooking.

KEWRA ESSENCE: This essential flavouring is derived from the shrub known as screw pine (*Pandanus tectorius*), which grows in the humid swampy backwater areas of South India and South East Asia. The flowers have an exquisite rose-like perfume. In Indian cooking, *kewra* essence is used to flavour sweet dishes. It is available in the form of *kewra* essence or *kewra* water at Indian grocers.

KIDNEY BEANS: The popular kidney-shaped red bean from the plant *Phaseolus vulgaris*. Kidney beans can be used in many types of cuisine: as an alternative to borlotti beans in Italian cooking, and as an alternative to pinto beans in Mexican-style cooking, or in stews, soups, and casseroles. Red kidney beans are known as *rajma* in India and are featured in the spicy chili-style dish of the same name popular in the Punjab. They are available at any grocery store or supermarket.

KRISHNA: The name for God given in the Sanskrit Vedic texts of India. Krishna is revered in the *Vedas* as the original form of the Godhead.

KUMERA (pronounced koomerer): A variety of sweet potato with a rich, orange colour, popular in New Zealand.

Marjoram

LAOS: (see **GALANGAL**)

LEMONGRASS: Used as a culinary herb is South East Asian cooking, especially Thai and Indonesian cuisine, lemongrass (*Cymbopogon citratus*) is a typical grass but has a bulbous base and a strong taste and smell of lemon. It is available in powdered form (called *Sereh* powder), in flakes, or sometimes fresh, from Asian grocery stores. Since very little is used at any one time, the dried flakes or powder are more practical to have on one's spice shelf.

LEMONS AND LIMES: Lemons (*Citrus limon*) and limes (*Citrus aurantifolia*) play a significant role in cuisines of the world.
Lemon juice is very much favoured as a souring agent in European and Eastern cuisines alike; the essential 'oil of lemon', which is concentrated in the rind or zest, is particularly well-liked in European cakes and sauces.
Limes are especially used in tropical countries, where they are more easily available. Lime juice, when used in cooking, gives a markedly different flavour to lemon juice, lime juice being more sour and slightly more bitter than lemon juice.
These juices also act as a preservative in cooked foods. Lemons and limes are wonderful sliced as garnishes, and, of course, are excellent thirst-quenchers. In serving an Indian-style meal, a wedge of lemon or lime is essential as an accompaniment.

LENTILS: Used extensively in cuisines of the world. Brown lentils (from the plant *Lens culinaris*) and red lentils (called masoor *dal* in India) are probably the most well-known. *Toovar dal* (*arhar dal*) is another lentil well-loved in Indian cooking. Lentils contain almost 25% protein, 54% carbohydrate and vitamin A, some of the B vitamins, and good amounts of minerals, including iron and calcium. Brown and red lentils are available at almost any supermarket or grocery store. *Toovar dal* is available at Indian grocery stores. (Note that due to their very high protein content, red lentils are not consumed by strict followers of the Vedic culture.)

LIMA BEANS: Popular in European cuisine, lima beans (*Phaseolus lunatas*), are also known as butter beans, and are available large or small. They are tasty additions to soups, stews, and salads and are featured in this book in *Lima Bean and Cheese Croquettes*. They are available at supermarkets and grocery stores.

LIME LEAVES: The fresh or dried leaves of the lime tree. They are used in South East Asian and, especially, Indonesian cooking. The leaves are used in rice, stews, and vegetable dishes to impart a pleasant lime taste.

MANGO POWDER: (see **AMCHOOR**)

MARJORAM: One of the most important of all kitchen herbs, it is used in virtually every type of European cuisine, although not very much used in Eastern cooking. Marjoram (*Majorana hortensis*) has a delicate, pleasant, sweet flavour with a slightly bitter, aromatic undertone. It is generally used in its dried form, for soup, stews, vegetable dishes, and sauces. As a fresh herb, it is delicious in salads.
Dried marjoram is available at any supermarket or grocer. Fresh marjoram is occasionally available at produce markets and at good greengrocers.

MASALA: A combination of herbs, spices, or

172

seasonings used in Indian cuisine. Some *masalas*, like Bengali *panch puran*, contain whole spices. Others, like *chat masala, garam masala, sambar masala*, or *rasam* powder, contain numerous powdered spices combined together. For details on *masalas*, see individual entries.

MEZZE: Middle Eastern hors d'oeuvres or appetizers. *Mezze* is essentially a Lebanese creation, but has spread throughout the Middle East. Delicious vegetarian *mezze* included in this book are fresh, round *Middle Eastern Breads (Pita)*; and dips such as *Chickpea and Sesame Dip (Hummus)*, *Lebanese Eggplant Dip (Babagannouj)*, and *Syrian Yogurt Cheese (Labneh)*. *Lebanese Bulgur-Wheat Salad (Tabbouleh)* invariably appears on the *mezze* banquet table, as do varieties of *Stuffed Vine Leaves (Dolmades)*, along with simple items such as slices of cucumber, olives, fresh raw or blanched vegetables, nuts, whole cooked chickpeas, and lemon wedges.

MINT: A widely used culinary herb. There are many species of mint, and classification is difficult because the species easily cross and hybridize.

Although spearmint (*Mentha spicata*) and peppermint (*Mentha piperata*) are the two most common mints, the round-leaved varieties of apple mint, Bowles mint, and pineapple mint (*Mentha rotundifolia*) are among the best mints for cooking.

Mint may be generally described as having a fresh, strong, sweet, and tangy flavour, with a cool after-taste. Mint is better used fresh rather than dried. In Indian cuisine, mint is commonly used in fresh chutneys (see *Mint Chutney*). Fresh mint also goes with many fruits and is excellent in fruit salads and fruit drinks such as *Lemon Mint and Whey Nectar*.

MOZZARELLA CHEESE: This famous Italian cheese was traditionally made from buffalo's milk, but these days it is more frequently made from cow's milk. It can be eaten fresh, but when hung for some time it becomes a little dry and is then specifically used for cooking. Mozzarella is a good melting cheese, making it a popular topping for pizzas. It can also be baked or batter-fried. It can be obtained at any good supermarket or grocery store.

MUNG BEANS: Protein-rich, green-skinned, oval beans commonly used for sprouting. Also known as 'green gram', whole green mung beans are excellent for stews and soups (see *Mung Bean and Tomato Soup*), as well as Indian dry-bean dishes. It is available at Indian or Asian grocers, or specialty stores.

MUNG BEAN SHOOTS: Sprouted, whole green mung beans. Popular in Chinese cooking, the mung beans are allowed to sprout until quite long. However, from a nutritional point of view, mung beans are best used when the beans have just sprouted and the shoot is less than 1 cm long. These are crisp in texture and bursting with nutrition. Mung bean shoots are rich in vitamins B, C, and E. Their protein content (mung bean shoots are 37% protein) is highly digestible; they are pleasantly sweet, low calorie, and inexpensive.

MUNG *DAL*: The pale-yellow beans from the plant *Phaseolus aureus*. Whether used with or without the husks, split mung beans are a popular food item in Indian cuisine. Mung *dal* is easy to digest, is high in protein, and cooks to a creamy purée in a short time. It is used extensively in soups, stews, and sauces throughout India. Split mung beans are also used in Thai and Vietnamese cooking (see *Vietnamese Sweet Mung Bean Cakes*). It is available at Indian or Asian grocery stores.

MUSTARD SEEDS: Of the many varieties of mustard, the three most prominent are the tiny round brownish-black seeds from the plant known as *Brassica nigra*, commonly known as black mustard; the purple-brown seed of *Brassica juncea*, commonly called brown mustard; and the yellow seeds from *Brassica alba*, known as white or yellow mustard.

Black and brown mustard seeds are often confused with each other. Brown mustard seeds (*Brassica juncea*) are commonly used as a spice seed in Indian cuisine, where they are known as *rai*. In South Indian Cuisine they are fried in hot oil or *ghee* to extract their nutty, pungent flavour before being added to soups, chutneys, or vegetable dishes. In Bengali cuisine, mustard seeds are one of the five ingredients in the whole spice blend known as *panch puran*.

Yellow mustard seeds (*Brassica alba*) are less pungent than the darker varieties and are commonly used in European cuisine as a pickling spice. They are strongly preservative, discouraging moulds and bacteria; hence their inclusion in pickles.

When mustard seeds are pounded, they form the basis of the immense varieties of commercial brands of the condiment known as mustard. Different varieties of mustard are made from different combinations of hulled and unhulled yellow or brown seeds. It is interesting to note that the pungency of mustard is due to an essen-

Nutmeg

Cloves

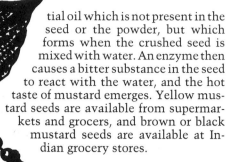

Pepper

tial oil which is not present in the seed or the powder, but which forms when the crushed seed is mixed with water. An enzyme then causes a bitter substance in the seed to react with the water, and the hot taste of mustard emerges. Yellow mustard seeds are available from supermarkets and grocers, and brown or black mustard seeds are available at Indian grocery stores.

NUTMEG: The fragrant nut found in the centre of the fruit of the densely foliated evergreen tree *Myristica fragrans*. The fleshy fruit of the nutmeg tree resembles an apricot. When it is ripe, it splits in half, revealing the beautiful, brilliant scarlet, net-like membrane, or avil, known as mace, which closely enwraps a brittle shell containing the glossy brown, oily nutmeg. Nutmeg is egg-shaped and is about 2.5 cm (1-inch) in diameter, with a sweet, warm, and highly spicy flavour.

Nutmeg is used in many cuisines of the world. It is often an ingredient in the North Indian spice blend known as *garam masala* and is used in cakes and sweet dishes. It is wonderful with pumpkin, squash, and sweet potato. In Italian cuisine it is very popular in spinach dishes and combines well with cheese. Nutmeg is also a common flavouring in the Levant and in various spicy dishes of South East Asia.

Whole nutmegs are best ground straight into the dish into which they are being used, as once grated, nutmeg quickly loses its flavour. Whole nutmegs are available at specialty stores and well-stocked supermarkets and grocery stores.

OATMEAL: The hulled oat grain that has been rolled or cut into flakes. There are three basic types: quick cook, or rolled oats, which generally has small flakes; hulled or gritted oatmeal; and steel cut oatmeal. Oatmeal is among the most nutritious of all the grains—it is 16.7% protein and is rich in inositol (one of the B-complex vitamins), iron, phosphorus, and thiamine. Oatmeal is generally used as porridge or muesli, but is also baked in breads and savoury dishes. It is available at any grocery store.

Red Chilies

OKRA: The rigid green seed pods of the plant *Hibiscus esculentus*. These elegantly curved and pointed pods are used as a vegetable in many cuisines of the world, notably North Indian, Middle Eastern, and Creole.

Its flavour resembles eggplant but with a somewhat mucilaginous texture. Choose crisp, fresh, green pods no longer than 10 cm (4

inches). Avoid shrivelled, limp, dull, or bruised specimens. Okra is available at quality greengrocers and produce markets.

OLIVE OIL: The oil extracted from the fruits of the Mediterranean tree *Olea europaea*.

The finest olive oil is cold-pressed from fresh ripe olives and has a pale-yellow or greenish colour and a very delicate flavour. Cruder versions of olive oil are second pressings made under heat. I prefer to have two grades of olive oil in the kitchen: mild, cold-pressed extra-virgin olive oil for salads and uncooked dishes, and a pure grade olive oil with a high smoking-point for cooking.

Choosing olive oil is much a matter of personal taste and preference. Olive oil is used in many cuisines of the world—not only in Mediterranean cooking. Good quality olive oil is available at specialty and Continental grocers.

OLIVES: The fruits of the semi-tropical evergreen tree *Olea europaea*. Used in all types of Mediterranean, Middle Eastern, European, and Creole cuisines, olives vary in size, colour, oil content, and flavour. Green olives are gathered unripe, whereas black olives are those which have been allowed to ripen. Crude olives straight from the tree are intensely bitter and quite inedible. They have to be washed to remove the bitterness, then pickled for some months in salt water until they resemble the olives as we know them.

See also: **KALAMATA OLIVES**.

ORANGE-BLOSSOM WATER: The fragrant water distilled from orange blossoms and used particularly in Middle Eastern cuisine. France produces and exports high-quality orange-blossom water, as does the Levant, particularly Beirut.

It can be used in savoury rices, sweets, and drinks and is featured in this book in *Middle Eastern Lemonade* and *Turkish Nut Pastries in Syrup (Baklava)*.

OREGANO: A piquant herb famous in Greek and Italian cuisine. Oregano is botanically confused with marjoram. In fact for many years both marjoram and oregano were known as *Marjorana hortensis*. There is still confusion today—oregano is still sometimes known as "Wild Marjoram".

Generally, what is purchased as oregano today is most probably *Origanum vulgare*, with a strong, piquant, sweet flavour and a pleasantly bitter, aromatic undertone.

Oregano is excellent with any tomato dish, especially pizza and varieties of tomato dishes that include pasta sauce. Its flavour marries well with basil. Oregano is available at any continental grocer, supermarket, or specialty shop.

PANCH PURAN: (see **FIVE SPICE**)

PANIR: (see **CURD CHEESE**)

PAPPADAM: Plain or spiced wafer-thin brittle disks made from dried *dal* paste that swell into thin tasty crispbreads when deep-fried or toasted over an open flame. Ranging from 7–25 cm (3–10 inches) in width, *pappadams* are popular served as accompaniments to a full meal, as snacks, or as party nibblers. They're available at Indian grocery stores.

PAPRIKA: The bright red powder made from the dried, sweet, chili-pepper pods of the many varieties of *Capsicum annuum*. Good paprika has a brilliant red colour and because it is not hot, it can be used in generous quantities, giving dishes a rich red hue. It is also very nutritious, having a high vitamin C content.

Paprika is the national spice of Hungary and is featured in Hungarian and Spanish as well as North Indian cuisines (where it is used in *dals* and sauces). It is available at grocery stores.

PARMESAN: The most famous of all the *grana*, or matured hard cheeses of Italy, Parmesan, or *Parmigiano*, takes at least two years to come to maturity, resulting in its traditional sharp flavour. Parmesan cheese should be bought in pieces to be freshly grated over sauces, pasta, or rice, or added to cooked dishes.

PARSLEY: One of the best known and most extensively used culinary herbs in western cuisine. There are numerous cultivated varieties of parsley, but the ornamental curled variety is the most popular as a garnish, and the flat-leaved parsley is most favoured in Italian and other Mediterranean cuisines. Both are varieties of *Petroselinum crispum*. Healthful parsley leaves, with their familiar mild, agreeable flavour, are an excellent source of vitamin C, iron, iodine, and other minerals. Parsley is appealing to the eye, nose, and taste, will sweeten the breath, and is a natural herbal deodorizer. It is a pleasant addition to an enormous variety of savoury dishes. It is available at produce markets, greengrocers, and supermarkets.

PASTA: The finest pasta is made from durum wheat, which is one of the hardest varieties of wheat. When making pasta from durum wheat, only the endosperm of the grain kernel is milled into semolina, which is then mixed with water to make the dough.

When preparing pasta dishes, note that the completed pasta should be tender without being soft and sticky—this is called *al dente*. Pasta comes in many shapes and sizes. Notable varieties used in this cookbook are as follows:
- *Conchiglie*—a shell-shaped pasta
- *Fettuccine*—a flat, ribbon noodle with a coiled, bird's-nest appearance
- *Lasagna*—flat sheets of pasta used for baking in layers
- *Linguine*—a very thin, narrow ribbon noodle
- *Penne rigate*—short, tubular, ridged pasta, like short macaroni, but with angled ends
- *Rigatoni*—a ridged short variety of macaroni
- *Risoni*—rice-shaped pasta used for soups
- *Spaghetti*—common string-like noodles of many varieties
- *Trenette*—narrow ribbon pasta similar to *linguine*
- *Vermicelli*—a thin variety of spaghetti

PEANUT OIL: Also known as ground-nut oil. The method of extraction is particularly important to the value of peanut oil. High-quality, more expensive peanut oil comes from cold pressing. Lesser-quality peanut oils are produced with the aid of chemical solvents. The oil is then refined and heated and treated with anti-oxidants. Cold pressed health-food store peanut oils are good substitutes for olive oil in salads, whereas the cheaper and more refined peanut oils usually sold at supermarkets are good for deep-frying, because peanut oil has a smoking point of up to 230°C/450°F and has a bland flavour.

PEPPER: The small, round berries of the woody perennial evergreen vine *Piper nigrum*. Black pepper, white pepper, and green pepper are all obtained from these same berries in different stages of maturity. For black pepper, the berries are picked whilst green, left in heaps to ferment, sun-dried, and allowed to shrivel and turn dark brown or black. Thus the whole berry, including the dark outer hull, forms what we know as black pepper.

White pepper is produced from fully ripened berries, which are greenish-yellow when picked and at the point of turning red. Then they are soaked in water, the outer hull is rubbed off, and the grey inner berries are sun-dried until they turn creamy white, to become what is known as white pepper.

Green peppercorns are soft, immature berries that have been picked and preserved in brine, or freeze dried.

Black pepper is characterized by a penetrating odour and a hot, biting, and extremely pungent flavour; milder-flavoured white pepper is generally appreciated in European cuisine. Either way, black and white pepper are used in practically every cuisine in the world. Although available pre-ground, discerning cooks prefer the superior flavour of freshly ground peppercorns, for which a pepper mill is an essential acquisition.

Rosemary

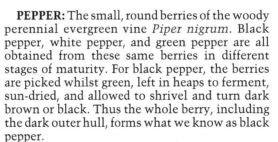

Parsley

175

Sage

Star Anise

PINTO BEANS: Protein-rich beans related to the kidney bean, from the well-known *vulgaris* family. Much-used in Mexican-style cuisine, it can be substituted with kidney beans if unavailable.

PIMIENTO: Skinned sweet red peppers of a small, elongated variety of *Capsicum annuum*. They are preserved in saltwater or sometimes in oil, and are used in Mediterranean cooking to add bright colours and sweet flavour, especially to salads. They also make an attractive garnish when drained and cut into strips.

PINENUT: Also known as pine kernel, *pignolia*, or *pinoli*. Pinenuts come from the stone pine (*Pinus pinea*), a beautiful Mediterranean pine tree. The pine cones are gathered, the seeds are shaken out and cracked, and the small white or cream-coloured kernels are extracted. Their delicious, delicate nutty taste has made them a very popular ingredient in Italian, Spanish, and Middle Eastern cuisine. They are available at specialty, Continental, or Middle Eastern grocers.

PITA: A lightly leavened round Middle Eastern bread with a soft crust and usually a hollow centre. Generally made without oil, it is baked in a very hot oven for a few minutes, where it puffs up, deflating when cooled. There are many versions throughout the Middle East, each one with a different name. The term *pita* has become a popular name for these breads in the West. Whether in Greece, Turkey, Lebanon, Syria, Morocco, Algeria, or Armenia, some version of round, slightly leavened bread is always available, especially for the famous *mezze*, or hor d'oeuvres.

POLENTA: A yellow maize or cornmeal grown in northern Italy, where it is regarded as a staple food. *Polenta* is graded according to its texture and is available fine-, medium-, or coarse-ground. It is available at most supermarkets and health food stores.

POPPY SEEDS: Two varieties of poppy seed are referred to here—black and white. Both are the seeds of the poppy plant *Papaver somniferum*.
The minute, kidney-shaped, bluish-black seeds have a pleasant nutty taste and crunchy texture. They are well-known in Middle Eastern and European cuisine as a topping for breads and cakes, or ground up and sweetened as a pastry filling.

White poppy seeds are much used in Indian cuisine. They are even smaller than black poppy seeds, have a similar flavour, and are creamy-white. When ground, they add special flavours to Bengali dishes. They are especially used as a thickener for sauces or gravies (flours are generally not used in Indian cuisine for this purpose).
Obtain black poppy seeds from any grocer or supermarket. White poppy seeds can be purchased at Indian Grocers.

PRASADAM: Food which has been offered to God before being eaten. *Prasadam* means 'God's mercy'. See introduction for more information.

RASAM POWDER: A South Indian spice blend used to flavour the famous *rasam*, a chili-hot soup dish made from *toovar* (*arhar*) *dal* lentils. Ingredients vary. The home-made *rasam* powder recipe contained in this book (see *Fiery South Indian Toor-Dal Soup*) contains mustard seeds, coriander seeds, dried hot red chilies, black peppercorns, fenugreek seeds, and cumin seeds. *Rasam* powder can be purchased ready-mixed in packets or tins from Indian grocery shops.

RICOTTA: Crumbly, soft white cheese made from the whey of cow's milk and popular in Italian cuisine. It is frequently used in cooking both sweet and savoury dishes in Italy, for, like curd cheese or cottage cheese, its mild, somewhat bland flavour combines well with other ingredients. It is available at selected supermarkets or specialty grocers.

ROSEMARY: The small, narrow, aromatic leaves of the evergreen shrub *Rosmarinus officinalis*. This fragrant seasoning herb with its clean, woody odour reminiscent of pine is popular in some European cuisines. Its strong, camphor-like taste is not always appreciated however, and it is easily over-used. Because whole leaves of dried rosemary are not pleasant to find in a dish, I find it useful to grind them to a powder before using. If fresh rosemary is available, whole sprigs can be added to a dish and removed whole at the completion of the cooking.

ROSE WATER: The diluted essence of rose petals, particularly from the highly scented species *Rosa damascena* and *Rosa centifolia*. It is widely used throughout the Middle East as a flavouring agent. In India it is especially used in the refreshing, icy-cold, sweet yogurt-based beverage known as *lassi*, in *Milk Balls in Rose Syrup* (*gulab jamun*), and in *rasgoolas*. It is available at Middle Eastern and Indian grocers.

SAMBAR POWDER: A zesty South Indian spice combination always added to the famous hot-and-sour *dal* dish called *Sambar*. Varieties of *sambar* powder are available, each with different combinations of ingredients. Varieties might contain ground, roasted red chilies, dried curry leaves, roasted and ground coriander, cumin, mustard and fenugreek seeds, black peppercorns, turmeric, sesame seeds, and toasted and finely powdered *chana dal*, *toovar dal*, and *urad dal*. *Sambar* powder (also called *sambar masala*) is available at Indian grocery stores.

SAMBAL OELEK: A hot condiment made from ground, fresh, hot red chilies, popular in Malay and Indonesian cuisine. It is often added to a dish for an extra-hot chili dimension, such as in *Malaysian Hot Noodles with Tofu* (*Mie Goreng*).

Available at Asian grocery stores. To make 2 teaspoons (10 ml) of your own *Sambal Oelek*, pound together 2 hot red chillies and ½ teaspoon (2 ml) salt.

SANTAN: (see **COCONUT MILK**)

SAFFLOWER OIL: The oil extracted from the seed of the tall, thistle-like safflower plant (*Carthamus tinctorius*). The seeds are husked and pressed and the oil extracted by hydraulic or chemical means. Safflower oil is low in saturated fatty acids, has a mild flavour, has a high smoking point, and is suitable as a salad oil or a deep-frying oil.

SAFFRON: The slender dried stigmas of the flowers of *Crocus sativus*, grown commercially in Spain, Kashmir, and China. When the plants bloom, the brilliant stigmas (the female organs of the plants) are hand-picked daily, just as the plants open in the early morning. About 210,000 dried stigmas, picked from about 70,000 flowers, yield one pound of saffron. Understandably, cost of saffron production is very high, and saffron is the world's most expensive spice. (At the time of writing, pure Spanish saffron is locally available at $3,655 per kilo.)

After picking, the saffron is dried in sieves over low heat, then stored immediately. The final product is a compressed, highly aromatic matted mass of narrow, thread-like, dark-orange to reddish-brown strands about 2.5 cm (1-inch) long.

Saffron has a pleasantly spicy, pungent, slightly bitter honey-like taste with such a potent colouring power that one part of its colouring component, known as *crocin*, is capable of colouring up to 150,000 parts of water unmistakably yellow.

Saffron has enjoyed immense popularity throughout the world for centuries. By the sixteenth century, for instance, saffron was being extensively cultivated in England as a culinary spice. Its popularity today is limited to mainly Indian, French, Middle Eastern, and Spanish cuisines.

The saffron strands should be soaked and ground or slightly dry-roasted and powdered before using.

A big pinch of saffron is sufficient to colour a whole dish, but be sure to purchase the real thing--saffron is often adulterated. And remember, there is no such thing as cheap saffron! Saffron is available at Indian grocers, gourmet stores, and large Chinese medical centres, where it is known as *hoong fa* (ask for the more expensive variety).

SEMOLINA: The cream-coloured cereal obtained from hard durum-wheat grains in the middle stages of flour milling when the wheat germ, bran, and endosperm are separated. The first millings of the endosperm are known as semolina.

Semolina is ground fine, medium, and coarse. Besides being used for making pasta in Italy, where semolina enjoys great popularity, it is also used in Indian cuisine, where it is known as *sooji*. It is simmered for fluffy sweet *halava* puddings or savoury vegetable dishes called *upma*. I find that medium- or coarse-ground semolina yields the best semolina *halava*.

Semolina is available at Indian, Italian, or specialty grocers and some supermarkets.

SESAME OIL: Two types of sesame oil are referred to here. One is expressed from the roasted seeds of the annual plant *Sesamum indicum*. It is much favoured as a flavouring agent in Chinese and Korean cooking. It has a low smoking-point and a delicious roasted-sesame flavour. Generally this delicate brown oil is added as a final seasoning to a cooked dish.

The golden oil expressed from the oil-rich unroasted sesame seeds has a slightly sweet smell and a clean taste. It has a higher smoking-point than roasted sesame oil and is used both as a salad oil and especially as a frying oil throughout the world, especially in Mexico and South India, where it is popular because it does not turn rancid, even in the hottest weather.

Chinese sesame oil is available at Asian grocery stores, and the cold-expressed pale sesame oil is available at health food stores or well-stocked grocers and supermarkets.

SESAME PASTE: A commonly used ingredient in Chinese cooking, not to be confused with *tahini*. Chinese sesame paste is made from whole, roasted, crushed sesame seeds. The oily, nutty-flavoured paste with a consistency of thick peanut butter has distinct smoky overtones and adds a special touch to savoury dishes. It is available at Asian grocery stores.

Tarragon

Saffron Crocus

Toovar dal

Turmeric

SESAME SEEDS: The seeds of the cultivated annual plant *Sesamum indicum*, grown predominantly in India and China. These flat, pear-shaped seeds are generally lightly roasted to bring out the nutty flavour and are popular in many cuisines of the world. In western cuisine they are scattered on bread and cakes before baking; they are ground into a delicious Middle Eastern confection called *halva*, and a semi-liquid paste called *tahini*; in Japanese cuisine they are roasted with sea salt and ground to a fine powder called *gomashio*, a versatile condiment; and they are popular in many regional Indian cuisines.

SICHUAN PEPPERCORNS: The dried red berries of the small, feathery-leaved, spiny tree *Xanthoxylum piperitum*, grown in Sichuan province of South Eastern China.

Sichuan peppercorns have a pungent smell, but only a faintly hot taste, and are an important ingredient in Chinese five-spice powder.

SNOWPEAS: The young, sweet pea pods of *Pisum saccaratum*, also called *mange-tout* in France. This delicately flavoured vegetable is a versatile cooking ingredient, especially in Chinese cooking, where it is stir-fried quickly to retain its flavour and colour. The pods should have their tops removed and their strings pulled away before use. They're available at Chinese grocers and supermarkets.

SPLIT PEAS: Skinned and split, green or yellow dried peas. The green ones are especially good for cooking to a creamy purée (see *Green Split-Pea Dal with Spinach and Coconut Milk*).

Yellow split peas can replace *toovar* or *chana dal* in a recipe. They are available at all supermarkets and grocery stores.

SRILA PRABHUPADA: The founder-*acharya* (spiritual master) of the International Society for Krishna Consciousness (ISKCON). Srila Prabhupada was the author of many spiritual texts and the world's most distinguished teacher of Vedic religion and thought. He guided his society and saw it grow to a worldwide confederation of hundreds of *ashramas*, schools, temples, institutes, and farm communities.

STAR ANISE: The dried, hard, brown, star-shaped fruit of the small evergreen tree *Illicium verum*. Star anise has a lico-rice-like flavour and odour and is an ingredient in the Chinese five-spice powder.

SUMAC: An important souring agent in Arab cuisine. The seeds of *Rhus corioria* are ground to a purple-red powder and used to add a sour, pleasantly astringent taste to recipes as a preferred substitute for lemon.

The extracted juice of the soaked seeds is used in salads and in some vegetable dishes to impart a tamarind-like flavour. *Sumac* has a pleasant, rounded, fruity sourness which is well worth experimenting with. It is available at Middle Eastern grocers.

TAHINI: A semi-liquid sesame butter used in Middle Eastern cuisine. This cream-grey paste has the consistency of runny peanut butter and is the basis of various salad dressings and *mezze* (entrées) throughout Greece, Cyprus, Lebanon, Jordan, and Syria, where it is known as *tahina*.

TAMARILLO: Sometimes called the tree tomato, this glossy plum-red egg-shaped fruit is a native to South America and the Peruvian Andes. It is now grown commercially in New Zealand. Tamarillos have a juicy, slightly acid flesh, and can be used raw, after peeling, for fruit salads or cooked in purées and chutneys. It is available at selected produce markets and greengrocers.

TAMARIND: The pulp extracted from the brown pods of the tamarind tree, *Tamarindus indica*.

The fresh pulp has a sour fruity taste and is popular in Indian and Indonesian cooking. Tamarind is available in different forms commercially. The crudest consists of blocks of partly dried, unpitted, broken, sticky, fibrous pods. They should be macerated in water to extract the sour brown tamarind juice, as should another form, in blocks of fibrous pulp without seeds. The most convenient is tamarind concentrate, which can be used straight from the jar. Tamarind makes excellent sweet-and-sour chutneys or sauces, and can be used in vegetable dishes and curries.

Tamarind in its various forms is available at Indian and South East Asian grocery stores.

TARRAGON: This famous gourmet culinary herb with long slender leaves and pungent, bittersweet, tangy flavour is popular in French cuisine, especially as one of the four fresh herbs found in *fines herbes* (along with parsley, chives, and chervil) and in butters, soups, sauces, creams, and salads. French tarragon (*Artemesia dracunculus*) is stronger in flavour than Russian tarragon (*Artemesia dracunculoides*). Tarragon is available at select greengrocers and produce markets.

THAI RICE: A long-grain, aromatic white rice

from Thailand. Sometimes called Jasmine rice, it cooks to large, soft, fluffy grains.

THYME: This attractive herb is grown in Mediterranean regions and Asia Minor. There are more than one hundred species of thyme, but common or garden thyme, *Thymus vulgaris*, is frequently used. Others include lemon, mint, orange, golden-lemon, caraway-scented, woolly-stemmed, and the silver thyme. Used fresh or dried, thyme imparts a distinctively warm, pleasant, aromatic flavour and is popular as one of the great European culinary herbs. It is used alongside bay and parsley in *bouquet garni*, and goes into many soups and vegetable dishes (especially potatoes, zucchini, eggplants, and sweet peppers). It is available fresh at selected greengrocers and dried at grocery stores and supermarkets.

TOFU: Soybean curd, or *tofu*, is used in Chinese, Japanese, Korean, and Indonesian cooking. This white, almost tasteless and odourless substance is produced from soya beans that have been successively crushed, boiled in water, strained, and pressed into a mould.
Tofu is low in calories and is cholesterol-free. High in protein, *tofu* is becoming increasingly popular in western kitchens.
Standard Chinese *tofu*, which is lightly pressed, is sold fresh in most Chinese grocers. It has the consistency of firm custard. A firmer variety of *tofu* is also available at Chinese shops. Japanese style *tofu* is the variety usually sold in health food shops in Australia. Being firmer, it is good for slicing, cubing, and deep-frying. Dried beancurd sheets and sticks are also used in Chinese cooking and are available at Chinese grocery shops.

TOOVAR DAL: Also called *arhar dal*, *toor dal*, or pigeon peas, these cream-coloured split lentils, which are paler in colour, flatter, and larger than yellow split peas, are widely used for cooking in Northern and Southwestern India. They have a delightful, slightly sweet flavour and are easy to digest, especially in the famous South Indian soup-like dishes *rasam* and *sambar*. *Toovar dal* is available at Indian grocers.

TORTILLA: A thin, round, flat bread made from white cornmeal, or masa. *Tortillas* are the national breads of Mexico and are cooked on a griddle. They're eaten fresh and are also the basis of Mexican dishes such as *Enchiladas* and *Tacos*.

TURMERIC: The rhizome, or underground stem, of the tropical herb *Curcuma longa*. The short, waxy, orange-yellow rhizomes are boiled, cleaned, sun-dried, and then ground to a fine, aromatic, yellowish powder that is used as an essential ingredient in Asian and, especially, Indian cooking. Turmeric adds a brilliant yellow colour to cooked dishes and imparts a slightly bitter, pungent flavour.
Used in vegetable, legume, bean, and *dal* dishes, it introduces colour and warmth to a dish, although overuse produces excessive colour and bitterness. Turmeric powder is available at Indian grocers and specialty stores.

TURNIP, preserved: (see *CHOY BOH*)

TAKUWAN: Japanese white daikon radish, pickled in rice bran and salt.

UMEBOSHI PLUM: Small, salted, pickled plum that is used in Japanese cooking. It has a dry, sour taste and is used to flavour rice and other foods.

URAD DAL: The split dried beans from the plant *Phaseolus mungo*. Whole *urad* beans are blackish-grey. Split *urad dal* are cream-white. Their shape resembles their close relative, split mung *dal*. They are used to prepare protein-rich purées and soups in Indian cuisine. Combined with grains and milk products, their protein value increases. In South Indian cooking they are fried in *ghee* or oil for use as nutty seasoning, and soaked and ground into dumplings, pancakes, and fried savouries. *Urad dal* is available at Indian grocery stores.

VANILLA: The pod of the climbing tropical orchid *Vanilla planifolia*. The vanilla flavouring material is obtained from the dried, cured, partially ripe pods. The white crystalline compound called vanillin, present only in the cured black pods, provides the delicately sweet, rich, spicy, and persistent aroma which characterises vanilla.
Whole vanilla beans are cooked with creams, custards, and sauces in French cuisine. The beans can be washed, dried and re-used. Vanilla sugar and pure vanilla essence are substitutes.
Vanilla beans are available at specialty grocers.

VEDIC CULTURE: Life-style based on the tenets of the four original scriptures of India, the Vedas.

VINE LEAVES: The leaves of the grape vine *Vitis vinifera*. The most popular use of vine leaves in vegetarian cookery is to stuff them with aromatic rice. The resultant little parcels are enjoyed in Middle Eastern and Mediterranean cuisines as *Dolma* or *Dolmades*. Vine leaves are obtained fresh in countries where grapes grow (leaves from any vine yielding

Vanilla

Thyme

179

edible grapes are suitable) or purchased preserved in water, salt, and citric acid in jars or plastic pouches from Greek or Middle Eastern grocery stores.

WATER CHESTNUTS: Fresh water chestnuts, with their crunchy, succulent texture and sweet, nutty taste, are a common delicacy in Asian cuisine. They are actually the edible root of an aquatic plant. The fresh water-chestnut has a tight skin; it should be peeled and sliced as required. If unavailable at good Chinese produce markets, tinned sliced water chestnuts sold at Chinese grocery stores are an acceptable (though inferior-tasting) substitute.

WHEY: The liquid by-product when milk is curdled in the curd-cheese-making process, or from yogurt when it is allowed to drain in a cheesecloth. It can be used in bread-making, in soups, or to cook vegetables. Allowed to sour, it can be used as an agent to curdle further batches of milk.

YEAST: Yeast used for baking commonly comes in two forms: compressed, or fresh, yeast; and dried or dehydrated yeast. When used in bread-making, both varieties produce enzymes which act on simple sugars to make carbon dioxide gas. This aerates the bread dough, causing it to rise, giving the bread its characteristic light texture.

YOGURT: This versatile and healthful cultured dairy product is a staple food found in many cuisines of the world. Its pleasantly tangy flavour and smooth, refreshing texture give it great appeal.

Yogurt appears in many dishes throughout this book, including *South Indian Yogurt Rice, Gujarati Yogurt Soup, South Indian Vegetable Combination, Mixed Vegetable and Yogurt Salad, Fresh Coconut Chutney, Savoury Dal Dumplings in Yogurt with Tamarind Sauce, Syrian Yogurt Cheese, Soft Cakes in Strawberry Yogurt, and Mango Yogurt Smoothie*. For information on how to prepare your own yogurt, refer to page one.

YOGURT CHEESE: (see **DEHIN**)

Directory of Recipes

182

General Index

About the Author

Since becoming a member of the International Society for Krishna Consciousness (ISKCON) in 1970, Kurma dasa has become one of the Hare Krishna movement's most celebrated chefs. As head chef at the famous Gopal's Vegetarian Restaurant in Melbourne, he has captivated tens of thousands of people with the delights of Vedic (traditional Indian) vegetarian cooking. Kurma is the inspiration and mainstay of Hare Krishna cooking throughout Australia, having generously shared his wealth of knowledge and skills with nearly a generation of Hare Krishna cooks.

For the last ten years, Kurma has been running regular vegetarian cooking courses for both beginners and advanced students. His 12-part television series, "Cooking with Kurma", is also enjoying great popularity throughout the world.

If you would like to correspond with him about the subject matter of this book, write; Kurma dasa, P.O. Box 125, Albert Park, Victoria 3206, Australia.

Hare Krishna Restaurants Around the World

ASIA

Bombay, India—Govinda's, Hare Krishna Land, Juhu 400 049/ Tel. 6206860

Calcutta, India—Russel St, Calcutta

Vrindaban, India—Krishna-Balaram Mandir, Bhaktivedanta Swami Marg, Raman Reti, Mathura Dist. 281 124/ Tel. 82478

Cebu, Phillippines—Govinda's, 26 Sanchiangko St.

Hong Kong—The Higher Taste Vegetarian Dining Club, 27 Chatam Road South, 6/F, Kowloon/ Tel. 739-6818

Kuala Lumpur, Malaysia—16-1 Jalan Bunusenam, Masjid India/ Tel. (3) 2986785

AUSTRALASIA

Australia

Adelaide—Crossways, 79 Hindley St., Adelaide, SA 5000/ Tel. (08) 272-0488

Brisbane—Crossways, First Floor, 99 Elizabeth St., Brisbane, QLD

Melbourne—Crossways, First Floor, 123 Swanston St., Melbourne, VIC 3000/ Tel. (03) 650 2939

Melbourne—Gopal's, First Floor, 139 Swanston St., Melbourne, VIC 3000/ Tel. (03) 650 1578

North Sydney—Gopal's, 180 Falcon St., North Sydney, NSW 2060/ Tel. (02) 955-6164

Perth—Gopal's, 129 Barrack St., Perth, WA 6000/ Tel. (09) 325-2168

Sydney—Govinda's Upstairs and Govinda's Take-away, 112 Darlinghurst Rd., Darlinghurst, NSW 2010/ Tel. (02) 357-5162

New Zealand

Auckland—Gopal's, First Floor, 291 Queen St./ Tel. (9) 303-4885

Christchurch—Gopal's, 143 Worcester St./ Tel. (3) 67-035

Fiji

Lautoka—Gopal's, Corner of Yasawa St. & Naviti St./ Tel. 62990

Suva—Gopals, 18 Pratt St./ Tel. 312259

Suva—Gopals, 37 Cumming St.

EUROPE

London, England—Govinda's, 9-10 Soho St./ Tel. (01) 437-3662

Milan, Italy—Govinda's, Via Valpetrosa 3/5, 20123 Milano/ Tel. (2) 862-417

Malmoe, Sweden—Higher Taste, Amiralsgatan 6, 21155 Malmoe/ Tel. (040) 970600

Rome, Italy—Govinda's, Via di San Simone 73/A, 00186 Roma/ Tel. (6) 654-1973

LATIN AMERICA

Belem, Para, Brazil—Sri Krsna Prasada, Av. Gentil Bittencourt, Passagem Mac Dowell, 96 (entre Dr. Morais e Benjamin Constant/ Tel. (091) 222-1886

Arequipa, Peru—Jerusalen 402/ Tel. 229523

Cuzco, Peru—Espaderos 128

Lima, Peru—Schell 634 Miraflores

NORTH AMERICA

Dallas, Texas, U.S.A.—Kalachandji's, 5430 Gurley Ave., 75223/ Tel. (214) 827-6330

Detroit, Michigan, U.S.A.—Govinda's, 383 Lenox Ave., 48215/ Tel. (313) 331-6740

Laguna Beach, California, U.S.A.—Gauranga's, 285 Legion St.,/ Tel. (714) 494-7029

Los Angeles, California, U.S.A.—Govinda's, 9624 Venice Blvd., Culver City, 90230/ Tel. (213) 836-1269

Ottawa, Ontario, Canada—Govinda's, 212 Somerset St. E., K1N 6V4/ Tel. (613) 233-1884

Philadelphia, Pennsylvania, U.S.A.—Govinda's, 529 South St., 19147/ Tel. (215) 829-0077

Provo, Utah, U.S.A.—Govinda's Buffet, 260 North University, 84601/ Tel. (801) 375-0404

St. Louis, Missouri, U.S.A.—Govinda's, 3926 Lindell Blvd., 63108/ Tel. (314) 535-8085

San Diego, California, U.S.A.—Govinda's, 3102 University Ave., 92104/ Tel. (619) 284-4826

San Francisco, California, U.S.A.—Govinda's, 86 Carl St., 94117/ Tel. (415) 753-9703

San Juan, Puerto Rico—Govinda, Tetuan 153, Viejo San Juan 00903/ Tel. (809) 725-4885

Toronto, Ontario, Canada—Govinda's Dining Room, 243 Avenue Rd., M5R 2J6/ Tel. (416) 922-5415

Vancouver, B.C, Canada—Hare Krishna Buffet, 5462 S.E. Marine Dr., Burnaby V5J 3G8/ Tel. (604) 433-9728

OTHER COUNTRIES

Abeokuta, Nigeria, Africa—Ibadan Rd., Obantoko, behind NET

Guatemala, Guatemala—Callejor Santandes a una cuadra abajo de Guatel, Panajachel Solola

La Paz, Bolivia—Restaurant Manjari, Calle Potosi 1315, esq. Colon

San Salvador, El Salvador—25 Avenida Norte 1132

Santa Cruz, Bolivia—Snack Govinda, Av., Argomosa (1° anillo), esq. Bolivar